Haskell Cookbook

Build functional applications using Monads, Applicatives, and Functors

Yogesh Sajanikar

BIRMINGHAM - MUMBAI

Haskell Cookbook

Copyright © 2017 Packt Publishing

First published: September 2017

Production reference: 1210917

Published by Packt Publishing Ltd.
Livery Place
35 Livery Street
Birmingham
B3 2PB, UK.

ISBN 978-1-78646-135-3

www.packtpub.com

Credits

Author
Yogesh Sajanikar

Reviewer
Fabian Linzberger

Commissioning Editor
Aaron Lazar

Acquisition Editor
Karan Sadawana

Content Development Editor
Siddhi Chavan

Technical Editor
Supriya Thabe

Copy Editor
Karuna Narayanan

Project Coordinator
Prajakta Naik

Proofreader
Safis Editing

Indexer
Francy Puthiry

Graphics
Abhinash Sahu

Production Coordinator
Nilesh Mohite

About the Author

Yogesh Sajanikar has received his bachelor's degree in Mechanical Engineering from Shivaji University, India, along with a gold medal and a master's degree in Production Engineering from the Indian Institute of Technology, Bombay, India.

Yogesh has an experience of more than 20 years, and he has extensively worked with Product Lifecycle Management (PLM) and Computer Aided Design (CAD) software development firms, and architected solutions for domains such as Construction and Shipping Domain.

Having hooked on to functional programming, he moved into the Finance domain and worked as an enterprise architect; he has also worked with Scala/F# and Haskell. Currently, he is working as a CTO for a startup. He has also started local Haskell meetups and has been an active participant in meetups and functional conferences.

Yogesh believes in the open source movement, and believes in giving back to the open source community.

I would like to sincerely thank my wife, Rashmi, for her constant encouragement and sacrifice; Atharva, my son, who has now decided to learn Haskell at an early age. I would like to take a moment to thank my mom, Geeta, and my late dad, Mukund, for enabling me in my life's journey.

Last, but nonetheless, I would sincerely thank my friends and colleagues at work. In the end, all the thanks to the wonderful staff at Packt, especially Siddhi and Supriya, who worked really hard to bring this book to reality. Their perseverance and pursuance really helped me complete the book despite the delays on my side.

About the Reviewer

Fabian Linzberger is a functional programming enthusiast and practitioner. He discovered Haskell in 2010 and it has been his favorite programming language ever since. You can find some of his code (some of it in Haskell) on GitHub (`https://github.com/lefant/`) or visit his personal homepage and check out his blog (`https://e.lefant.net/`).

www.PacktPub.com

For support files and downloads related to your book, please visit www.PacktPub.com.

Did you know that Packt offers eBook versions of every book published, with PDF and ePub files available? You can upgrade to the eBook version at www.PacktPub.com and as a print book customer, you are entitled to a discount on the eBook copy. Get in touch with us at service@packtpub.com for more details.

At www.PacktPub.com, you can also read a collection of free technical articles, sign up for a range of free newsletters and receive exclusive discounts and offers on Packt books and eBooks.

https://www.packtpub.com/mapt

Get the most in-demand software skills with Mapt. Mapt gives you full access to all Packt books and video courses, as well as industry-leading tools to help you plan your personal development and advance your career.

Why subscribe?

- Fully searchable across every book published by Packt
- Copy and paste, print, and bookmark content
- On demand and accessible via a web browser

Customer Feedback

Thanks for purchasing this Packt book. At Packt, quality is at the heart of our editorial process. To help us improve, please leave us an honest review on this book's Amazon page at `https://www.amazon.com/dp/1786461358`.

If you'd like to join our team of regular reviewers, you can e-mail us at `customerreviews@packtpub.com`. We award our regular reviewers with free eBooks and videos in exchange for their valuable feedback. Help us be relentless in improving our products!

Table of Contents

Preface

Functional programming has been gaining lot of momentum recently. We are seeing different paradigms of functional programming creeping into imperative languages such as C++, C#, and Python. There are languages such as Scala that try to offer best of both worlds, that is, object-oriented programming and functional programming.

As Haskell is a pure and non-strict language, and strictly separates pureness from effect-full computations, it really stands out among these languages. Its strong theoretical basis, such as an elaborate type system, combined with concise and expressive syntax, gives Haskell a unique flavor. It really helps in programming declaratively by specifying what rather than how! In this book, we will focus on practical aspects of the language.
Haskell Cookbook is meant for programmers who have a programming background. Most of the readers should be acquainted with an imperative language, such as Java/Python or C++.

This cookbook can be logically divided into two parts, the first five chapters serve as building blocks for programming in Haskell. These chapters cover syntactical and semantic details of the language by describing how to use and define functions and data types. In these chapters, we also cover type classes and the Functor, Applicative, and Monads concepts.
The last seven chapters will introduce you to the practical aspects of usage of Haskell and its rich set of libraries. These chapters will take you through containers in Haskell and backend development (developing with database) to frontend development (web framework). The last three chapters focus on advanced concepts, such as doing parallel and distributed programming in Haskell.

Each recipe is self-sufficient, and, wherever possible, the recipe will try to build a concept (such as Monad) from scratch, before moving on to a recipe that will use the concept from the existing library. This is especially true in the first five chapters.
Use this book to dive into Haskell and Functional Programming in general. Start building small toy programs by using recipes, and move on to bigger programs to create your own web application or a distributed system. Even if you are not planning to use Haskell in your day-to-day work, I can assure you that it will change the way you look at programming, even when programming with other languages.

This book is not possible without encouragements from my family and the constant pursuance and perseverance of the staff at Packt. These people believed in me even when I was delayed or transgressed.

What this book covers

Chapter 1, *Foundations of Haskell*, introduces you to Haskell and helps you setup the environment for Haskell using the stack as a tool. In this chapter, you will write your first Haskell program, and then analyze its parts.

Chapter 2, *Getting Functional*, warms you up to Haskell by introducing recursion, maps, filters, and folds. It ends up by implementing a prime sieve.

Chapter 3, *Defining Data*, explores the rich data types that Haskell provides. You will be exposed to product and sum types. This chapter further introduces standard type classes in Haskell.

Chapter 4, *Working with Functors, Applicatives, and Monads*, dives deeper into Haskell by exploring the rich type classes and their instances. The recipes in this chapter allow the reader to build their own monad, and introduces IO monad.

Chapter 5, *More about Monads*, builds on the previous chapter by further creating and using monad transformers, and finally building a parser with Attoparsec.

Chapter 6, *Working with Common Containers and Strings*, looks at common containers and introduces Foldable and Traversals. In this chapter, you will also cook your own container and test it using Quickcheck. This chapter also looks at an alternate representation of String, that is, Text and ByteString.

Chapter 7, *Working with Relational and NoSQL Databases*, uses the Haskell based model declaration template and queries using persistent library. We will also use redis to work with NoSQL databases.

Chapter 8, *Working with HTML and Templates*, works with the Heist template framework along with the Blaze HTML library to create composable HTML documents.

Chapter 9, *Working with Snap Framework*, explores various web application development aspects, such as routing, templating, authentication, and sessions using the Snap Framework.

Chapter 10, *Working with Advanced Haskell*, introduces you to advanced concepts such as Existentially Quantified Type, Rank-N-Type, type family, and GADT.

Chapter 11, *Working with Lens and Prism*, explores the lens library to look at the concept of Lens and Prism. This chapter explains the concept of lens by building one itself. The rest of the chapter explains rich features of the Lens library.

Chapter 12, *Concurrent and Distributed Programming in Haskell*, introduces the building blocks of concurrent programming, such as IORef, MVar, and STM. The later part introduces Cloud Haskell to create distributed applications.

What you need for this book

- You will need a fairly recent operating system, such as Windows, Linux, or Mac OS.
- You should set up the stack tool from https://www.haskellstack.org/. Use the Stack setup to download GHC (Haskell Compiler) on your machine. Stack is an extremely useful tool to work with different versions of GHC and packages.
- You will need a good editor. Vi and Emacs have very good support for Haskell. Eclipse and Sublime also have support for Haskell.

Who this book is for

This book is targeted at readers who wish to learn the Haskell language. If you are a beginner, *Haskell Cookbook* will get you started. If you are experienced, it will expand your knowledge base. A basic knowledge of programming will be helpful.

Sections

In this book, you will find several headings that appear frequently (Getting ready, How to do it, How it works, There's more, and See also).

To give clear instructions on how to complete a recipe, we use these sections as follows:

Getting ready

This section tells you what to expect in the recipe, and describes how to set up any software or any preliminary settings required for the recipe.

How to do it...

This section contains the steps required to follow the recipe.

How it works...

This section usually consists of a detailed explanation of what happened in the previous section.

There's more...

This section consists of additional information about the recipe in order to make the reader more knowledgeable about the recipe.

See also

This section provides helpful links to other useful information for the recipe.

Conventions

In this book, you will find a number of text styles that distinguish between different kinds of information. Here are some examples of these styles and an explanation of their meaning.

Code words in text, database table names, folder names, filenames, file extensions, pathnames, dummy URLs, user input, and Twitter handles are shown as follows: "Conditionally import `Prelude`, hiding the `reverse` function."

A block of code is set as follows:

```
reverse :: [a] -> [a]
reverse xs = reverse' xs []
where
  reverse' :: [a] -> [a] -> [a]
  reverse' [] rs = rs
  reverse' (x:xs) rs = reverse' xs (x:rs)
```

When we wish to draw your attention to a particular part of a code block, the relevant lines or items are set in bold:

```
main-is: Main.hs
default-language: Haskell2010
build-depends: base >= 4.7 && < 5
  , mtl
  , containers
```

Any command-line input or output is written as follows:

```
stack build
stack exec -- state-monad
```

New terms and **important words** are shown in bold.

Warnings or important notes appear like this.

Tips and tricks appear like this.

Reader feedback

Feedback from our readers is always welcome. Let us know what you think about this book--what you liked or disliked. Reader feedback is important for us as it helps us develop titles that you will really get the most out of.

To send us general feedback, simply e-mail feedback@packtpub.com, and mention the book's title in the subject of your message.

If there is a topic that you have expertise in and you are interested in either writing or contributing to a book, see our author guide at www.packtpub.com/authors.

Customer support

Now that you are the proud owner of a Packt book, we have a number of things to help you to get the most from your purchase.

Downloading the example code

You can download the example code files for this book from your account at http://www.packtpub.com. If you purchased this book elsewhere, you can visit http://www.packtpub.com/support and register to have the files e-mailed directly to you.

You can download the code files by following these steps:

1. Log in or register to our website using your e-mail address and password.
2. Hover the mouse pointer on the **SUPPORT** tab at the top.
3. Click on **Code Downloads & Errata**.
4. Enter the name of the book in the **Search** box.
5. Select the book for which you're looking to download the code files.
6. Choose from the drop-down menu where you purchased this book from.
7. Click on **Code Download**.

Once the file is downloaded, please make sure that you unzip or extract the folder using the latest version of:

- WinRAR / 7-Zip for Windows
- Zipeg / iZip / UnRarX for Mac
- 7-Zip / PeaZip for Linux

The code bundle for the book is also hosted on GitHub at `https://github.com/PacktPublishing/HaskellCookbook`. We also have other code bundles from our rich catalog of books and videos available at `https://github.com/PacktPublishing/`. Check them out!

Errata

Although we have taken every care to ensure the accuracy of our content, mistakes do happen. If you find a mistake in one of our books--maybe a mistake in the text or the code--we would be grateful if you could report this to us. By doing so, you can save other readers from frustration and help us improve subsequent versions of this book. If you find any errata, please report them by visiting `http://www.packtpub.com/submit-errata`, selecting your book, clicking on the **Errata Submission Form** link, and entering the details of your errata. Once your errata are verified, your submission will be accepted and the errata will be uploaded to our website or added to any list of existing errata under the Errata section of that title.

To view the previously submitted errata, go to `https://www.packtpub.com/books/content/support` and enter the name of the book in the search field. The required information will appear under the **Errata** section.

Piracy

Piracy of copyrighted material on the Internet is an ongoing problem across all media. At Packt, we take the protection of our copyright and licenses very seriously. If you come across any illegal copies of our works in any form on the Internet, please provide us with the location address or website name immediately so that we can pursue a remedy.

Please contact us at copyright@packtpub.com with a link to the suspected pirated material.

We appreciate your help in protecting our authors and our ability to bring you valuable content.

Questions

If you have a problem with any aspect of this book, you can contact us at questions@packtpub.com, and we will do our best to address the problem.

1
Foundations of Haskell

In this chapter, we will cover the following recipes:

- Getting started with Haskell
- Working with data types
- Working with pure functions and user-defined data types
- Working with list functions

Introduction

We all love programs! On one side, there are surgical programming languages such as C and C++, which can solve the problem with clinical efficiency. This can be good and bad at the same time. A very experienced programmer can write a very efficient code; at the same time, it is also possible to write code that is unintelligible and very difficult to understand. On the other side, there are programs that are elegant, composable, and not only easier to understand, but also easier to reason with, such as Lisp, ML, and Haskell.

It is the second kind of programs that we will be looking at in this book. Not that efficiency is not important to us, nor does it mean that we cannot write elegant programs in C/C++. However, we will concentrate more on expressiveness, modularity, and composability of the programs. We will be interested more on the *what* of the program and not really on the *how* of the program.

Understanding the difference between *what* and *how* is very critical to understand the expressiveness, composability, and reasoning power of functional languages. Working with functional languages involves working with expressions and evaluations of expressions. The programmer builds functions consisting of expressions and composes them together to solve a problem at hand. Essentially, a functional programmer is working towards construction of a function to solve the problem that they are working on.

We will look at a program written in Haskell. The program adds two integers and returns the result of addition as follows:

```
add :: Int -> Int -> Int
add a b = a + b
```

Here, the `add` function takes two arguments, which are applied to the expression on the right-hand side. Hence, the expression `add a b` is equivalent to `a + b`. Unlike programming languages such as C/C++, `add a b` is not an instruction, but *expressions* and *application* of the values a and b to the expression on the right-hand side and the value of the expression. In short, one can say that `add a b` *is bound to value of the expression* `a + b`. When we call `add 10 20`, the expression is applied to the values `10` and `20`, respectively. In this way, the `add` function is equivalent to a value that evaluates to an expression to which two values can be applied.

The functional program is free to evaluate the expression in multiple ways. One possible execution in a functional context is shown in the following diagram. You can see that **add a b** is an expression with two variables **a** and **b** as follows:

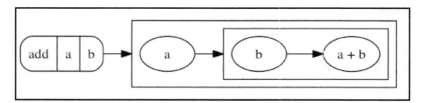

When value **10** is bound to variable **b**, the expression substitutes the value of **b** in the expression on the right-hand side:

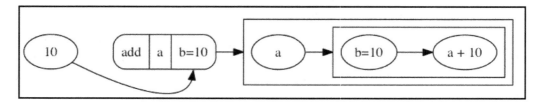

Now, the whole expression is reduced to an expression in **a**:

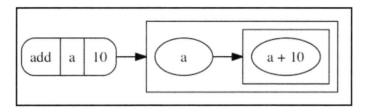

When value **20** is bound to variable **a**, the expression again substitutes the value of **a** in the expression on the right-hand side:

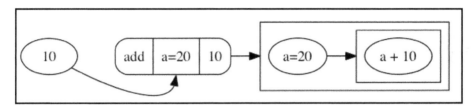

Finally, the expression is reduced to a simple expression:

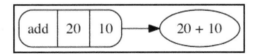

Note that in the expression add a b, a and b can both be expressions. We can either evaluate the expressions before substitution, or we can substitute the expressions first and then reduce them. For example, an expression add (add 10 20) 30 can be substituted in the expression a + b as follows:

```
add (add 10 20) 30 = (10 + 20) + 30
```

Alternatively, it can be substituted by evaluating `add 10 20` first and then substituting in the expression as follows:

```
add (add 10 20) 30 = add (10 + 20) 30
                   = add 30 30
                   = 30 + 30
```

The first approach is called **call by name**, and the second approach is called **call by value**. Whichever approach we take, the value of the expression remains the same. In practice, languages such as Haskell take an intelligent approach, which is more geared towards efficiency. In Haskell, expressions are typically reduced to weak-headed normal form in which not the whole expression is evaluated, but rather a selective reduction is carried out and then is substituted in the expression.

Getting started with Haskell

In this recipe, we will work with **Glasgow Haskell Compiler** (**GHC**) and its interpreter GHCi. Then, we will write our first Haskell program and run it in the interpreter.

 We will use GHC throughout the book. GHC (`https://www.haskell.org/ghc/`) is the most widely used Haskell compiler. GHC supports Haskell 2010 language specifications (`https://wiki.haskell.org/Definition`). The current book is based on Haskell 2010 specifications. GHC supports an extensive range of language extensions.

How to do it...

We will install Stack, a modern tool to maintain different versions of GHC and to work with different packages. Perform the following steps:

1. Install Stack. Visit `https://docs.haskellstack.org/en/stable/README/` and follow the instructions for your operating system.
2. Check that Stack works for your system by running the command `stack --version` at the command prompt.

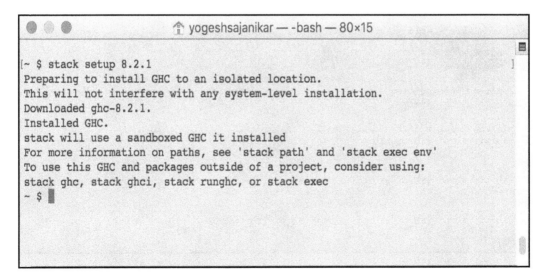

```
● ● ●              ⌂ yogeshsajanikar — -bash — 80×24
[~ $ stack --version
Version 1.4.0 x86_64
Compiled with:
- Cabal-1.24.2.0
- Glob-0.7.14
- HUnit-1.5.0.0
- MonadRandom-0.5.1
- QuickCheck-2.9.2
- SHA-1.6.4.2
- StateVar-1.1.0.4
- aeson-1.0.2.1
- aeson-compat-0.3.6
- annotated-wl-pprint-0.7.0
- ansi-terminal-0.6.2.3
- ansi-wl-pprint-0.6.7.3
- array-0.5.1.1
- asn1-encoding-0.9.4
- asn1-parse-0.9.4
- asn1-types-0.3.2
- async-2.1.1
- attoparsec-0.13.1.0
- auto-update-0.1.4
- base-4.9.1.0
- base-compat-0.9.1
```

Check the latest GHC version by visiting `https://www.haskell.org/ghc/`. Set up GHC on your box by providing the GHC version number:

```
● ● ●              ⌂ yogeshsajanikar — -bash — 80×15

[~ $ stack setup 8.2.1
Preparing to install GHC to an isolated location.
This will not interfere with any system-level installation.
Downloaded ghc-8.2.1.
Installed GHC.
stack will use a sandboxed GHC it installed
For more information on paths, see 'stack path' and 'stack exec env'
To use this GHC and packages outside of a project, consider using:
stack ghc, stack ghci, stack runghc, or stack exec
~ $ █
```

3. If you have already set up GHC on your box, then you will see the following output:

4. Pick up your editor. You can set up your favorite editor to edit Haskell code. Preferable editors are Emacs, Vi, and Sublime. Once you have picked up your favorite editor, ensure that the executables for the editor remain in your path or note down the full path to the executable.

Let's create a new project, `hello`. Create the new project `hello` by running the following command in the command prompt in an empty directory:

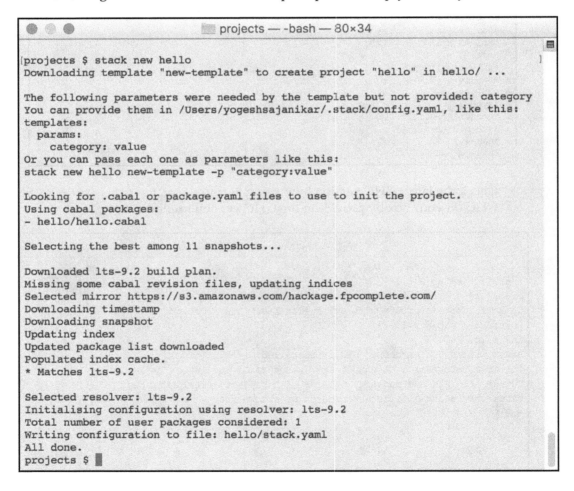

```
projects $ stack new hello
Downloading template "new-template" to create project "hello" in hello/ ...

The following parameters were needed by the template but not provided: category
You can provide them in /Users/yogeshsajanikar/.stack/config.yaml, like this:
templates:
  params:
    category: value
Or you can pass each one as parameters like this:
stack new hello new-template -p "category:value"

Looking for .cabal or package.yaml files to use to init the project.
Using cabal packages:
- hello/hello.cabal

Selecting the best among 11 snapshots...

Downloaded lts-9.2 build plan.
Missing some cabal revision files, updating indices
Selected mirror https://s3.amazonaws.com/hackage.fpcomplete.com/
Downloading timestamp
Downloading snapshot
Updating index
Updated package list downloaded
Populated index cache.
* Matches lts-9.2

Selected resolver: lts-9.2
Initialising configuration using resolver: lts-9.2
Total number of user packages considered: 1
Writing configuration to file: hello/stack.yaml
All done.
projects $ ▊
```

Stack will select the latest package resolver. Stack will create a folder with the project name.

5. Change to project directory (`hello`) and run `stack setup`. When run from the new project directory, Stack automatically downloads the corresponding GHC and sets it up.

6. Compile and build the project:

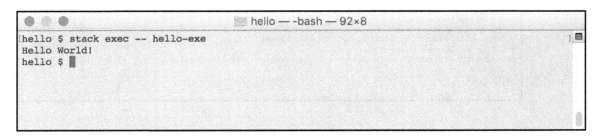

```
hello $ stack build
hello-0.1.0.0: configure (lib + exe)
Configuring hello-0.1.0.0...
hello-0.1.0.0: build (lib + exe)
Preprocessing library hello-0.1.0.0...
[1 of 1] Compiling Lib              ( src/Lib.hs, .stack-work/dist/x86_64-osx/Cabal-1.24.2.0/build/Lib.o )
Preprocessing executable 'hello-exe' for hello-0.1.0.0...
[1 of 1] Compiling Main             ( app/Main.hs, .stack-work/dist/x86_64-osx/Cabal-1.24.2.0/build/hello-e
xe/hello-exe-tmp/Main.o )
Linking .stack-work/dist/x86_64-osx/Cabal-1.24.2.0/build/hello-exe/hello-exe ...
hello-0.1.0.0: copy/register
Installing library in
/Users/yogeshsajanikar/projects/haskell/haskell_cookbook/Ch_1-Foundations_of_Haskell/projects/hello/.stack-
work/install/x86_64-osx/lts-9.2/8.0.2/lib/x86_64-osx-ghc-8.0.2/hello-0.1.0.0-KwseWZXCZphlLcfBbJuRhm
Installing executable(s) in
/Users/yogeshsajanikar/projects/haskell/haskell_cookbook/Ch_1-Foundations_of_Haskell/projects/hello/.stack-
work/install/x86_64-osx/lts-9.2/8.0.2/bin
Registering hello-0.1.0.0...
hello $
```

7. You can now run the project using the following command:

```
hello $ stack exec -- hello-exe
Hello World!
hello $
```

8. You should see the reply `someFunc` printed on the console. It means that the program compilation and execution was successful.

9. Inspect the `hello` project by opening an explorer (or file finder) and exploring the `hello` directory:

- The project contains two main directories, `app` and `src`. The library code goes into the `src` folder, whereas the main executable producing code goes into the `app` folder.
- We are interested in the `app/Main.hs` file.

10. Now, we will set an editor. You can set the editor by defining environment variable `EDITOR` to point to the full path of the editor's executable.

11. Run the GHC interpreter by opening the command prompt and traversing to the `hello` project directory. Then, execute the command `stack ghci`. You will see the following output:

```
                           hello — ghc ‹ stack ghci — 92×19
[hello $ stack ghci
The following GHC options are incompatible with GHCi and have not been passed to it: -thread
ed
Configuring GHCi with the following packages: hello
Using main module: 1. Package `hello' component exe:hello-exe with main-is file: /Users/yoge
shsajanikar/projects/haskell/haskell_cookbook/Ch_1-Foundations_of_Haskell/projects/hello/app
/Main.hs
GHCi, version 8.0.2: http://www.haskell.org/ghc/  :? for help
Loaded GHCi configuration from /Users/yogeshsajanikar/.ghc/ghci.conf
[1 of 1] Compiling Lib              ( /Users/yogeshsajanikar/projects/haskell/haskell_cookbo
ok/Ch_1-Foundations_of_Haskell/projects/hello/src/Lib.hs, interpreted )
Ok, modules loaded: Lib.
[2 of 2] Compiling Main             ( /Users/yogeshsajanikar/projects/haskell/haskell_cookbo
ok/Ch_1-Foundations_of_Haskell/projects/hello/app/Main.hs, interpreted )
Ok, modules loaded: Lib, Main.
Loaded GHCi configuration from /private/var/folders/hj/t11zhf4x31n8zclw3ph6gphw0000gn/T/ghci
4494/ghci-script
*Main Lib> ▮
```

Set an editor if you haven't done so already. We are using Vi editor:

```
*Main Lib> :set editor gvim
```

12. Open the `Main.hs` file in the editor:
    ```
    *Main Lib> :edit app/Main.hs
    ```

    This will open the `app/Main.hs` file in the window:

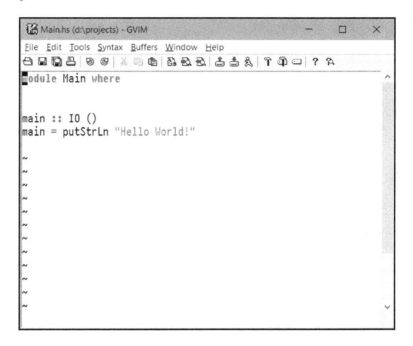

13. Enter the following source in the editor:

    ```
    module Main where

    -- Single line comment!
    main :: IO ()
    main = putStrLn "Hello World!"
    ```

14. Save the source file and exit. You will see that GHCi has successfully loaded the saved file:

```
[2 of 2] Compiling Main
( d:\projects\hello\app\Main.hs, interpreted )
Ok, modules loaded: Lib, Main.
*Main>
```

You can also load the file by running :load app/Main.hs in the command prompt.

15. Now, you can run the main function that we have defined in the source file, and you will see the Hello World message:

```
*Main> main
Hello World!
```

Exit the GHCi by running :quit in the prompt.

16. You can now rebuild and run the program by running the following commands:

```
stack build
stack exec -- hello-exe
```

You will again see the output Hello World as shown in the following screenshot:

```
hello — -bash — 92×8
[hello $ stack exec -- hello-exe
Hello World!
hello $
```

How it works...

This recipe demonstrated the usage of Stack to create a new project, build it, set up the corresponding GHC version, build the project, and run it. The recipe also demonstrated the use of the Haskell command prompt, aka GHCi, to load and edit the file. GHCi also allows us to run the program in the command prompt.

The recipe also shows the familiar Hello World! program and how to write it. The program can be interpreted in the following way.

Dissecting Hello World

We will now look at different parts of the Main.hs program that we just created to understand the structure of a typical Haskell program. For convenience, the screenshot of the program is attached here:

```
● ● ●        Main.hs (~/projects/haskell/haskell_cook...1-Foundation...
1 module Main where
2
3 -- Single line comment!
4 main :: IO ()
5 main = putStrLn "Hello World!"
6 █
~
~
~
~
~
                                        6,0-1         All
```

The first line means that we are defining a module called Main. The source that follows where is contained in this module. In the absence of any specifications, all the functions defined in the module are exported, that is, they will be available to be used by importing the Main module.

The line number **3** (in the screenshot) that starts with -- is a comment. -- is used to represent a single-line comment. It can appear anywhere in the source code and comments on everything until the end of the line.

The next line is this:

```
main :: IO ()
```

This is a declaration of a function. :: is a keyword in Haskell, and you can read :: as *has type*. IO is a higher order data type as it takes a parameter (IO is a special data type called **IO monad**; we will see more of it at the later). () is an empty tuple and is a parameter to IO. An empty tuple in Haskell is equivalent to *Unit Type*. One can say that it is equivalent to void in imperative languages.

Hence, main :: IO () should be interpreted as follows:

```
main has a type IO ()
```

The next line actually defines the function:

```
main = putStrLn "Hello World"
```

It simply means that main is a function whose value is equivalent to an expression on the right-hand side, putStrLn "Hello World".

The putStrLn is a function defined in Prelude, and you can look up the type of the function by entering the following command in the prompt:

```
Prelude> :type putStrLn
putStrLn :: String -> IO ()
```

Here, putStrLn has a type String -> IO (). It means that putStrLn is a function that, when applied and when the argument is of String type, will have the resultant type IO (). Note how it matches with our type declaration of the main function.

The function declaration in the source code in Haskell is not compulsory, and the Haskell compiler can figure out the type of the function all by itself by looking at the definition of the function. You can try this by again editing the source file and removing declaration.

To edit the same file again, you can just issue the :edit command without any parameter. GHCi will open the editor with the previously opened file. To reload the file again, you can issue the :reload command and GHCi will load the file.

Now, you can verify the type of main function by issuing :t main (:t is equivalent to :type). Verify that the type of main is IO ().

There's more...

If you visit the Stack website at `https://www.stackage.org/`, you will notice that Stack publishes nightly packages and **Long Term Support** (**LTS**) packages. While creating a new project, Stack downloads the latest LTS package list. It is also possible to provide the name of the LTS package explicitly by providing `stack new —resolver lts-9.2`.

In the project directory, you will notice two files:

- `<project>.yaml`
- `<project>.cabal`

The YAML file is created by Stack to specify various things, including LTS version, external packages, and so on. The `.cabal` file is the main project file for the Haskell package. The cabal is the tool that Stack uses internally to build, package, and so on. However, there are several advantages of using Stack as Stack also supports pre-built packages and manages cabal well. Furthermore, Stack also supports the Docker environment.

Working with data types

In this recipe, we will work with basic data types in Haskell. We will also define our own data types.

How to do it...

1. Create a new project `data-types` using Stack new data types. Change into the directory `data-types` and build the new project using `stack build`.

    In the command prompt, run `stack ghci`. You will see the prompt. Enter this `=:type (5 :: Int) =:` command:

    ```
    *Main Lib> :type (5 :: Int)
      (5 :: Int) :: Int
    ```

    `:type` is a GHCi command to show the type of the expression. In this case, the expression is 5. It means that the expression `(5 :: Int)` is `Int`. Now, enter this `:type 5` command:

    ```
    *Main Lib> :type 5
      5 :: Num t => t
    ```

2. GHCi will interpret 5 as 5 :: Num t => t, which means that Haskell identified 5 as some numerical type t. Num t => t shows that the type is t and that it has an extra qualification, Num. Num t denotes that t is an instance of a type class Num. We will see type classes later. The Num class implements functions required for numerical calculation. Note that the result of :type 5 is different from :type (5::Int).

3. Now, enter :type (5 :: Double). You will see (5 :: Double) :: Double. Do the same thing with 5::Float:

```
*Main Lib> :type (5 :: Double)
(5 :: Double) :: Double
```

Note the difference between 5, 5::Int, 5::Float, and 5::Double. Without a qualification type (such as :: Int), Haskell interprets the type as a generic type Num t => t, that is, 5 is some type t, which is a Num t or numerical type. Now enter following boolean types at the prompt:

```
*Main Lib> :type True
True :: Bool
*Main Lib> :type False
False :: Bool
```

True and False are valid boolean values, and their type is Bool. In fact, True and False are the only valid Bool values in Haskell. If you try 1 :: Bool, you will see an error:

```
*Main Lib> 1 :: Bool

<interactive>:9:1: error:
* No instance for (Num Bool) arising from the literal
  '1'
* In the expression: 1 :: Bool
  In an equation for 'it': it = 1 :: Bool
```

Haskell will complain that 1 is a numerical type and Bool is not a numerical type, which would somehow represent it (value 1).

4. Now, type :type 'C' in the prompt. GHCi will report its type to be 'C' :: Char. Char is another data type and represents a Unicode character. A character is entered within single quotes.

5. Get more information about each type. To do this, you can enter `:info <type>` in the prompt:

```
*Main Lib> :info Bool
data Bool = False | True
-- Defined in 'ghc-prim-0.5.0.0:GHC.Types'
instance Bounded Bool -- Defined in 'GHC.Enum'
instance Enum Bool -- Defined in 'GHC.Enum'
instance Eq Bool -- Defined in 'ghc-prim-0.5.0.0:GHC.Classes'
instance Ord Bool -- Defined in 'ghc-prim-0.5.0.0:GHC.Classes'
instance Read Bool -- Defined in 'GHC.Read'
instance Show Bool -- Defined in 'GHC.Show'
```

This will show more information about the type. For `Bool`, Haskell shows that it has two values `False | True` and that it is defined in `ghc-prim-0.5.0.0:GHC.Types`. Here, `ghc-prim` is the package name, which is followed by its version `0.5.0.0` and then Haskell tells that `GHC.Types` is the module in which it is defined.

How it works...

We have seen four basic types `Int`, `Double`, `Char`, and `Float`. More information about these types is given in the following table:

Type	Description	Remarks
Int	Fixed precision integer type	Range [-9223372036854775808 to 9223372036854775807] for 64-bit Int.
Float	Single precision (32-bit) floating point number	
Double	Double precision (64-bit) floating point number	
Char	Character	
Bool	Boolean values	True or False

Note that all types start with a capital letter.

In previous sections of this recipe, when we ran the command :info Bool, at GHCi prompt, Haskell also showed various instances of information. It shows more about the behavior of the type. For example, instance Eq Bool means that the type Bool is an instance of some type class Eq. In Haskell, type class should be read as a type that is associated with some behavior (or function). Here, the Eq type class is used in Haskell for showing equality.

There's more...

You can get more information about type classes by exploring :info Eq. GHCi will tell you which types have instances of the Eq type class. GHCi will also tell you which are the methods defined for Eq.

Working with pure functions and user-defined data types

In this recipe, we will work with pure functions and define simple user-defined data types. We will represent a quadratic equation and its solution using user-defined data types. We will then define pure functions to find a solution to the quadratic equation.

Getting ready

1. Create a new project quadratic using the following command:

```
stack new quadratic
```

Change into the project folder.

2. Delete src/Lib.hs and create a new file src/Quadratic.hs to represent the quadratic equation and its solution.

3. Open the `quadratic.cabal` file, and in the section library, replace `Lib` by `Quadratic` in the tag `exposed-modules`:

```
library
  hs-source-dirs:      src
  exposed-modules:     Quadratic
  build-depends:       base >= 4.7 && < 5
  default-language:    Haskell2010
```

How to do it...

1. Open `Quadratic.hs` and add a module definition to it:

```
module Quadratic where
```

2. Import the standard module `Data.Complex` to help us represent a complex solution to the quadratic equation.

3. Define the data type to represent the quadratic equation:

```
data Quadratic = Quadratic { a :: Double, b :: Double,
  c :: Double }
  deriving Show
```

This represents the quadratic equation of the form $a*x2+b*x+c=0a*x2+b*x+c=0$. a, b, and c represent the corresponding constants in the equation.

4. Define the data type for representing the root:

```
type RootT = Complex Double
```

This represents that the complex data type parameterized by `Double`. `RootT` is synonymous to type `Complex Double` (similar to `typedef` in C/C++).

5. A quadratic equation has two roots, and hence we can represent both the roots as follows:

```
import Data.Complex
  type RootT = Complex Double
  data Roots = Roots RootT RootT deriving Show
```

6. Implement the solution. We will take a top-down approach to create a solution. We will define a top-level function where we will implement a function assuming lower level details:

```
roots :: Quadratic -> Roots
```

This shows that the `roots` function takes one argument of type `Quadratic`, and returns `Roots`.

7. Implement three cases mentioned next:

```
-- | Calculates roots of a polynomial and return set of roots
roots :: Quadratic -> Roots

-- Trivial, all constants are zero, error roots are not defined
roots (Quadratic 0 0 _) = error "Not a quadratic polynomial"

-- Is a polynomial of degree 1, x = -c / b
roots (Quadratic 0.0 b c) = let root = ( (-c) / b :+ 0)
                            in Roots root root

-- b^2 - 4ac = 0
roots (Quadratic a b c) =
let discriminant = b * b - 4 * a * c
in rootsInternal (Quadratic a b c) discriminant
```

We have referred to the `rootsInternal` function, which should handle case **A**, B, and **C** for the case **III**.

8. Implement the `rootsInternal` function to find all roots of the quadratic equation:

```
rootsInternal :: Quadratic -> Double -> Roots
-- Discriminant is zero, roots are real
rootsInternal q d | d == 0 = let r = (-(b q) / 2.0 / (a q))
                                 root = r :+ 0
                             in Roots root root

-- Discriminant is negative, roots are complex
rootsInternal q d | d < 0 = Roots (realpart :+ complexpart)
(realpart :+ (-complexpart))
where plusd = -d
  twoa = 2.0 * (a q)
  complexpart = (sqrt plusd) / twoa
  realpart = - (b q) / twoa

-- discriminant is positive, all roots are real
```

```
rootsInternal q d = Roots (root1 :+ 0) (root2 :+ 0)
where plusd = -d
  twoa = 2.0 * (a q)
  dpart = (sqrt plusd) / twoa
  prefix = - (b q) / twoa
  root1 = prefix + dpart
  root2 = prefix - dpart
```

Open `src/Main.hs`. We will use the `Quadratic` module here to solve a couple of quadratic equations. Add the following lines of code in `Main.hs`:

```
module Main where

import Quadratic
import Data.Complex

main :: IO ()
main = do
  putStrLn $ show $ roots (Quadratic 0 1 2)
  putStrLn $ show $ roots (Quadratic 1 3 4)
  putStrLn $ show $ roots (Quadratic 1 3 4)
  putStrLn $ show $ roots (Quadratic 1 4 4)
  putStrLn $ show $ roots (Quadratic 1 0 4)
```

9. Execute the application by building the project using `stack build` and then executing with `stack exec - quadratic-exe` in the command prompt. You will see the following output:

```
Roots ((-2.0) :+ 0.0) ((-2.0) :+ 0.0)
Roots ((-1.5) :+ 1.3228756555322954) ((-1.5) :+
(-1.3228756555322954))
Roots ((-1.5) :+ 1.3228756555322954) ((-1.5) :+
(-1.3228756555322954))
Roots ((-2.0) :+ 0.0) ((-2.0) :+ 0.0)
Roots ((-0.0) :+ 2.0) ((-0.0) :+ (-2.0))
```

How it works...

A quadratic equation is represented by `ax^2 + bx + c = 0`. There are three possible cases that we have to handle:

Case	Condition	Root 1	Root 2	Remarks
I	`a = 0` and `b = 0`	ERROR	ERROR	
II	`a = 0`	`x = -c/b`	Not applicable	Linear equation
III	a and b are non-zero, `delta = b2 - 4ac`			
III-A	`delta = 0`	`-b/(2a)`	`-b/(2a)`	Perfect square
III-B	`delta > 0`	`(-b+sqrt(delta))/(2a)`	`(-b-sqrt(delta))/(2a)`	Real roots
III-C	`delta < 0`	`(-b+sqrt(delta))/(2a)`	`(-b-sqrt(delta))/(2a)`	Complex roots

We will define a module at the top of the file with the `Quadratic` module where the name of the module matches file name, and it starts with a capital letter. The `Quadratic` module is followed by the definition of module (data types and functions therein). This exports all data types and functions to be used by importing the module.

We will import the standard `Data.Complex` module. The modules can be nested. Many useful and important modules are defined in the base package. Every module automatically includes a predefined module called **Prelude**. The Prelude exports many standard modules and useful functions. For more information on base modules, refer to `https://hackage.haskell.org/package/base`.

The user-defined data is defined by the keyword data followed by the name of the data type. The data type name always start with a capital letter (for example, data `Quadratic`).

Here, we will define `Quadratic` as follows:

```
data Quadratic = Quadratic { a :: Double, b ::
  Double, c :: Double  }
  deriving Show
```

There are several things to notice here:

- The name on the left-hand side, `Quadratic`, is called **type constructor**. It can take one or more data types. In this case, we have none.
- The name `Quadratic` on the right-hand is called **data constructor**. It is used to create the value of the type defined on the left-hand side.
- `{a :: Double, b :: Double, c :: Double }` is called the **record syntax** for defining fields. `a`, `b` and `c` are fields, each of type `Double`.
- Each field is a function in itself that takes data type as the first argument and returns the value of the field. In the preceding case, `a` will have the function type `Quadratic -> Double`, which means `a` will take the value of type `Quadratic` as the first argument and return the field `a` of type `Double`.
- The definition of data type is followed by deriving `Show`. `Show` is a standard type class in Haskell and is used to convert the value to `String`. In this case, Haskell can automatically generate the definition of `Show`. However, it is also possible to write our own definition. Usually, the definition generated by Haskell is sufficient.

We will define root as type `Complex Double`. The data type `Complex` is defined in the module `Data.Complex`, and its type constructor is parameterized by a type parameter a. In fact, the `Complex` type is defined as follows:

```
data Complex a = a :+ a
```

There are several things to notice here. First, the type constructor of `Complex` takes an argument a. This is called **type argument**, as the `Complex` type can be constructed with any type a.

The second thing to note is how the data constructor is defined. The data constructor's name is not alphanumeric, and it is allowed.

Note that the data constructor takes two parameters. In such a case, data constructor can be used with infix notation. That is, you can use the constructor in between two arguments.

The third thing to note is that the type parameter used in the type constructor can be used as a type while defining the data constructor.

Since our quadratic equation is defined in terms of `Double`, the complex root will always have a type `Complex Double`. Hence, we will define a type synonym using the following command:

```
type RootT = Complex Double
```

We will define two roots of the equation using the following command:

```
data Roots = Roots RootT RootT deriving Show
```

Here, we have not used the record syntax, but just decided to create two anonymous fields of type `RootT` with data constructor `Roots`.

The `roots` function is defined as follows:

```
roots :: Quadratic -> Roots
```

It can be interpreted as the `roots` function has a type `Quadratic -> Roots`, which is a function that takes a value of type `Quadratic` and returns a value of type `Roots`:

- **Pattern matching**: We can write values by exploding data constructor in the function arguments. Haskell matches these values and then calls the definition on the right-hand side. In Haskell, we can separate the function definition using such matching. Here, we will use pattern matching to separate cases I, II, and III, defined in the preceding section. The case I can be matched with value (`Quadratic 0 0 _`) where the first two zeros match fields a and b, respectively. The last field is specified by `_`, which means that we do not care about this value, and it should not be evaluated.
- **Raising an error**: For the first case, we flag an error by using function error. The function error takes a string and has a signature (`error :: String -> a`) which means that it takes a `String` and returns value of any type a. Here, it raises an exception.
- **let .. in clause**: In the case II as mentioned in the preceding section, we use `let ... in` clause.

  ```
  let root = ( (-c) / b :+ 0)
  in Roots root root
  ```

Here, the `let` clause is used to bind identifiers (which always start with a lowercase letter; so do function names). The `let` clause is followed by the `in` clause. The `in` clause has the expression that is the value of the `let...in` clause. The `in` expression can use identifiers defined in `let`. Furthermore, `let` can bind multiple identifiers and can define functions as well.

We defined `rootsInternal` as a function to actually calculate the roots of a quadratic equation. The `rootsInternal` function uses pattern guards. The pattern guards are explained as follows:

- **Pattern guards**: The pattern guards are conditions that are defined after a vertical bar | after the function arguments. The pattern guard defines a condition. If the condition is satisfied, then the expression on the right-hand side is evaluated:

  ```
  rootsInternal q d | d == 0 = ...
  ```

  In the preceding definition, `d == 0` defines the pattern guard. If this condition is satisfied, then the function definition is bound to the expression on the right-hand side.

- **where clause**: The `rootsInternal` function also uses the `where` clause. This is another form of the `let...in` clause:

  ```
  let <bindings>
  in <expression>
  ```

  It translates to the following lines of code:

  ```
  <expression>
  where
  <bindings>
  ```

In `Main.hs`, we will import the `Quadratic` module and use the functions and data type defined in it. We will use the do syntax, which is used in conjunction with the `IO` type, for printing to the console, reading from the console, and, in general, for interfacing with the outside world.

The `putStrLn` function prints the string to the console. The function converts a value to a string. This is enabled because of auto-definition due to deriving `Show`.

We will use a data constructor to create values of `Quadratic`. We can simply specify all the fields in the order such as, Quadratic 1 3 4, where a = 1, b = 3, and c = 4. We can also specify the value of `Quadratic` using record syntax, such as Quadratic { a = 10, b = 30, c = 5 }.

Things are normally put in brackets, as shown here:

```
putStrLn (show (roots (Quadratic 0 1 2)))
```

However, in this case, we will use a special function $, which simplifies the application of brackets and allows us to apply arguments to the function from right to left as shown:

```
putStrLn $ show $ roots (Quadratic 0 1 2)
```

Source formatting

You must have also noticed how the Haskell source code is formatted. The blocks are indented by white spaces. There is no hard and fast rule for indenting; however, it must be noted that there has to be a significant white space indent for a source code block, such as the `let` clause or the `where` clause. A simple guideline is that any block should be indented in such a way that it is left aligned and increases the readability of the code. A good Haskell source is easy to read.

Working with list functions

In this recipe, we will work with the `list` data type in Haskell. The `list` function is one of the most widely used data types in Haskell.

Getting ready

Use Stack to create a new project, `list` functions, and change into the project directory. Build the project with `stack build`.

Remove the contents of `src/Lib.hs` and add the module heading:

```
module Lib where
```

How to do it...

1. Create an empty list:

   ```
   emptyList = []
   ```

2. Prepend an element to the list:

   ```
   prepend = 10 : []
   ```

3. Create a list of five integers:

```
list5 = 1 : 2 : 3 : 4 : 5 : []
```

4. Create a list of integers from 1 to 10:

```
list10 = [1..10]
```

5. Create an infinite list:

```
infiniteList = [1..]
```

6. This is the head of a list:

```
getHead = head [1..10]
```

7. This is the tail of a list:

```
getTail = tail [1..10]
```

8. This is all but the last element:

```
allbutlast = init [1..10]
```

9. Take 10 elements:

```
take10 = take 10 [1..]
```

10. Drop 10 elements:

```
drop10 = drop 10 [1..20]
```

11. Get n^{th} element:

```
get1331th = [1..] !! 1331
```

12. Check if a value is the element of the list.

```
is10element = elem 10 [1..10]
```

13. Do pattern matching on the list. Here we check whether the list is empty or not:

    ```
    isEmpty [] = True
    isEmpty _ = False
    ```

14. Do more pattern matching. Here we do pattern matching on elements present in the list.

    ```
    isSize2 (x:y:[]) = True
    isSize2 _ = False
    ```

15. Concatenate two lists:

    ```
    cat2 = [1..10] ++ [11..20]
    ```

16. String is actually a list. Check this by creating a list of characters:

    ```
    a2z = ['a'..'z']
    ```

17. Since string is a list, we can use all list functions on string. Here we get the first character of a string:

    ```
    strHead = head "abc"
    ```

18. Zip two lists:

    ```
    zip2 = zip ['a'..'z'] [1.. ]
    ```

19. Open app/Main.hs and use the preceding functions from the list, and also print values:

    ```
    module Main where

    import Lib

    main :: IO ()
    main = do
      putStrLn $ show $ (emptyList :: [Int])
      putStrLn $ show $ prepend
      putStrLn $ show $ list5
      putStrLn $ show $ list10
      putStrLn $ show $ getHead
      putStrLn $ show $ getTail
      putStrLn $ show $ allbutlast
      putStrLn $ show $ take10
      putStrLn $ show $ drop10
      putStrLn $ show $ get1331th
    ```

```
putStrLn $ show $ is10element
putStrLn $ show $ isEmpty [10]
putStrLn $ show $ isSize2 []
putStrLn $ show $ cat2
putStrLn $ show $ a2z
putStrLn $ show $ strHead
```

20. Build the project using `stack build` and run it using stack run `list-functions-exe`. Note that `Main` does not use the `infiniteList` snippets and does not print them.

How it works...

List is defined as follows:

```
data [] a = []          -- Empty list or
    | a : [a]    -- An item prepended to a list, is also a list
```

There are two data constructors. The first data `[]` constructor shows an empty list, and a list with no elements is a valid list. The second data constructor tells us that an item prepended to a list is also a list.

Also, notice that the type constructor is parameterized by a type parameter `a`. It means that the list can be constructed with any type `a`.

List creation

The first three snippets in the previous section are created using list's data constructors. The third example shows recursive application of the second constructor.

Enumerated list

The fourth and fifth snippets show how to create a list from enumerated values. Enumerated values are those that implement type class `Enum` and are implemented by ordered types such as `Int`, `Double`, `Float`, `Char`, and so on. The enumerated type allows us to specify a range using `'..'` (for example, `1..10`, which means numerals 1 to 10, including `10`). It is also possible to drop the to value. For example, `1..` will create an infinite list. It is also possible to specify an increment by specifying consecutive values. For example, `1,3,..10` will expand to `1, 3, 5, 7, 9` (note that the last value `10` is not part of it as it does not belong to the sequence).

Head and tail of a list

From the definition of a list, any element, when prepended to a list, is also a list. For example, 1:[2,3] is also a list. Here, 1 is called the head of the list, and 2 is called the tail of the list.

The functions head and tail return head and tail, respectively, of the list. The snippets 6 and 7 show an example of head and tail. Head has a signature – head :: [a] -> a and tail has a signature :: [a] -> [a].

Operations on a list

Once we have a list, we can do various operations, such as the following ones:

- init :: [a] -> [a]: Take all but the last element of the list. This is shown in snippet 8.
- take :: Int -> [a] -> [a]: Take, at the most, the first *n* elements of the list (shown as the Int argument). If the list has less than *n* elements, then it will consume the entire list. This is shown in snippet 9.
  In snippet 9, we worked on an infinite list and took only the first 10 elements. This works in Haskell, because in Haskell, nothing is evaluated until computation needs a value. Hence, even if we have an infinite list, when we take the first 10 elements, only 10 elements of the list are evaluated. Such things are not possible in strict languages. Haskell is not a strict language.

- drop :: Int -> [a] -> [a]: Similar to take, but the drop function drops the first *n* elements. It will drop the whole list if the list has less than *n* elements. If we operate on an infinite list, then we will get an infinite list back. Snippet 10 shows an example of drop.

Indexed access

The function names in Haskell do not necessarily start with alphabets. Haskell allows us to use a combination of other characters as well. Many collections, including list, define !! as an indexing function. Snippet 11 uses this.

The function !! takes a list and an index *n*, and returns the nth element, starting 0. The signature of !! is (!!) :: Int -> [a] -> a.

It is important to note that an access to an indexed element in the list is not random. It is sequential and is directly proportional to the index value. Hence, care should be taken to use this function.

Checking whether an element is present

The elem function checks whether a given element is present in the list. The elem function must be able to equate itself with another of its own type. This is done by implementing type Eq class, which allows checking whether two values of a type are equal or not.

Pattern matching on list

Once we know that a list has two data constructors, we can use them in the function argument for pattern matching. Hence, we can use [] for empty list matching, and we can use x:y:[] to match two elements followed by an empty list.

In the snippet 13, we used an empty list pattern for checking whether a list is empty or not.

In the snippet 14, we used x:y:[] to check whether the list has length 2 or not. This might not be a very good thing if we want to check the larger size. There, we might use the length function to get the size of the list. However, be aware of the fact that the length function is not a constant time function, but proportional to the size of the list.

List concatenation

It is possible to concatenate two lists by using the ++ function. The running time of this function is directly proportional to the size of the first list.

Strings are lists

It is important to note that the type String in Haskell is implemented as a list of Char:

```
type String = [Char]
```

Hence, all list operations are valid string operations as well. The snippets 17 and 18 show this by applying list functions on String. Since list is not a random access collection and operations such as concatenation are not constant time operations, strings in Haskell are not very efficient. There are libraries such as text that implement strings in a very efficient way.

There's more...

The preceding list of operations on Haskell list is not exhaustive. You can refer to the Data.List module in the base package (which is installed as a part of GHC). It provides documentation to all the functions that operate on list.

2
Getting Functional

In this chapter, we will look at the following recipes:

- Working with recursive functions
- Reversing a list - Recursive worker function pattern
- Creating maps and filters
- Working with laziness and recursion
- Working with folds
- Sorting a list
- Implementing merge sort
- Implementing Eratosthenes Sieve

Introduction

In functional programming, functions are first class values. It means that functions can be returned as values, and one can pass functions as arguments. In this chapter, we will start with recursive functions and gradually move to higher order functions, functions that take other functions as arguments. Our goal is to be able to write functions that are correct and tested. Haskell is a lazy language. We can take advantage of this fact, and write interesting and compact functions to take advantage of its laziness.

We will start with recursive functions, and see how recursion works. We will then move to tail recursive functions. We will explore a useful *worker* pattern while working with tail recursion. Next we will take advantage of laziness while calculating Fibonacci numbers recursively.

We will then work with maps and filters, which are very useful in many situations. We will then move to *folds*, which are important generalizations of recursions. We will move to more complex examples, such as implementing a bottoms-up merge sort, and a recursive implementation of Eratosthenes Sieve for finding out prime numbers.

Working with recursive functions

In this recipe, we will calculate fibonacci numbers by writing a simple recursive function. Fibonacci numbers are the numbers appearing in the fibonacci sequence.

Fibonacci numbers are calculated as follows:

$F_n = F_{n-1} + F_{n-2}$

We need to provide the first two seed fibonacci numbers in the sequence so that we can calculate the next set of fibonacci numbers. We will seed the sequence with 0 and 1. Our sequence will look like this:

0, 1, 1, 2, 3, 5, 8, 13, 21, 34, 55, 89, 144 ....

We will start indexing with 0. Hence, the 0th fibonacci number is 0, 1st fibonacci number is 1, .. 5th fibonacci number is 5 ... and so on.

Getting ready

Create a new project, fibonacci, using stack with the simple template:

```
stack new fibonacci simple
```

This will create a `fibonacci` directory and will add only `Main.hs` in the `src` folder. If you build the project, it will create the executable `fibonacci`. The default implementation will print `hello world`.

How to do it...

1. Open `src/Main.hs`. The file will define the `Main` module with the function `main :: IO ()`.

2. Here is the module definition. Add declaration of our function, `fib`. The function takes an integer to denote the index of the fibonacci number and returns the fibonacci number at the given index:

    ```
    fib :: Integer -> Integer
    ```

3. Handle the base cases using pattern matching and pattern guards. We have three cases:

  • Case I--Index is negative. This is an error case:

    ```
    fib n | n < 0 = error "invalid index"
    ```

  • Case II--Index is zero. We provide the 0th value as a seed value:

    ```
    fib 0 = 0
    ```

  • Case III-- Index is one. We provide the 1st value as the seed value:

    ```
    fib 1 = 1
    ```

4. Handle the generic case, that is, calculate the nth fibonacci number from the $n\text{-}1^{th}$ and $n\text{-}2^{th}$ numbers by writing a simple recursive definition:

    ```
    fib n = fib (n-1) + fib (n-2)
    ```

5. Modify the `main` function to use the `fib` function to print fibonacci numbers at indices 0, 1, 5, 10, and 20:

```
main :: IO ()
main = do
  putStrLn $ "f(0) = " ++ show (fib 0)
  putStrLn $ "f(1) = " ++ show (fib 1)
  putStrLn $ "f(5) = " ++ show (fib 5)
  putStrLn $ "f(10) = " ++ show (fib 10)
  putStrLn $ "f(20) = " ++ show (fib 20)
```

6. Build the project and run it:

```
stack build
stack exec fibonacci
```

7. You should see following output. Verify that we have indeed printed the correct results. You can to refer the fibonacci sequence at `https://oeis.org/A000045`:

```
f(0) = 0
f(1) = 1
f(5) = 5
f(10) = 55
f(20) = 6765
```

How it works...

The heart of the definition is as follows:

```
fib n = fib (n-1) + fib (n-2)
```

Simple recursion involves calling the same function we are defining. In the definition of `fib n`, we will call `fib (n-1)` and `fib (n-2)` and add their results.

The evaluation of the fibonacci number by this recursive definition is shown in the following diagram. The diagram shows the evaluation of **fib 5**. Note how at each stage, the `fib` function gradually reduces the argument and recursively calculates the value of the 5th fibonacci number:

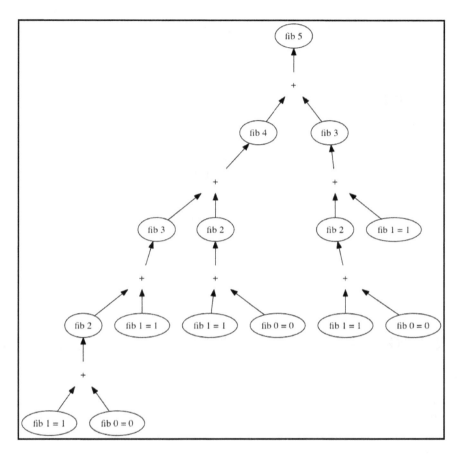

The preceding function is a simple recursive function. One can also implement mutually recursive functions. For example, we can implement functions isEven and isOdd that check whether a number is even or odd, respectively, in a mutually recursive way. We will use 1 and 2 as seed values for odd and even tests, respectively. In a mutually recursive function definition, one function, f1, calls the other function, f2, whereas the other function, f2, calls this function, f1:

```
isEven 2 = True
isEven n = isOdd (n-1)
isOdd 1 = True
isOdd n = isEven (n-1)
```

Note how recursive calls are made. Each recursive call is breaking down the problem into a smaller problem. Also, at a certain stage, one has to handle a basic condition to avoid infinite recursion.

There's more...

The recursive functions are sometimes ridiculously easy to write, and lead to a very simple and elegant function definition. However, one has to exercise caution to avoid infinite recursion and even a long recursion. For example, the evaluation of **fib 5**, as shown in the preceding diagram, denotes that each fibonacci value is calculated multiple times. **fib 2** is called three times, **fib 3** is called twice, and **fib 4** is calculated once.

The preceding implementation of the fibonacci number is very simple and looks very elegant. However, values are calculated multiple times, and in fact, the evaluation order for calculating the nth fibonacci number is directly proportional to the fibonacci series itself. Hence, if you try to evaluate the fibonacci number more than 100th index, it will not complete the execution.

Reversing a list - Recursive worker function pattern

In the previous recipe, we saw implementation using a simple recursive definition. In this recipe, we will use a commonly found recursive function implementation pattern called **worker pattern**.

The list does not have random access. We have to access elements of a list sequentially to be able to do something with it. When reversing a list, we need to remember this fact.

Getting ready

Create a new project, `reverse`, using Stack and the `simple` template. Also, build the project:

```
stack new reverse simple
stack build
```

How to do it...

1. Change directory to `reverse`, and open `src/Main.hs`. This file defines the `Main` module.

2. Conditionally import `Prelude`, hiding the `reverse` function:

   ```
   import Prelude hiding (reverse)
   ```

    Note that `Prelude` is imported automatically unless it is explicitly imported. Since we will write our own `reverse` function, we need to hide the `reverse` function while importing `Prelude`.

3. Write the signature of a `reverse` function:

   ```
   reverse :: [a] -> [a]
   ```

   This function takes a list of any type, `a`, and returns the reversed list.

4. Implement the `reverse` function using recursion:

   ```
   reverse :: [a] -> [a]
   reverse xs = reverse' xs []
   where
     reverse' :: [a] -> [a] -> [a]
     reverse' [] rs = rs
     reverse' (x:xs) rs = reverse' xs (x:rs)
   ```

   Note that we have a written `recursive` function. However, this recursive function is an internal function `reverse'` that takes two arguments.

5. Use the `reverse` function in `main` to test it. Here, we will check whether the function has successfully reversed the list [1..10]:

   ```
   main :: IO ()
   main = do
   let inp = [1..10]
     rs = reverse inp
     putStrLn $ "Reverse of " ++ (show inp) ++ " is " ++ (show rs)
   ```

6. If you build the project using `stack build` and execute it with the command `stack exec reverse`, you will see the following output:

   ```
   Reverse of [1,2,3,4,5,6,7,8,9,10] is [10,9,8,7,6,5,4,3,2,1]
   ```

How it works...

The `reverse` function is implemented as follows:

```
reverse xs = reverse' xs []
```

Here, we used an internal `reverse'` function with an extra argument.

The internal function `reverse'` is a worker function that actually does the work. Its signature is as follows:

```
reverse' :: [a] -> [a] -> [a]
```

It takes two arguments--the first one is the list that needs to be reversed and the second argument is where we store the result, that is, the **reversed list**. The recursion is implemented for the worker function `reverse'`.

There are two base cases for the input list:

- Case I--List is empty--Here, we will simply return the second argument, which is where we have stored the result:

```
reverse' [] rs = rs
```

- Case II--List is not empty--The first element of the list is taken and is added at the start of the result list. The recursion is called with the input list, without the first element, and the result list, where we have added the first element taken from the input:

```
reverse' (x:xs) rs = reverse' xs (x:rs)
```

We need to give an initial value for the result list when we call `reverse'` in the `reverse` function. The initial value has to be an empty list `[]`.

We can verify that the implementation works by running the `reverse'` function ourselves:

- Case I--List is empty--The `reverse'` function will be called as follows:

```
reverse' [] []
```

Since the input is an empty list, we will simply return the result `[]`. This is the correct result!

- Case II--List is not empty--Let's take a sample list [1,2,3,4,5] and pass it to the reverse' function and carry out the steps ourselves. The reverse' function will be called as follows:

```
reverse' [1,2,3,4,5] []
```

As per our implementation, since the input is a non-empty list, we will take the first element and add it to the result list, and continue with the recursion. Hence, the recursed call will look like this:

```
reverse' [2,3,4,5] [1]
```

The recursion will continue this way until the input list is empty, which is case I, and we will simply return the result list:

```
reverse' [3,4,5] [2,1]
= reverse' [4,5] [3,2,1]
= reverse' [5] [4,3,2,1]
= reverse' [] [5,4,3,2,1] -- Input is empty, return the result
= [5,4,3,2,1]
```

As you have noticed, the reverse' function takes N steps, where N is the number of elements in the input list. This pattern, where we use a worker function and store the result as an argument, is called a **worker pattern**.

There's more...

The interesting thing about this solution is that it uses an internal function that does the recursion. The result of the recursion is stored as an argument. When a special case is hit (such as the list being empty in our example), the result of the recursion is returned.

The recursion is **tail recursion**. It means that whenever we recurse, we ensure that the last function that is evaluated is exactly the same function that we are defining. In our example, we always called reverse' function as a top expression. The compiler optimizes the tail recursive functions such that they are executed in constant space and without adding them to stack.

The following diagram shows how a tail recursive function works. The diagram shows how a tail recursive *reverse'* function works. You can see that at each step, the recursion does the same operation till it reaches a point where recursion can be stopped. Since each operation in a tail recursion is same, the compiler can run recursion without incurring an overhead on stack. Please refer to the following diagram:

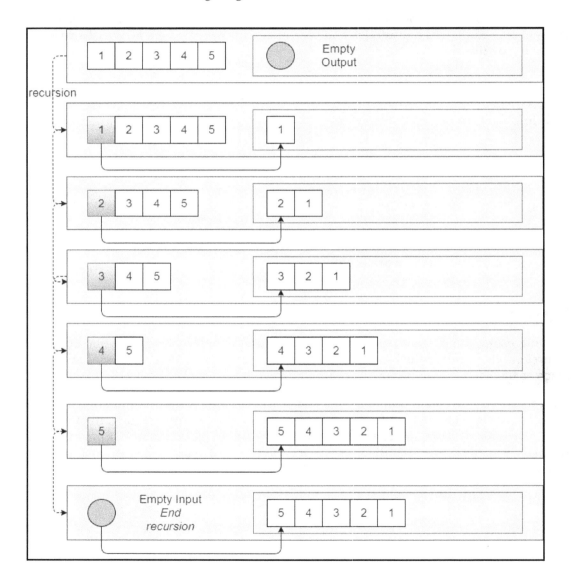

The following snippet to calculate the length of a list will highlight this fact:

- Implementation without tail recursion:

```
length [] = 0
length (_:xs) = 1 + length xs
```

- Implementation with tail recursion:

```
length xs = length' xs 0
  where
  length' [] len = len
  length' (_:xs) len = length' xs (1+len)
```

Creating maps and filters

In this recipe, we will continue working with recursive functions. In addition to recursion, we will introduce higher order functions. Higher order functions are functions that take other functions as an argument. Higher order functions introduce a layer of abstraction over other functions. If you see a certain pattern repeated over and over again, then you might have hit a situation that can be abstracted as a higher order function.

Though provided by default by Haskell's `Prelude` module, we will write our own version of two important higher order functions, `map` and `filter`.

Getting ready

Using `stack`, create a new project, `map-filter`, using the `simple` template. Change to the project folder and build the application:

```
stack new map-filter simple
stack build
```

How to do it...

1. Open `src/Main.hs`, and import `Prelude`, hiding two functions `map` and `filter`. These are the very functions we will implement:

```
import Prelude hiding (map, filter)
```

2. Write the declaration of `map`. A `map` is a function that takes a function, applies it to each member of the list, and returns the transformed list:

    ```
    map :: (a -> b) -> [a] -> [b]
    ```

Note the brackets around `(a -> b)`. It denotes that it is a function that takes an argument of type `a` and returns a value of type `b`. Without the brackets, Haskell will interpret the function declaration differently.

The `map` function takes two arguments and a return value, as described:

-   The first argument `(a -> b)` is a transformer function
-   The second argument `[a]` is a list of `a`
-   The return type of the function is a list of `b`, `[b]`

3. Handle different cases to define `map`. The input list can be empty. Handle this case first. For the empty list, we do not need any transformation:

    ```
    map mapper [] = []
    ```

4. When the input list is non-empty, we will take the first element of the list. Apply the mapping function to it and finally, put it in front of the mapped remaining list using recursion:

    ```
    map mapper (x:xs) = mapper x : map mapper xs
    ```

    Note that the preceding definition is not tail recursive. We can also write a tail recursive version of `map`. We will call it `map'` using the worker pattern as follows:

    ```
    map' :: (a -> b) -> [a] -> [b]
    map' mapper xs = map1 xs []
    where
      map1 [] rs = reverse rs
      map1 (x:xs) rs = map1 xs (mapper x : rs)
    ```

5. Let's implement `filter` now. The **filter** function, as the name suggests, filters the elements of the input list using the given criteria. The criteria is given in terms of a function that checks whether an element of the list qualifies for the criteria. If the element qualifies, the function should return `True` for each such element which satisfies the criteria.

6. The criteria should work with the element of the input list. Its type is (a -> Bool). The input is a list [a]. The return type is the subset of the input list, so the return type should also be [a]. Write down the declaration of the filter function:

```
filter :: (a -> Bool) -> [a] -> [a]
```

7. When the input list is empty, we do not have to do anything:

```
filter f [] = []
```

8. When the input list is non-empty, we will check the first element with the criteria function f. Then, put it in front of the filtered list, which is obtained by applying the filter to the remaining of the list:

```
filter f (x:xs)
 | f x = x : filter f xs
 | otherwise = filter f xs
```

9. Note that the preceding implementation is not tail-recursive. We can also implement a tail-recursive version of filter `filter'` as follows:

```
filter' :: (a -> Bool) -> [a] -> [a]
filter' f xs = filter1 xs []
where
 filter1 [] rs = reverse rs
 filter1 (x:xs) rs
 | f x = filter1 xs (x : rs)
 | otherwise = filter1 xs rs
```

10. Now, we will use map and filter, which we defined earlier. In the main function, we will use map, its tail-recursive version map', filter, and its tail-recursive version filter'. We will take [1..10] as input, and apply the square function on each element of the list using map and map'. We will then filter the *odd* elements of the same list using filter and filter':

```
main :: IO ()
main = do
let input = [1..10]
  squares = map (\x -> x * x) input
  squares' = map' (\x -> x * x) input
  odds = filter odd input
  odds' = filter' odd input
  putStrLn "Squaring [1..10]"
  putStrLn "Squares using map"
  putStrLn (show squares)
  putStrLn "Squares using tail recursive map"
  putStrLn (show squares')
  putStrLn "Filtering odd numbers in [1..10]"
  putStrLn "Using filter"
  putStrLn (show odds)
  putStrLn "Using tail recursive filter"
  putStrLn (show odds')
```

11. If you run the executable, you will see the following output:

```
map-filter — -bash — 41×38
map-filter $ stack exec map-filter
Squaring [1..10]
Squares using map
[1,4,9,16,25,36,49,64,81,100]
Squares using tail recursive map
[1,4,9,16,25,36,49,64,81,100]
Filtering odd numbers in [1..10]
Using filter
[1,3,5,7,9]
Using tail recursive filter
[1,3,5,7,9]
```

How it works...

In this recipe, we have worked with two functions, *map* and *filter*. These functions are described in the next section.

Map function

In the recipe, we have implemented map in two ways. Both implementations are described here as follows:

- The map function is defined as *map f (x:xs) = f x : map f xs*. Here, the mapping function f is applied to the first element, and then we will recurse using the remaining list and then join the result. Suppose the input list is [1,2,3,4,5], and we apply f to it. Then, our map will work in the following way. (Note that the function f is categorically not defined concretely to simplify the explanation of **map**.) As you can see, the result list keeps expanding towards the right (for example, f 1 : <rest of the list expanded here>):

```
map f [1,2,3,4,5] = f 1 : map f [2,3,4,5]
          = f 1 : (f 2 : map f [3,4,5])
          = f 1 : (f 2 : (f 3 : map f [4,5]))
          = f 1 : (f 2 : (f 3 : (f 4 : map f [5])))
          = f 1 : (f 2 : (f 3 : (f 4 : (f 5 : map f []))))
          = f 1 : (f 2 : (f 3 : (f 4 : (f 5 : []))))
          -- reducing further
          = f 1 : f 2 : f 3 : f 4 : f 5 : []
```

- The tail recursive function map' is defined using the worker pattern. Instead of building a stack during recursion such as implemented in preceding section, it builds the argument. The worker function map1 that is used by map' is shown here:

```
map' f [1,2,3,4,5] = map1 [1,2,3,4,5] []
          = map1 [2,3,4,5] [f 1]
          = map1 [3,4,5] [f 2, f 1]
          = map1 [4,5] [f 3, f 2, f 1]
          = map1 [5] [f 4, f 3, f 2, f 1]
          = map1 [] [f 5, f 4, f 3, f 2, f 1]
          -- When input is empty, the result is reversed and
          returned
          = [f 1, f 2, f 3, f 4, f 5]
```

- In the tail-recursive version, the list builds up, but in the reversed order. Hence, when we return the final value, we have to reverse the list.

Filter function

The `filter` function is implemented similarly to *map*. However, there are some differences, which are given as follows:

- The filter behavior is similar to `map` as explained earlier. However, notice the use of multiple pattern guards:

```
filter f (x:xs)
 | f x = x : filter f xs
 | otherwise = filter f xs
```

- Each guard is evaluated, and if it is evaluated to `True`, then the expression on the right-hand side is evaluated.
- Note the use of `otherwise` in the guard. The function `otherwise` always evaluates to `True` and is used to represent default behavior when everything in the guard evaluates to `False`.

 We have used the library function `odd` to test whether a number is odd. Also, notice the use of `let` in the do block. In the do block, `let` is used to bind identifiers to value. This `let` function is different from the `let..in` block.

There's more...

We have implemented two very commonly used higher order functions in Haskell. You will notice subtle differences between recursive and tail-recursive functions. There is another important difference that must be highlighted. The non-tail-recursive version of `map` and `filter` can work with the `infinite` list because the first element is evaluated and the rest of the list is evaluated only when it is required. In, for the tail-recursive version, the whole list has to be evaluated, as we need to push the whole list in to the result argument and then reverse it.

You can also refer to the Hackage source of `Data.List` and its implementation of map and filter.

Working with laziness and recursion

So far, we have seen a simple recursion; recursion using worker pattern. Haskell adds laziness to the mix. We can use laziness to our advantage while working with recursion.

In this recipe, we will again calculate the fibonacci number. However, this time, we will do it with infinite lists. By taking advantage of Haskell's laziness to evaluate an expression only when it is required, we can really create a linear time algorithm $(O(n))$ for the fibonacci number.

Getting ready

Create a new project, `fibonacci-infinite`, by running Stack. Change into the project directory and build it using Stack:

```
stack new fibonacci-infinite simple
stack build
```

How to do it...

1. Open `src/Main.hs` in an editor. After the module definition, we will add the definition for our fibonacci number.

2. Add the function declaration for `fib`. Let's assume that we have an infinite list of fibonacci numbers, `fiblist`. Finding the nth fibonacci number in the list is easy using the `List index function (!!)`:

   ```
   fib :: Int -> Integer
   fib n = fiblist !! n
   ```

3. Implement the function `fiblist`. The function `fiblist` is obviously a list of integers. Define `fiblist` as follows:

   ```
   fiblist :: [Integer]
   fiblist = 0 : 1 : zipWith (+) fiblist (tail fiblist)
   ```

4. This is an efficient implementation $(O(n))$ of the fibonacci number calculator. We can test it by calculating the 10000th fibonacci number:

   ```
   main :: IO ()
   main = do
     let fib10k = fib 10000
     putStrLn $ "10000th fibonacci number is " ++ (show fib10k)
   ```

5. If you build and run the application, it will print a very large number (thanks to big integer support in Haskell):

6. You can check whether our number is correct by checking the 1000th fibonacci number at `http://www.bigprimes.net/archive/fibonacci/10000/`.

How it works...

The preceding implementation looks deceptively simple, and it works! This is one of the highlights of Haskell. It provides a very elegant language construct to write such compact and meaningful programs in.

The heart of `fiblist` is the use of the `zipWith` function. The `zipWith` has the following signature:

```
zipWith :: (a -> b -> c) -> [a] -> [b] -> [c]
```

The `zipWith` function takes a function `f` and two lists. The `zipWith` function takes out an element from each list and applies the funcion `f` on these two elements. The `zipWith` function recursively continues this operation until either of the input lists are exhausted. In fact, `zipWith` is implemented in `Prelude` as follows:

```
zipWith f [] _ = [] -- Either input is empty, the result is empty
zipWith f _ [] = [] --
zipWith f (x:xs) (y:ys) = f x y : zipWith xs ys
```

Let's see how `fiblist` is able to represent an infinite number of fibonacci numbers. `fiblist` is defined as follows:

```
fiblist = 0 : 1 : zipWith (+) fiblist (tail fiblist)
```

The first two elements are the initial fibonacci numbers, 0, and 1, respectively. The rest of the elements are evaluated only when asked for. Otherwise, it remains as an *unevaluated* expression. For example, if we need to evaluate `fiblist` until five fibonacci numbers, it will be done as follows. The inputs to `zipList` is `fiblist` itself and the tail of `fiblist` (all but the first element). Since the first two elements are already there, we can use them. Hence, they are the only numbers highlighted in the initial `fiblist` expression. Hence, using Haskell's laziness carefully and cleverly, we can write an elegant routine to calculate fibonacci numbers:

```
fiblist = 0 : 1 : zipWith (+) [0,1...] [1,...]
-- Use first two elements of the list passed to zipWith and add
  them
    = 0 : 1 : (0 + 1) : zipWith (+) [1,1...] [1,..]
-- zipWith now recurses to process remaining elements of fiblist
-- and tail of fiblist.
    = 0 : 1 : 1 : (1 + 1) : zipWith (+) [1,2..] [2..]
-- Thus zipWith keeps on supplying elements to fiblist, and it
itself uses -- this list to evaluate further.
    = 0 : 1 : 1 : 2 : (1 + 2) : zipWith (+) [2,3...] [3..]
    = 0 : 1 : 1 : 2 : 3 : (2 + 3) : zipWith (+) [3, 5...] [5...]
    = 0 : 1 : 1 : 2 : 3 : 5 : zipWith (+) [3, 5...] [5..]
```

Note how `zipWith` uses initial values to evaluate and feed fibonacci numbers to itself.

The evaluation of lazy list can be shown graphically here:

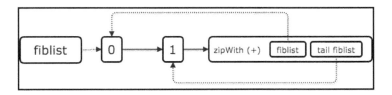

Working with folds

In this recipe, we will look at two of the most important high-order functions, called *foldr* and *foldl*. These functions carry out the following activities:

- Abstract iterative process over a collection such as a list
- Give a way to work with each of the elements within the collection
- Give a way to summarize elements and combine them with user-supplied values

Depending on the way elements are combined, the functions are called *foldr (fold right)* or *foldl (fold left)*. Many higher order functions such as *map* or *filter* can be expressed in terms of *foldr* or *foldl*.

In this recipe, we will write `sum` and `product` functions to calculate the sum and product of numbers in the input list respectively. We will also use folds to implement *map* and *filter*.

Getting ready

Use Stack to create a new project, `folds`, with the `simple` template, and build it, after changing directory to the project folder:

```
> stack new folds simple
> stack build
```

How to do it...

1. Open `src/Main.hs` and add the following definitions to it. For each function such as `sum`, we will create two versions--`sumr`, which uses `foldr`, and `suml`, which uses `foldl`.

2. Use both, right and left folds to sum up the numerical contents of a list to write functions `sumr` and `suml` as follows:

   ```
   sumr :: Num a => [a] -> a
   sumr xs = foldr (+) 0 xs

   suml :: Num a => [a] -> a
   suml xs = foldl (+) 0 xs
   ```

3. Similarly, use right and left folds to calculate product of all elements in the list. This should results in functions `productr` and `productl` respectively:

   ```
   productr :: Num a => [a] -> a
   productr xs = foldr (*) 1 xs

   productl :: Num a => [a] -> a
   productl xs = foldl (*) 1 xs
   ```

4. Define `map` using the folds `mapr` and `mapl`:

```
mapr :: (a -> b) -> [a] -> [b]
mapr f xs = foldr (\x result -> f x : result) [] xs

mapl :: (a -> b) -> [a] -> [b]
mapl f xs = foldl (\result x -> f x : result) [] xs
```

 Note how an anonymous function is defined (`\x result -> f x : result`). This is called `lambda` function. Its syntax is `\ arg1 arg2 ... -> <body of the lambda>`. The backslash `\'` is an abbreviation of the Greek letter lambda!

5. Define the filter using the `folds filterr` and `filterl`:

```
filterr :: (a -> Bool) -> [a] -> [a]
filterr f xs = foldr filtered [] xs
where
  filtered x result
  | f x        = x : result
  | otherwise = result
  filterl :: (a -> Bool) -> [a] -> [a]
  filterl f xs = foldl filtered [] xs
where
    filtered result x
    | f x = x : result
    | otherwise = result
Test the functions that we defined in the main function:
main :: IO ()
main = do
let input = [1..10]
  square x = x * x
putStrLn "Calculating sum of [1..10]"
putStrLn "  Using foldr"
putStrLn (show $ sumr input)
putStrLn "  Using foldl"
putStrLn (show $ suml input)

putStrLn "Calculating product of [1..10]"
putStrLn "  Using foldr"
putStrLn (show $ productr input)
putStrLn "  Using foldl"
putStrLn (show $ productl input)

putStrLn "Squaring [1..10] using map"
putStrLn "  Using foldr"
putStrLn (show $ mapr square input)
```

```
putStrLn "  Using foldl"
putStrLn (show $ mapl square input)

putStrLn "Filtering odd elements [1..10] using filter"
putStrLn "  Using foldr"
putStrLn (show $ filterr odd input)
putStrLn "  Using foldl"
putStrLn (show $ filterl odd input)
```

6. Build the project using `stack build` and run it. You should see the following output:

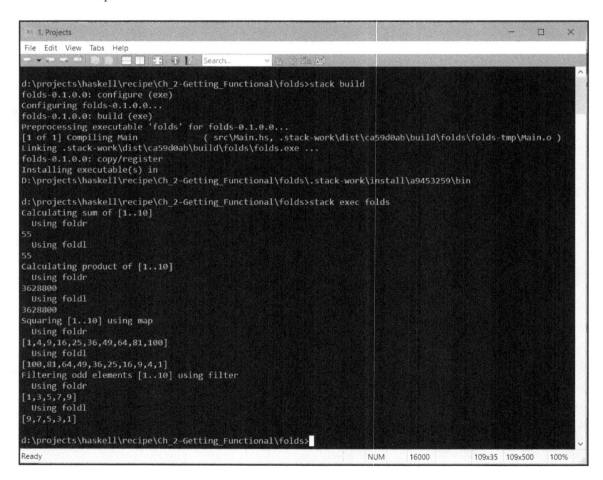

How it works...

Foldr has a type declaration as shown here:

```
foldr :: Foldable t => (a -> b -> b) -> b -> t a -> b
```

Whereas, foldl has a type declaration as shown here:

```
foldl :: Foldable t => (b -> a -> b) -> b -> t a -> b
```

The part of the declaration Foldable t denotes that folds can be implemented by any data type that would declare itself to be Foldable (Foldable is a type class). In the context of list, the preceding function can be adapted as follows:

```
foldr :: (a -> b -> b) -> b -> [a] -> b
foldl :: (b -> a -> b) -> b -> [a] -> b
```

Foldr takes three arguments, which are described here:

- (a -> b -> b): This is the function that takes the element of type a of the list (or Foldable), another value of type b, and produces b
- b: This is the default value that needs to be applied when we exhaust the input list (or Foldable)
- [a]: This is the input list (or Foldable)
- b: This is the result type

Foldr expression evaluation can be shown by taking an example. Let's take sumr as an example. We will find the sum of [1..5] and show how foldr evaluates it:

```
sumr [1..5] = foldr (+) 0 [1..5]
-- take the first element, use (+) to add this to
-- result of foldr applied to tail of the list
        = (+ 1 (foldr (+) 0 [2..5]))
-- Applying above step repeatedly...
        = (+ 1 (+ 2 (foldr (+) 0 [3..5])))
        = (+ 1 (+ 2 (+ 3 (foldr (+) 0 [4,5]))))
        = (+ 1 (+ 2 (+ 3 (+ 4 (foldr (+) 0 [5])))))
        = (+ 1 (+ 2 (+ 3 (+ 4 (+ 5 (foldr (+) 0 []))))))
-- The input is exhausted, this is where we use the supplied value
 0
        = (+ 1 (+ 2 (+ 3 (+ 4 (+ 5 0)))))
-- Now we can reduce the expression, starting with the innermost
bracket
        = (+ 1 (+ 2 (+ 3 (+ 4 5))))
        = (+ 1 (+ 2 (+ 3 9)))
```

```
            = (+ 1 (+ 2 12))
            = (+ 1 14)
            = 15 -- This is our result
```

Note how `foldr` keeps folding from the right-hand side. Actually, the preceding expression is equivalent to `(1 + (2 + (3 + (4 + (5 + 0))))))`. The chain of combining function `(+)` groups towards right.

Similarly, `foldl` takes three arguments, which are described here:

- `(b -> a -> b)`: This is the function that takes the value of result type b, an element of type a of the list (or `Foldable`), and produces b
- b: This is the default value that needs to be applied when we exhaust the input list (or `Foldable`)
- `[a]`: This is the input list (or `Foldable`)
- b: This is the result type

We will explain *foldl* using an example. Let's take the same input `[1..5]` and take its sum using `suml`, which is implemented using `foldl`:

```
suml [1..5] = foldl (+) 0 [1..5]
-- We start with initial value and combine it with first element
            = foldl (+) (+ 0 1) [2..5]
-- Repeating the process
            = foldl (+) (+ (+ 0 1) 2) [3..5]
            = foldl (+) (+ (+ (+ 0 1) 2) 3) [4,5]
            = foldl (+) (+ (+ (+ (+ 0 1) 2) 3) 4) [5]
            = foldl (+) (+ (+ (+ (+ (+ 0 1) 2) 3) 4) 5) []
-- We exhausted the input, and we have result ready..
            = (+ (+ (+ (+ (+ 0 1) 2) 3) 4) 5)
-- Reducing
            = (+ (+ (+ (+ 1) 2) 3) 4) 5)
            = (+ (+ (+ 3) 3) 4) 5)
            = (+ (+ 6) 4) 5)
            = (+ 10 5)
            = 15
```

Note how the expression reduces from the left-hand side. The chain of combining functions `(+)` gathers towards the left.

`productl`, `productr`, `mapl`, and `mapr` can be similarly explained.

There's more...

The functions `suml` and `sumr` produce similar results because the combining function `(+)` is commutative, that is, a + b = b + a. However, when applied to `map` and `filter`, the results are different for `mapr` and `mapl`. This is because the list concatenation operator used for `mapr` and `mapl` is not commutative. Hence, the application of concatenation `(:)` to `foldr` and `foldl` produces different results. In fact, `foldl` would produce a reversed list. It is shown here (with elements `[1..3]`):

```
-- Note both foldr and foldl are passed a function that adds an
element to the list.
foldr (:) [] [1..3] = 1 : foldr [] [2..3]
                    = 1 : 2 : foldr [] [3]
                    = 1 : 2 : 3 : []
                    = [1,2,3] -- Produces same list

foldl (\result x -> x : result) [1..3] = foldl (1 : []) [2..3]
                                       = foldl (2 : 1 : []) [3]
                                       = foldl (3 : 2 : 1 : []) []
                                       = 3 : 2 : 1 : []
                                       = [3,2,1]
```

Sorting a list

In this recipe, we will write a pseudo-quick sort using recursion. We call it pseudo-quick sort because it looks deceptively such as quick sort, but does not have a performance anywhere near it.

Getting ready

Use Stack to create a new project, `pseudo-qsort`, with the `simple` template and build it, after changing directory to the project folder:

```
> stack new pseudo-qsort simple
> stack build
```

How to do it...

1. Open `src/Main.hs` and write the `qsort` implementation. The `qsort` involves the following:
   - Choosing an element of the list to be sorted
   - Using the chosen element as a pivot, divide the input list into two parts:
     - Subset of the list smaller than the pivot element
     - Subset of the list greater than or equal to the pivot element
   - Recursively sorting two parts in a similar way

2. In Haskell, we can implement a method like quick sort quite easily. `Ord a` in the `qsort` declaration signifies that the elements of the list `[a]` can be compared for inequality, and it is possible to use the operators <, >, <=, and >=:

```
qsort :: Ord a => [a] -> [a]
qsort [] = []
qsort (x:xs) = qsort ys ++ [x] ++ qsort zs
where
    ys = filter (\y -> y < x) xs
    zs = filter (\z -> z >= x) xs
```

3. Test quick sort using a randomly shuffled list (in the sample, we will take ten elements within the range `0..10`):

```
main :: IO ()
main = do
let input = [5,2,3,1,7,9,8,4,6,0]
  sorted = qsort input
  putStrLn $ "input: " ++ (show input)
  putStrLn $ "sorted: " ++ (show sorted)
```

4. When built and executed, the program should produce the following output:

How it works...

The crux of the preceding code lies in the following line:

```
qsort ys ++ [x] ++ qsort zs
```

In the preceding statement, notice the following:

- We choose the first element of the list, x as the pivot.
- The list is then split into two parts ys and zs using the filter function.
- ys is the list of elements less than x, and zs is the list of elements greater than or equal to x.
- We recursively sort ys and zs, and combine the two parts and pivot to create a sorted list. We will use list concatenation (++) to do this.

At the outset, the implementation looks like an exact qsort. However, a closer look reveals that we use the filter function to partition the elements in the list. The filter function is an $O(n)$ function. In the worst case, the performance of our algorithm will be $O(n^2)$, a far cry from the qsort specifications.

There's more...

You might have noticed the lack of random access in the list. This is true for many functional collections in Haskell. Even if you have random access, the persistence in Haskell means that we cannot modify the element in place without sacrificing purity. Hence, it can be seen that at times, the functional algorithms are a tad bit slower than their imperative counterparts. However, designed carefully, we can almost always match the performance of imperative language with the elegance of functional programming.

Implementing merge sort

In this recipe, we will implement merge sort. The merge sort that we are implementing is *bottoms-up* merge sort. In bottoms-up merge sort, we start by sorting pairs of elements in the list. Then, gradually, we start merging them in pairs, until we have only one left.

Getting ready

Use Stack to create a new project, merge-sort, with the simple template and build it, after changing the directory to the project folder:

```
> stack new merge-sort simple
> stack build
```

How to do it...

1. Open src/Main.hs; we will implement merge sort here.
2. We will start with the implementation of two utility functions; group2 and merge.
3. The group2 function is used to divide the input list in pairs. We will ensure that the pairs are sorted in the result. A single element is considered sorted:

```
-- Group elements in groups of twos, but when we group it we keep
them
-- sorted.
group2 :: Ord a => [a] -> [[a]]
group2 [] = []
-- A single element is already sorted.
group2 (x:[]) = [[x]]
```

```
-- Create groups of two and sort them
group2 (x:y:xs) = (sortPair x y) : group2 xs
where
  sortPair x y | x >= y    = y : x : []
               | otherwise = x : y : []
```

4. The `merge` function is used to merge two input lists. It is assumed that the input lists are already sorted. While merging, we look at the elements of two input lists one by one, and put them in correct order.

```
-- Assume that two lists are sorted, and merge them in the
increasing
-- order.
merge :: Ord a => [a] -> [a] -> [a]
merge [] ys = ys   -- If one of the input is empty, the other
list is the result.
merge xs [] = xs
merge (x:xs) (y:ys)   -- Compare heads of inputs while merging.
Continue recursively
| x >= y    = y : merge (x:xs) ys
| otherwise = x : merge xs (y:ys)
```

5. We will continue merging until we have only one list left. We will use the worker pattern for recursion. We will implement an internal function `mergeStep'` to merge adjacent lists:

```
mergeSort :: Ord a => [a] -> [a]
mergeSort xs = mergeSort' (group2 xs)
where
  mergeSort' :: Ord a => [[a]] -> [a]
  mergeSort' [] = []
  mergeSort' (xs:[]) = xs
  mergeSort' xss = mergeSort' (mergeStep' xss)
  mergeStep' :: Ord a => [[a]] -> [[a]]
  mergeStep' [] = []
  mergeStep' (xs:[]) = [xs]
  mergeStep' (xs:ys:xss) = (merge xs ys) : mergeStep' xss
```

6. Test the implementation:

```
main :: IO ()
main = do
let input = [5,2,3,1,7,9,8,4,6,0]
sorted = mergeSort input
putStrLn $ "input: " ++ (show input)
putStrLn $ "sorted: " ++ (show sorted)
```

7. Run the program, and check the output:

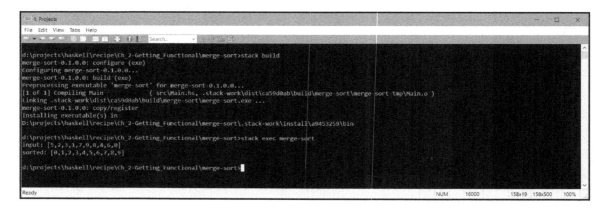

How it works...

The `mergeSort` function is implemented in terms of a worker function `mergeSort'`. This function is given a grouped list. This grouped list is a pairwise sorted list of lists created from input using the function `group2`. If `mergeSort'` receives an empty list, or a list with a single element (single list inside a list), then it returns it as a result.

If `mergeSort'` receives a lists of list that contains more than one list, then it calls `mergeStep'` to pairwise merge adjacent lists to create another list of lists.

This can be shown graphically as follows:

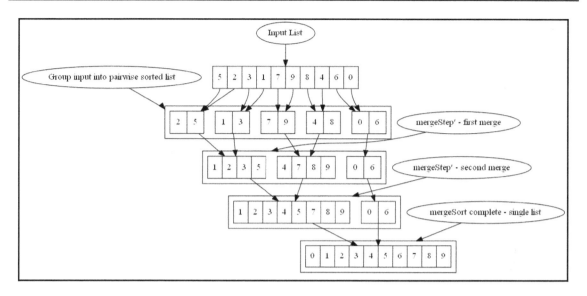

Implementing Eratosthenes Sieve

In this recipe, we will look at a prime number calculator called **Eratosthenes Sieve**. It is an old algorithm for finding prime numbers. The prime numbers are found by crossing out composite numbers. The sieve works as follows:

1. Start with 2, a known prime. Strike out all the numbers that are multiples of 2.
2. Start with the next unmarked number, which will be the next prime (since it is not divided by any prime before). Repeat the procedure of marking all the multiples.
3. Repeat the procedure.

For more information, visit https://en.wikipedia.org/wiki/Sieve_of_Eratosthenes.

Getting ready

Create a new project, eratosthenes, using the simple Stack template. Change into the project directory and build it:

```
stack new eratosthenes simple
stack build
```

How to do it...

1. Open `src/Main.hs`; we will add our prime number generator here.

2. We will start with 2 as the initial prime number and continue with only odd numbers; this will remove all the factors of 2.

3. We will assume that there are infinite prime numbers. We can write a list of primes as follows:

```
primes :: [Integer]
primes= 2 : filterMultiples allMultiples [3,5..]
where
   allMultiples = mergeMultiples $ map multiples primes
   multiples i = map (i*) [i..]
```

Here, `allMultiples` are all multiples of all the primes; `filterMultiples` will weed out all those multiples from the list of odd numbers `[3,5..]`. All multiples are found out by lazily going over the primes that we are calculating and finding multiples of each.

4. We need to implement `filterMultiples` to weed out composites, `merge` to merge two list of multiples, and `mergeMultiples` to recursively merge all multiples of primes:

```
filterMultiples :: Ord a => [a] -> [a] -> [a]
filterMultiples (f:fs) (x:xs) | f < x       = filterMultiples fs
(x:xs)
   | f > x       = x : filterMultiples (f:fs) xs
   | otherwise = filterMultiples fs xs

merge :: Ord a => [a] -> [a] -> [a]
merge (x:xs) (y:ys) | x < y      = x : merge xs      (y:ys)
               | x > y      = y : merge (x:xs) ys
               | otherwise = x : merge xs      ys

mergeMultiples :: Ord a => [[a]] -> [a]
mergeMultiples ((x:xs):xss) = x : merge xs (mergeMultiples xss)
```

5. Finally, we can test our prime numbers by checking the 1000th prime number (https://en.wikipedia.org/wiki/List_of_prime_numbers#The_first_1000_prime_numbers):

```
main :: IO ()
main = do
let prime1k = take 1000 primes
```

```
prime1kth = prime1k !! 999
putStrLn $ "1000th prime number is " ++ (show prime1kth)
```

6. If you build the project and run it, then you should see the 1000th prime number:

How it works...

The preceding algorithm is inspired by Richard Bird's list-based algorithm for the sieve. The algorithm carefully uses laziness, recursion, and infinite lists to create an infinite list of prime numbers. The following diagram will help you visualize the algorithm:

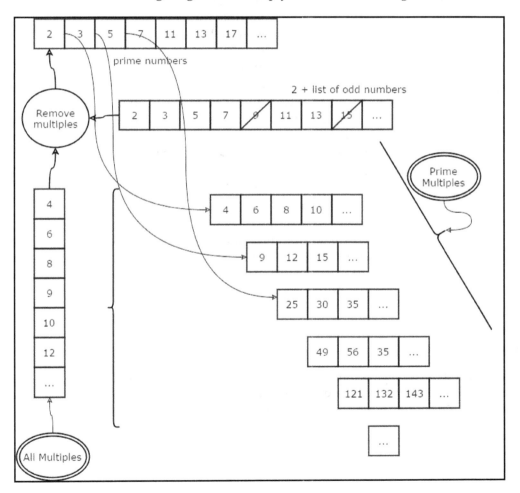

In the implementation, we carry out following steps:

- We will start with a prime 2. Then we construct an infinite list of primes 2--
  `filterMultiples allMultiples [3,5..]`. The
  `filterMultiples` function remove all the multiples of primes from the infinite
  list of odd numbers.
- The `allMultiples` function is interesting; it lazily creates a list of multiples for
  each prime number currently in the sieve and merges them. Notice the following
  points in the implementation:
  - We will take advantage of this laziness and use the fact that the
    first number is already calculated (it is the number 2). We will use
    this number to find multiples of 2 (4, 6, 8...). We will also use the
    fact that the first element of the multiples list will always be less
    than the first element of the remaining multiples. This is because
    we are filtering with primes, which are arranged in the increasing
    order (2, 3, 5..), and the first multiple of the ith prime will always be
    less than the $(i+1)^{th}$ prime. This is shown in the diagram.
  - This simplifies the merging, as we always take the first multiple as
    the first element in the merged list of multiples and then resume
    with merging the remaining list. Merging is done recursively.
  - This helps in lazily defining prime numbers as we can take exactly
    one multiple of a single prime number before continuing with
    search for the next one.
  - The next prime number is found when we remove multiples from
    the list of odd numbers and reach a stage where every remaining
    multiple in the multiples list is greater than the element in the list
    of odd numbers. We will term this number as a prime number and
    thus, continue our quest for prime numbers.

There's more...

This version is inspired by Richard Bird's list-based implementation. For this
implementation and other implementations of prime number sieve, refer to `https://www.`
`cs.hmc.edu/~oneill/papers/Sieve-JFP.pdf`.

3
Defining Data

In this chapter, we will look at following recipes:

- Defining a product type
- Defining a sum type
- Defining a binary tree and traversing it
- Defining data with functions
- Using Maybe
- Using Either
- Working with type classes
- Working with Monoid

Introduction

In the last chapter, we looked at functions, recursions, and higher order functions. In this chapter, we will look at another important aspect of the Haskell language. The data types in Haskell are very expressive and are used to express very intuitive data structures. We have seen that Haskell works by reducing or computing the values from expressions (which are formed by applying functions to values and so on). For each value, there is some type associated with it. In fact, we can also say that each type represents a collection or a set of values.

In this chapter, we will look at basic algebraic types. The term **algebraic** type came from the association between the values of a type and algebraic operations such as sum and product. We will also look at recursively defined types, where the type is included in the definition of the type itself. We will also look at parametric types. Moreover, we will look at two often used types in Haskell (`Maybe` and `Either`).

Finally, we will introduce the concept of type class. We will explain the very basic classes in Haskell, which are `Show`, `Eq`, `Ord`, and `Read`. We will also show how we can create an instance of a `monoid`, another very useful type class.

Defining a product type

In this recipe, we will look at product types. We will define simple data types with two parameters, and then will do different experiments with it.

Getting ready

Create a new project called `product-type` using the `simple` Stack template:

```
stack new product-type simple
```

Change the working directory to product-type.

How to do it...

1. Open `src/Main.hs` for editing.
2. Add the following data definitions for product types:

```
data Product1 = Product1 Bool deriving Show
data Product2 = Product2 Bool Bool deriving Show
data Product3 a = Product3 a Bool deriving Show
data Product4 a b = Product4 a b deriving Show
```

3. Change the `main` function to use the product types defined earlier to create instances, and print their values:

```
main :: IO ()
main = do
putStrLn "Product1: Simple product type"
putStrLn $ show $ Product1 True
putStrLn $ show $ Product1 False

putStrLn "Product2: Product type with two fields"
putStrLn "Product2 has two boolean fields. Each one can take
 two values each"
putStrLn $ show $ Product2 True True
putStrLn $ show $ Product2 True False
putStrLn $ show $ Product2 False True
putStrLn $ show $ Product2 False False

putStrLn "Product3: Product type with two fields, one
    parametric (Int)"
putStrLn "Cardinality of Product3 is cardinality of Int
    multipled by two"
putStrLn $ "which is " ++ (show (2 * (fromIntegral (maxBound ::
    Int) - fromIntegral (minBound :: Int) + 1)))
let product3 = Product3 10 True :: Product3 Int
putStrLn $ show product3

putStrLn "Product4: Product type parametrized by two types (Int
    Bool)"
putStrLn "Hence is equivalent to Product3 in these parameters"
putStrLn $ show $ (Product4 10 True :: Product4 Int Bool)
```

4. Build and run the project:

```
stack build
stack exec -- product-type
```

You should see the following output:

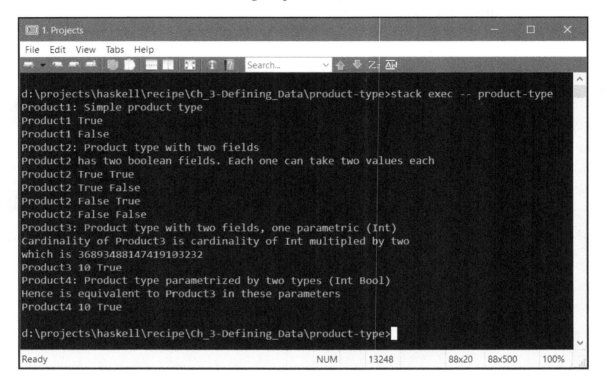

How it works...

1. We defined `Product1` with one data constructor `Product1 :: Bool ->`
   `Product1`. How many values can we construct for `Product1`? Since it takes Bool,
   it can have two values `Product1 True` and `Product1 False`. This is the
   simplest product type that we have defined.

2. Next, we defined a data type `Product2`. `Product2`'s constructor takes two Bool values. For `Product2`, we can construct four values. Please refer to the following table:

Product2 fields	Bool	Bool
Product2	True	True
Product2	True	False
Product2	False	True
Product2	False	True

Note that we have four values for `Product2`. Also, note that we constructed `Product2` by adding one more `Bool` field to `Product1`. For each possible value of `Product1`, we have two possible values for the added field in `Product2`. Hence, the total number of possible values for `Product2` is equal to the product of possible values for each field that it has. This is why a data type with multiple fields is called a **product type**.

3. Next, we created a parametric data type `Product3`. `Product3` takes a data type a and has an additional Bool field. In the example, we constructed an instance of `Product3 Int`. This type has two fields, one of type `Int` and another of type `Bool`. We already know that `Bool` has only two possible values. To find the possible values of `Int`, we used `maxBound` and `minBound` to get maximum and minimum values of `Int` (we have to specify type for `maxBound`, and `minBound`, for example, `minBound::Int`, to signify that we are interested in the minimum bounding value for type `Int`). Maximum `Int` value is 9223372036854775807, and minimum `Int` value is -9223372036854775808. Hence, cardinality of `Int` is 18446744073709551616. Since for each `Int` value we can have two `Bool` values, the total number of possible values for `Product3` is twice the amount, that is, 36893488147419103232.

4. For `Product4`, the type takes two type arguments, a and b. In the example, we use `Int` and `Bool` as type arguments. Hence, the number of possible values for `Product4 Int Bool` is same as `Product3 Int`.

Defining a sum type

The sum types are equivalent to variant (or union in C). However, sum type in Haskell is much more than that. It is also called **tagged union**. The simplest sum type is Bool, which can take two values True and False. In this recipe, we will define simple sum types and use them in our example.

Getting ready

Create a project called sum-type using the Stack simple template:

```
stack new sum-type simple
```

How to do it...

1. Open src/Main.hs for editing.

2. Add the following data type for representing the days in a week:

```
data Days = Sunday | Monday | Tuesday | Wednesday | Thursday |
Friday | Saturday deriving Show
```

3. Now, add the Variant type that takes five type arguments:

```
data Variant a b c d e = Variant0
                | Variant1 a
                | Variant2 b
                | Variant3 c
                | Variant4 d
                | Variant5 e
                deriving Show
```

4. Now, use the preceding types in our main function:

```
main :: IO ()
main = do
putStrLn $ "Sum Type 1 : Showing days of the week"
putStrLn $ show [Sunday, Monday, Tuesday, Wednesday, Thursday,
Friday, Saturday]
putStrLn $ "Days type can have only 7 values"
putStrLn ""
putStrLn "Sum Type 2 : Variant with 5 possible data
constructors"
```

```
putStrLn "Each constructor contribues number of possible
values"
putStrLn "of types a, b, c, d, e or f"

let v0 = Variant0 :: Variant Int Float Double Char String
    v1 = Variant1 10 :: Variant Int Float Double Char String
    v2 = Variant2 11.0 :: Variant Int Float Double Char String
    v3 = Variant3 12.0 :: Variant Int Float Double Char String
    v4 = Variant4 'A' :: Variant Int Float Double Char String
    v5 = Variant5 "Haskell" :: Variant Int Float Double Char String

putStrLn "Showing all variants"
putStrLn $ show [v0,v1,v2,v3,v4,v5]
putStrLn "Variant0 has only one value, however its type is
completely qualified"
```

5. Now, build and run the project:

```
stack build
stack exec -- sum-type
```

The following output should be generated:

```
● ● ●                    🖿 sum-type — -bash — 94×14
[sum-type $ stack exec -- sum-type
Sum Type 1 : Showing days of the week
[Sunday,Monday,Tuesday,Wednesday,Thursday,Friday,Saturday]
Days type can have only 7 values

Sum Type 2 : Variant with 5 possible data constructors
Each constructor contribues number of possible values
of types a, b, c, d, e or f
Showing all variants
[Variant0,Variant1 10,Variant2 11.0,Variant3 12.0,Variant4 'A',Variant5 "Haskell"]
Variant0 has only one value, however its type is completely qualified
sum-type $ ▊
```

How it works...

1. First, we defined a data type called Days. It has seven alternative values (Sunday to Saturday). The Days type can take, at the most, seven values.

2. Next, we defined a data type called `Variant`. The `Variant` data type is classified by five type arguments. In the example, we used `Int`, `Float`, `Double`, `Char`, and `String`. The data type defines constructors `Variant1` ... `Variant5` with a field each corresponding to one type. At the same type, we also have a constructor `Variant0`, which does not have a field at all. Hence, the number of possible types that `Variant` can take is the sum of all possible values that each type can take. Additionally, we have to add one value for `Variant0`.

3. Since the number of possible values is the sum of all alternatives, this is called **sum type**.

4. Note that sum type is not generally found in languages such as C/C++ and so on. The union is the closest that one can have to sum type in these languages.

Defining a binary tree and traversing it

In this recipe, we will look at a data type that is recursively defined. We will define a binary tree and then explore functions to traverse it.

Getting ready

Create a new project `binary-tree-traverse` using the `simple` Stack template. Change into this directory:

```
stack new binary-tree-traverse simple
```

How to do it...

1. Open `src/Main.hs`; we will be using this file for our recipe.
2. Define a binary tree data type:

```
data BinaryTree a = Leaf
  | BinaryTree { left :: BinaryTree a
               , val :: a
               , right :: BinaryTree a }
  deriving Show
```

3. Write the `helper` functions `empty`, `singleton`, and `node` to create an empty tree and a tree with a single node, and compose the two trees with a value to create a new tree:

```
empty :: BinaryTree a
empty = Leaf

singleton :: a -> BinaryTree a
singleton x = BinaryTree Leaf x Leaf

node :: BinaryTree a -> a -> BinaryTree a -> BinaryTree a
node l x r = BinaryTree { left = l, val = x, right = r }
```

4. Define in-order depth first traversal for the binary tree:

```
dfTraverse :: BinaryTree a -> [a]
dfTraverse Leaf = []
dfTraverse tree = dfTraverse (left tree) ++ [val tree] ++
dfTraverse (right tree)
```

5. Now, define breadth first traversal for the binary tree:

```
bfTraverse :: BinaryTree a -> [a]
bfTraverse Leaf = []
bfTraverse tree = bfTraverse1 [tree] [] []
where
  bfTraverse1 [] [] xs = reverse xs
  bfTraverse1 [] q xs = bfTraverse1 (reverse q) [] xs
  bfTraverse1 (Leaf:ts) q xs = bfTraverse1 ts q xs
  bfTraverse1 (t:ts) q xs = bfTraverse1 ts (right t:left t:q)
  (val t:xs)
```

6. Create a sample tree.

```
sampleTree :: BinaryTree Int
sampleTree = node l 1 r
where
  l = node ll 2 rl
  r = node lr 3 rr
  ll = node lll 4 rll
  rl = node lrl 5 rrl
  lr = node llr 6 rlr
  rr = node lrr 7 rrr
  lll = singleton 8
  rll = singleton 9
  lrl = singleton 10
  rrl = singleton 11
```

```
llr = singleton 12
rlr = singleton 13
lrr = singleton 14
rrr = singleton 15
```

7. Now use the sample tree for traversal. Do both breadth first as well as depth first traversal.

```
main :: IO ()
main = do
let tree = sampleTree
inorder = dfTraverse tree
bfs = bfTraverse tree
putStrLn "In order depth first traversal"
print inorder
putStrLn "Breadth first traversal"
print bfs
```

8. Build and run the project:

```
stack build
stack exec -- binary-tree-traverse
```

9. The output should print the following:

How it works...

1. The binary tree can either be empty (no value, no children) or can have exactly two child trees and a value.
2. The binary tree is parameterized by a type argument. The type argument denotes the type of the value that each node stores.

3. The binary tree is defined as a sum type. Following are the alternatives for the sum type:
    1. The empty tree is denoted by data constructor `Leaf`.
    2. The binary tree node is a product type (`BinaryTree`) implemented using record syntax, with the following fields:
        - **left**: This denotes the left binary tree
        - **val**: This indicates the value of the node
        - **right**: This denotes the right binary tree
    3. Since `left` and `right` are of type `BinaryTree`, this is a recursively defined data type.

4. The `helper` function *empty* creates an empty tree, which is just a leaf without any value `BinaryTree Leaf`.

5. The `singleton` function creates a `node` with two empty child trees.

6. The `node` function takes in `left` and `right` binary trees, along with a value.

7. It is also possible to create values of `BinaryTree` by directly using data constructors. However, many a times it is easier to use `helper` functions such as the ones we defined.

8. The sample tree that is created in the main function looks like this:

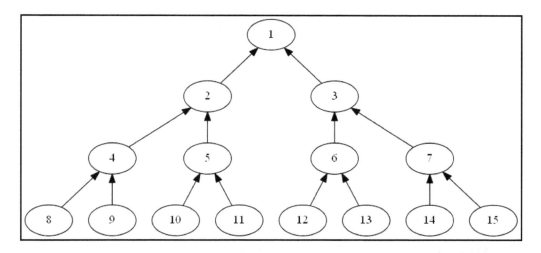

9. The recipe defines two traversals--**depth first** traversal and **breadth first** traversal. Both traversal functions return a list of values stored in the tree in the order of their traversal.

10. The depth first traversal function defines in-order depth traversal. In the in-order depth first traversal following the steps are as follows:
    1. The left tree is traversed.
    2. Then, the parent node is visited.
    3. Then, the left tree is traversed again.

11. The depth first traversal function `dfTraverse` uses two cases:
    1. The tree is empty (that is, it has value `Leaf`). In this case the empty list is returned, as there is no value to visit.
    2. The tree has a left tree, a value, and a right tree. In this case, we recursively call traversal for left tree and then append to it the value of the node and the result of right node traversal. Can you define pre-order and post-order traversal?

    If we traverse the sample tree shown in the preceding diagram, we should get the list
    [8,4,9,2,10,5,11,1,12,6,13,3,14,7,15].

12. In the breadth first traverse, all the node values at the same level are visited before visiting the nodes in the next level.

13. The breadth first traversal function `bfTraverse` is implemented using a worker pattern. It uses the worker, `bfTravers1`:
    1. `bfTravers1` assumes that it is already traversing a set of nodes in the breadth first order at a certain level.
    2. As it visits nodes, it collects both children and pushes them in a queue.
    3. When the input set of nodes is exhausted, the queue is reversed and passed to `bfTraverse1` in a recursion. The queue reversal is required, as the queue is implemented as a list, and the newest element is added and removed from the front of the list.
    4. The breadth first order for the sample tree, created in our recipe, should be as follows:
    [1,2,3,4,5,6,7,8,9,10,11,12,13,14,15]

Defining data with functions

So far, we looked at data types that take the values of other data types (both `simple` or `complex`). Since Haskell functions are also treated as first-class values, we can also use functions in our data type definition. In this recipe, we will define two data types that use functions as one of the field.

The first data type encapsulates a function f :: a -> b, whereas the second data type is an interesting recursive structure.

Getting ready

Use the simple stack template to create a new project called data-type-with-function, and change into this directory:

```
stack new data-type-with-function simple
```

How to do it...

1. Open src/Main.hs for editing.

2. Add a new data type Func a b to represent the function f :: a -> b:

```
newtype Func a b = Func (a -> b)
```

3. Add a compose function. The compose function takes in two functions and composes them together by giving an output of the first function to the next one:

```
compose :: Func a b -> Func b c -> Func a c
compose (Func f) (Func g) = Func (g . f)
```

4. Now, add a apply function; this takes our data type Func and applies an argument to it:

```
apply :: Func a b -> a -> b
apply (Func f) a = f a
```

5. Now, define a data type called Fix; it takes a function as an argument and tries to recursively define it by applying itself to the function:

```
newtype Fix f = Fix (f (Fix f))
```

6. Now, define a type Ghost; it takes an argument. However, it does not use it in its definition:

```
data Ghost a = Ghost deriving Show
```

7. We will now use these types in the `main` function. We will define two functions—square, which squares a given number, and `sqrti`, which is the square root for an integer. We will wrap them in our `Func` data type and compose them. As a result of the application of the composition, we should get the same integer back.

8. Next, we will use the `Fix` data type in conjunction with `Ghost` to see how `Fix` recursively applies function f along with itself.

9. The `main` function should be written as follows:

```
main :: IO ()
main = do
  let square x = x * x
  sqrti = floor . sqrt . fromIntegral

  let squareF = Func square
  sqrtF = Func sqrti

  let idF = compose squareF sqrtF

  putStrLn "Composing square and square root functions"
  putStrLn "is an identity. Applying a value should not change
  it"
  print $ apply idF 3

  let x = Ghost
  y = Fix x
  Fix z = y

  putStrLn "Original value is "
  print x
  putStrLn "After fixing, "
  print z
```

10. Build and execute the project:

```
stack build
stack exec -- data-type-with-function
```

The output should look like this:

How it works...

1. The first data type Func takes two arguments, a and b. The data definition simply encapsulates it inside as Func (a -> b). Here, (a -> b) represents the function type that takes a as an argument and produces a value of type b.

2. The function compose simply extracts the functions encapsulated in Func a b and Func b c and composes them with the (.) function.

   > The function (.) is called **function composition**, and it is used to compose functions without having to specify. It can be simply defined as (.) g f x = g (f x). Also, note when we use function composition, we do not have to specify an argument to the function. This is called a **point-free** style of programming. At times, a point-free style may be clearer to understand.

3. The apply function extracts the function and applies an argument to it.

4. The Fix data type is interesting. It is recursive and special because it applies the type argument to itself in its definition. Look carefully at the data type in our usage of Fix at every step. Note that the type argument a that Fix needs is not a simple type. It is a type that needs another type argument to it. You can inspect this by running the following lines of code:

```
*Main> :i Fix
type role Fix nominal
newtype Fix (f :: * -> *) = Fix (f (Fix f))
-- Defined at src\Main.hs:13:1
```

5. The (f :: * -> *) data type in the GHCi output indicates that f is a type that needs another type as an input to it.

   First, we will define x as a binding to the type Ghost and create a value of Fix by applying x to it:

   ```
   let x = Ghost
   y = Fix x
   ```

6. Then, we will try to extract the field value in the definition of Fix, that is, the underlined part of the definition Fix f (Fix f). We can do that using the following code:

   ```
   let Fix z = y
   ```

7. Then, if we check the type of z, then we get the following output:

   ```
   *Main> :t z
   z :: Ghost (Fix Ghost)
   ```

   This can be surprising, but we can visually show this definition:

   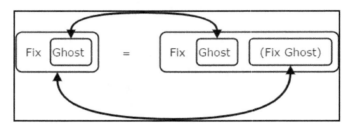

   The type Ghost that we passed to Fix is applied to itself, Fix Ghost. Thus, it produces a recursive type.

    The Fix type is inspired by its function counterpart fix :: (a -> a) -> a. It represents a fixed point and is a very useful function to understand recursion. For more information, you can visit https://en.wikibooks.org/wiki/Haskell/Fix_and_recursion.

8. Finally, the Ghost type looks curious too. It takes a type argument but does not use it in its definition. Hence, this is called a **Phantom Type**. Phantom Types are very useful in programs as we can use them to add a type annotation to our definition.

Using Maybe

Maybe is a sum type very often used to indicate a NULL value or nothing. In fact, it is a very type-safe way of representing a NULL value. Explicitly saying that we have either a value or nothing makes our life simpler during programming steps, which can fail, and we may not want to continue.

In this recipe, you will learn to use the Maybe data type.

Getting ready

Create a new project called using-maybe using the simple stack template. Change into the directory and build the solution:

```
stack new using-maybe simple
stack build
```

How to do it...

1. Open src/Main.hs. We will experiment in the main function in this file. Replace the main function with following content:

```
main :: IO ()
main = do
putStrLn "Using Maybe"
```

2. Continue in the same function. Start defining various values of Maybe. Maybe is a sum type that may contain a value. The data constructor Just takes the value, whereas the constructor Nothing represents the absence of any value. Define three instances of the Maybe value, representing integral values 10, 2, and 0:

```
let i = Just 10 :: Maybe Int
j = Just 2 :: Maybe Int
z = Just 0 :: Maybe Int
```

3. Note the indentation. Since it is part of the same function main, the indentation should match the putStrLn "Using Maybe" line.

4. Use the `isJust` function to check if the `Maybe` value does contain some value. Use `isNothing` to check the absence of any value in the `Maybe` data:

```
putStrLn $ "Does (Just 10) represent a value? " ++ (show $
isJust i)
putStrLn $ "Does (Nothing) represent a value? " ++ (show $
isJust Nothing)
putStrLn $ "Does (Nothing) is really Nothing? " ++ (show $
isNothing Nothing)
```

5. A singleton list is a list that contains a single element. The functions `listToMaybe` and `maybeToList` convert a singleton list to `Maybe` and `Maybe` to a singleton list, respectively. The empty list corresponds to `Nothing`, whereas the list with an element will put the the value of the element into `Maybe`:

```
putStrLn ""
putStrLn $ "Singleton List and Maybe interoperability"
putStrLn $ "Converting list [10] to Maybe : " ++ (show $
listToMaybe [10])
putStrLn $ "Converting empty list to Maybe (Nothing) : " ++
(show $ (listToMaybe [] :: Maybe Int))
putStrLn $ "Converting Maybe (Just 10) to list : " ++ (show $
maybeToList (Just 10))
putStrLn $ "Converting Maybe (Nothing) to list : " ++ (show $
maybeToList (Nothing :: Maybe Int))
```

6. Use function `maybe :: b -> (a -> b) -> Maybe a -> b`. The `Maybe` function takes a default value `b` and an function `(a -> b)`. If the `Maybe` value is `Nothing`, it uses the default value `b`. Otherwise, it uses the function `(a -> b)` to transform the `Maybe` value `a` to `b`:

```
putStrLn ""
putStrLn "Using default value for a transformation using
'maybe'"
putStrLn $ "Use NULL if Nothing, and convert a value to string
if Maybe holds a value"
let defaultNull = "NULL"
convertToString = maybe defaultNull show
null = convertToString Nothing
something = convertToString (Just 10)
putStrLn $ "Converting Nothing to String : " ++ null
putStrLn $ "Converting a value to String : " ++ something
```

7. Here, we will use the default value `NULL` and convert a `Maybe` value to `String`. If `Maybe` contains some value, it is converted to its string representation using `show`. Otherwise, `NULL` is printed.

8. Let's now look at using `Maybe` in an example to illustrate the usage of `Maybe`. Define a separate function `safeOperation`, which defines a safe binary operation. If a certain condition is met, then we will evaluate the result as `Nothing`. We will use it to represent division by zero in the function `safeDiv`:

```
safeOperation :: Num a => (a -> a -> Bool) -> (a -> a -> a) ->
Maybe a -> Maybe a -> Maybe a
-- If any of the input is Nothing, then the output is Nothing
safeOperation _ _ Nothing _ = Nothing
safeOperation _ _ _ Nothing = Nothing
-- If the condition is met, then the result is nothing.
safeOperation c _ (Just i) (Just j) | c i j = Nothing
-- Normally call the operation
safeOperation c op (Just i) (Just j) = Just (i `op` j)

-- Safe division, the condition is satisfied when denominator is
zero
safeDiv :: Maybe Int -> Maybe Int -> Maybe Int
safeDiv = safeOperation divCondition div
where
 divCondition _ 0 = True
 divCondition _ _ = False
```

9. Use the function `safeDiv` in the `main` function to check the result of division by zero. Append the following to the `main` function shown earlier. We will illustrate both legal division (that is, division by a non-zero number) and illegal division (that is, division by zero). When divided by zero, we should get `Nothing`:

```
putStrLn ""
putStrLn $ "Getting value from (Just 10) = " ++ (show $
fromJust i)
putStrLn $ "Safe Division - 10 / 2"
let safeAnswer1 = safeDiv i j
putStrLn $ "Answer is " ++ (show safeAnswer1)
putStrLn ""
putStrLn $ "Safe Division by Zero - 10/0"
let safeAnswer2 = safeDiv i z
putStrLn $ "Answer is " ++ (show safeAnswer2)
```

10. We can also define the safe division using the monadic do notation. Define the function `safeDiv1` separately in the file `src/Main.hs`:

```
safeDiv1 :: Maybe Int -> Maybe Int -> Maybe Int
safeDiv1 i j = do
  xi <- i
  xj <- j
  if 0 == xj
    then
    Nothing
  else
    return (xi `div` xj)
```

11. Note the use of `return` and `(<-)`. Use `safeDiv1` in the `main` function. Add the following lines to the `main` function:

```
putStrLn ""
putStrLn $ "We can also use - do notation"
let safeAnswer3 = safeDiv1 i z
putStrLn $ "Safe Division by Zero using do notation - 10 / 0 =
" ++ (show safeAnswer3)
```

12. Finally, use `mapMaybe`. This function is similar to `map`, except that it takes a function that produces the values of `Maybe`. All `Nothing` values are filtered out, and all remaining values are extracted in the list:

```
putStrLn ""
let evens = mapMaybe (\x -> if odd x then Nothing else (Just
  x)) [1..10]
putStrLn $ "Filtering out odd elements - mapMaybe (\\a -> if
  odd a then Nothing else (Just a)) [1..10] = " ++ (show evens)
```

13. In the preceding example, we will filter out odd numbers in the given input. For each odd value in the input list, we will produce `Nothing`; otherwise, we will just print `Just x` (where x is the input value).

14. Build the project and execute it:

```
stack build
stack exec -- using-maybe
```

15. You should see the following output:

```
●  ●  ●                          using-maybe — -bash — 106×30
Yogeshs-MBP:using-maybe yogeshsajanikar$ stack exec -- using-maybe
Using Maybe
Does (Just 10) represent a value? True
Does (Nothing) represent a value? False
Does (Nothing) is really Nothing? True

Singleton List and Maybe interoperability
Converting list [10] to Maybe : Just 10
Converting empty list to Maybe (Nothing) : Nothing
Converting Maybe (Just 10) to list : [10]
Converting Maybe (Nothing) to list : []

Using default value for a transforamtion using 'maybe'
Use NULL if Nothing, and convert a value to string if Maybe holds a value
Converting Nothing to String : NULL
Converting a value to String : 10

Getting value from (Just 10) = 10
Safe Division - 10 / 2
Answer is Just 5

Safe Division by Zero - 10/0
Answer is Nothing

We can also use - do notation
Safe Division by Zero using do notation - 10 / 0 = Nothing

Filtering out odd elements - mapMaybe (\a -> if odd a then Nothing else (Just a)) [1..10] = [2,4,6,8,10]
Yogeshs-MBP:using-maybe yogeshsajanikar$
```

How it works...

The data type `Maybe` is defined as follows:

```
data Maybe a = Just a
     | Nothing
```

This is a sum type, which either represents a value, using the `Just` data constructor, or `Nothing`. The various functions such as `isJust`, `isNothing`, `fromJust`, `listToMaybe`, and `maybeToList` are used to check or extract the values from `Maybe`.

The interesting function to note is `safeOperation`. This illustrates the main usage of `Maybe`. The `Maybe` value `Nothing` denotes a *failure* of some kind in an operation. As a result, all the remaining operations should produce `Nothing`. This saves us the effort of checking the result of an operation at every step. The safe operation signature is shown here:

```
safeOperation :: Num a => (a -> a -> Bool) -> (a -> a -> a) ->
Maybe a -> Maybe a -> Maybe a
```

The first argument (`a -> a -> Bool`) denotes a condition. If this condition is evaluated to `True`, then the result produced is `Nothing`. The second argument (`a -> a -> a`) denotes an actual operation that works on two inputs of type `a` and produces an output of type `a`. The third and fourth arguments are of the `Maybe` type. They are the actual arguments passed to the `safeOperation` function. If any one of these arguments equals `Nothing`, the result is `Nothing`. Otherwise, if the condition is not `True`, the second argument (`a -> a -> a`) is used to carry out the actual underlying operation.

Using this function, we can convert a binary operation such as division and convert it to safe operations. At any point of time, if the condition is met or if any of the input is `Nothing`, all the operations produced thereafter are `Nothing`.

We also used the `monadic` notation to represent the safe division. This is interesting. The `do` notation allows us to extract values of `Maybe` using (`<-`), and then, we use `return` to represent `Just`. However, we will reserve the explanation for the next chapter where we will discuss the use and implementation of doing notation in detail.

Using Either

Similar to `Maybe`, another data type that is used often in Haskell is `Either`. While `Maybe` decides to `map` something or nothing, `Either` goes with two types and keeps either of them. In this recipe, we will construct a safe division using the `Either` data type and will see how we can represent the error messages in a better way.

Getting ready

Use the following command to create a new project called `using-either` using the `simple` template:

```
stack new using-either simple
```

Change into the newly created project directory.

How to do it...

1. Open src/Main.hs.

2. Import the Data.Either module:

```
import Data.Either
```

3. Define safe division, handling the division by zero case:

```
safeDiv :: Either String Int -> Either String Int -> Either
String Int
safeDiv (Left e) _ = Left e   -- Any Left _ is an error, we
produce the same
safeDiv _ (Left e) = Left e   -- error as a result.
safeDiv (Right i) (Right j) | j == 0 = Left "Illegal Operation:
Division by Zero"
safeDiv (Right i) (Right j) = Right (i `div` j)
```

4. Use safe division in the main function to illustrate usage of Either:

```
main :: IO ()
main = do
let i = Right 10 :: Either String Int
j = Right 2 :: Either String Int
z = Right 0 :: Either String Int

putStrLn $ "Safe division : 10 / 2 = " ++ (show $ safeDiv i j)
putStrLn $ "Safe division : 10 / 0 = " ++ (show $ safeDiv i z)
```

5. Build and execute the project:

```
stack build
stack exec -- using-either
```

6. You should see the following output:

```
using-either$ stack exec — using-either
Safe division : 10 / 2 = Right 5
Safe division : 10 / 0 = Left "Illegal Operation: Division by Zero"
using-either$
```

How it works...

The `Either` data type has two data constructors and is defined as a sum type as follows:

```
data Either a b = Left a | Right b
```

In our recipe, we used `Either String Int`, where the right value is of the `Int` type and the left value is of the `String` type. In many practical examples, the `Left` value is used as an error value and the `Right` value is used as an intended result value.

In the function `safeDiv`, we stored the error value in `Left` as a `String` and stored the result in the `Right` value.

Like `Maybe`, `Either` appears in many libraries on package and is a popular choice to represent result values with error, if any.

Working with type classes

In this recipe, you will learn about type classes. The type classes provide a common behavior across data types. In this way, a type class abstracts the common behavior and can be implemented by a variety of data. One can relate type classes to *interface* in C# or C++.

So far, whenever we defined data types we derived the data types from the *Show* type class without providing any explicit implementation for the type. In such cases, the default implementation is provided by GHC. In this recipe, we will provide explicit implementation for the standard Haskell type classes `Show`, `Read`, `Enum`, `Eq`, and `Ord`.

Getting ready

Create a new project called `working-with-type-classes` using the `simple` stack template and change into the working directory:

```
stack new working-with-type-classes simple
```

How to do it...

1. Open `src/Main.hs` for editing. We will use this file for using type classes.

2. Define a data type `Month` to describe a month in a year:

```
data Month = January | February | March | April | May | June
    | July | August | September | October | November |
    December deriving Show
```

   Note that we have still used automatic derivation from `Show`. We will illustrate `Show` later in the recipe.

3. Next, implement the `Enum` class. The `Enum` class is responsible for generating a list of consecutive integers and expressions such as `[1..10]`. The `Enum` class provides this behavior by associating with `Integer`. Create an instance of the `Enum` class for the data type `Month`. Essentially, we need to implement two functions, `toEnum` and `fromEnum`, to convert from and to `Integers`:

```
instance Enum Month where
    toEnum 0 = January
    toEnum 1 = February
    toEnum 2 = March
    toEnum 3 = April
    toEnum 4 = May
    toEnum 5 = June
    toEnum 6 = July
    toEnum 7 = August
    toEnum 8 = September
    toEnum 9 = October
    toEnum 10 = November
    toEnum 11 = December
    toEnum n = toEnum $ n `rem` 12

    fromEnum January = 0
    fromEnum February = 1
    fromEnum March = 2
    fromEnum April = 3
    fromEnum May = 4
    fromEnum June = 5
    fromEnum July = 6
    fromEnum August = 7
    fromEnum September = 8
    fromEnum October = 9
    fromEnum November = 10
    fromEnum December = 11
```

4. Implement the `equality` type class for our data type `Month`. It gives an ability to check equality among the values of our data type `Month`. Define the function `(==)`. We will use the previous definition of `Enum` to convert the values to `Integer` and then compare them:

```
instance Eq Month where
m1 == m2 = fromEnum m1 == fromEnum m2
```

5. Now, implement the `Ord` type class. `Ord` stands for ordere, and it gives the ordering among the values of our the data type `Month`. We need to define a function `compare` and return the values of data type `Ordering`. We will again use the fact that we have already implemented the `Enum` type class and that `Integers` already implement the `Ord` type class. Hence, we will convert the values of `Month` to integers and then invoke its `compare` method:

```
instance Ord Month where
 m1 `compare` m2 = fromEnum m1 `compare` fromEnum m2
```

Note how we implemented the `compare` function using the in-fix notation.

6. So far we have implemented a data type (in this, and earlier recipes) which uses auto implementation for `Show` provided by the compiler, GHC. Now, we will implement a data type where we provide explicit implementation for `Show` and `Read`. Implement a data type, `RoseTree`, which is a n-ary tree.

```
data RoseTree a = RoseTree a [RoseTree a]
```

7. Now, implement the `Show` type class. For `Show`, we have to implement a function `show :: a -> String`:

```
toString :: Show a => RoseTree a -> String -> String
toString (RoseTree a branches) =
( "<<" ++) . shows a . ('[':) . branchesToString branches .
(']':) . ( ">>" ++)
where
 branchesToString [] r = r
 branchesToString (x:[]) r = branchesToString [] (toString x ""
  ++ r)
 branchesToString (x:xs) r = branchesToString xs (',' :
  toString x "" ++ r)
```

Use the preceding function to implement `Show`:

```
instance Show a => Show (RoseTree a) where
show tree = toString tree ""
```

8. Now, implement a type class `Read`. The `Read` class does the reverse of the type class `Show`; it reads the `String` value returned by `Show` and converts it back to a value of a type. Here, we will implement an instance of type class for `RoseTree`:

```
instance Read a => Read (RoseTree a) where
readsPrec prec ('<':'<':s) =
 case readsPrec prec s of
[(a,t)] -> case readList t of
[(as,ts)] -> case ts of
('>':'>':ss) -> [(RoseTree a as, ss)]
  _ -> []
  _ -> []
  _ -> []
readsPrec prec _ = []

readList xs =
 let readList' ('[':ys) rs =
      case readsPrec 0 ys of
       [(r,zs)] -> readList' zs (r:rs)
       _ -> readList' ys rs

 readList' (',':ys) rs =
      case readsPrec 0 ys of
       [(r,zs)] -> readList' zs (r:rs)
       _ -> []

 readList' (']':ys) rs = [(rs,ys)]
 readList' _ _ = []

 in readList' xs []
```

9. Now, use the implementation in the `main` function to use the preceding type classes:

```
main :: IO ()
main = do
putStrLn "Enumerating months"
putStrLn $ show [January ..December]
putStrLn "Enumerating odd months"
putStrLn $ show [January,March .. December]
putStrLn $ "Equating months, January with itself : "
++ (show $ January == January)
++ " and January with February : "
++ (show $ January == February)
putStrLn $ "Using /= function"
putStrLn $ "Not equating months, January with itself : "
++ (show $ January /= January)
++ " and January with February : "
++ (show $ January /= February)
putStrLn $ "Comparing months, January with itself : "
++ (show $ January `compare` January)
++ " and January with February : "
++ (show $ January `compare` February)

putStrLn ""
putStrLn "Creating a tree"

let singleton = RoseTree 10 []
tree = RoseTree 10 [RoseTree 13 [RoseTree 11 []], RoseTree 7
[], RoseTree 5 [RoseTree 3 []]]

putStrLn ""
putStrLn $ "Showing singleton tree : " ++ show singleton
putStrLn $ "Showing tree : " ++ show tree

putStrLn ""
putStrLn $ "Read what you show -- show (read (show tree) )"
putStrLn $ "Singleton Tree - " ++ show (read (show singleton) ::
RoseTree Int)
putStrLn $ "Tree - " ++ show (read (show tree) :: RoseTree Int)
```

10. Build and run the application:

```
stack build
stack exec -- working-with-type-classes
```

11. The output should look like this:

```
● ● ●                          working-with-type-classes — -bash — 119×20
working-with-type-classes$ stack exec -- working-with-type-classes
Enumerating months
[January,February,March,April,May,June,July,August,September,October,November,December]
Enumerating odd months
[January,March,May,July,September,November]
Equating months, January with itself : True and January with February : False
Using /= function
Not equating months, January with itself : False and January with February : True
Comparing months, January with itself : EQ and January with February : LT

Creating a tree

Showing singleton tree : <<10[]>>
Showing tree : <<10[<<5[<<3[]>>]>>,<<7[]>>,<<13[<<11[]>>]>>]>>

Read what you show -- show (read (show tree) )
Singleton Tree - <<10[]>>
Tree - <<10[<<5[<<3[]>>]>>,<<7[]>>,<<13[<<11[]>>]>>]>>
working-with-type-classes$
```

How it works...

Type classes provide a very good abstraction for defining common behavior across data types. For example, the Eq type class is defined as follows:

```
class Eq a where
  (==) :: a -> a -> Bool
  (/=) :: a -> a -> Bool
```

The preceding type class defines a set of behavior for type a. The behavior is a set of functions. The Eq class specifies two functions, equality (==) and non-equality (/=). Both functions take two arguments of type a and return Bool.

The standard Haskell provides definition for both (==) and (/=) as follows:

```
  x == y = not (x /= y)   -- Note the definition of (==) by in-fix
notation.
  x /= y = not (x == y)
```

You can see that the behavior of equality is defined in terms of non-equality and vice versa. To be able to provide a meaningful definition for our data type, it should be sufficient to provide definition for either `(==)` or `(/=)`, as the default definition then would call another operator. In our case, we will provide the definition for `(==)` by converting the value to `Int` using the `Enum` class. The definition of `Eq` requires the creation of instance as follows:

```
instance Eq Month where
   (==) month1 month2 = (fromEnum month1) == (fromEnum month2)
```

The definition of `Show` and `Read` needs more attention. `Show` needs a function `show :: a -> String`. The string concatenation function `(++)` is proportional to the size of the string on the left-hand side, and hence is not efficient. To alleviate this problem, we will write a function `toString :: a -> String -> String`. It uses the second argument to accumulate the values converted to string and is similar to a worker pattern. The `Read` class similarly needs a definition of `readsPrec`. The `readsPrec` returns the type `ReadS`, which is equivalent to `String -> [(a, String)]`. The input is the `String` representation of the data type, and the result value is a singleton list (list with only one item), with a tuple. The result tuple contains the value of the data type and remaining string (after converting to the value). This allows us to continue parsing using the remaining tree. In the definition of the `Read` instance for `RoseTree`, we will define a function `readsPrec`, which starts by scanning the string for initial <<, which marks the start of `RoseTree`. Also, note the instance of `Read` for `RoseTree`:

```
instance Read a => Read (RoseTree a) where
```

This indicates that the `Read` instance of `RoseTree` a is defined only if the `Read` instance for a is also defined.

Working with Monoid

Monoid is an important and very useful type class. A Monoid assumes two behaviors:

1. There is a default or empty value of the data type.
2. Given two values of the data type, they can be combined to create a single value.

The simplest example of a Monoid is `Integer`. We can define an empty value of an `Integer` as 0. We can then use `addition` as an operation to combine two `Integers`. In this recipe, we will define a data type `Option` and define an instance for Monoid.

Getting ready

Create a new project called `working-with-monoid` with the `simple` template using Stack:

```
stack new working-with-monoid simple
```

Change into the newly created project directory.

How to do it...

1. Start editing `src/Main.hs`. Add `import Data.Monoid` at the top. This module contains the definition of the `Monoid` type class.

2. Define a data type `Option`. The data contains a Boolean field and a list of `String`:

```
data Option = Option { boolOption :: Bool, selections ::
[String] }
    deriving Show
```

3. Define the instance of `Monoid`. The `Monoid` class needs to define at minimum two functions, `mempty` and `mappend`:

```
instance Monoid Option where
mempty = Option False []
(Option b1 s1) `mappend` (Option b2 s2) = Option (b1 || b2) (s1
++ s2)
```

4. Use the `Option` data type and its `Monoid` instance in the `main` function:

```
main :: IO ()
main = do
putStrLn "Define default options"
let defaultOptions = mempty :: Option
putStrLn (show defaultOptions)
let option1 = defaultOptions `mappend` (Option True [])
  option2 = option1 `mappend` (Option False ["haskell"])
  option3 = option2 `mappend` (Option True ["cookbook"])

putStrLn $ "Adding True flag - " ++ show option1
putStrLn $ "Adding False flag, and selection \"haskell\" - "
++ show option2
putStrLn $ "Adding True flag, and selection \"cookbook\" - "
++ show option3
```

```
putStrLn $ "Contatenating all options"
putStrLn $ "Concatenation Result - "
  ++ show (mconcat [defaultOptions, option1, option2 ])
```

5. Build and execute the project:

```
stack build
stack exec -- working-with-monoid
```

6. You should see the following output:

```
● ● ●                        working-with-monoid — -bash — 119×14
working-with-monoid$ stack exec -- working-with-monoid
Define default options
Option {boolOption = False, selections = []}
Adding True flag - Option {boolOption = True, selections = []}
Adding False flag, and selection "haskell" - Option {boolOption = True, selections = ["haskell"]}
Adding True flag, and selection "cookbook" - Option {boolOption = True, selections = ["haskell","cookbook"]}
Contatenating all options
Concatenation Result - Option {boolOption = True, selections = ["haskell"]}
working-with-monoid$
```

How it works...

The Monoid class is defined as follows:

```
class Monoid a where
  mempty :: a
  mappend :: a -> a -> a
  mconcat :: [a] -> a
```

The mempty function defines a default value. The mappend function defines that as a result of combining two values of a, we will get a single value of type a. mconcat indicates that we can combine all the values in the list to produce a single value of type a. To define a Monoid instance, we need to define at least mempty and mappend functions:

Laws of Monoid--The monoid instance should follow this law:

- **mappend x mempty** = x (Appending the default value should not change the value)

- **mappend mempty x** = x (Appending a value to the default value is the same as value)

- **mappend x (mappend y z)** = mappend (mappend x y) z (Associativity)

- **mconcat xs** = foldr mappend mempty (Contatenation is equivalent to foldr with mempty as default value and mappend as combining operation)

For the Option data type, we defined mempty to be an Option with a False Boolean flag and an empty list of selections. When appended, we used the OR operation to combine boolean values, and selection strings are appended. You can confirm that this follows all laws of Monoid.

Monoids are very useful and appear at many places while programming. In fact, sometimes, there can be more than two definitions for a Monoid. For example, we can define Monoid for an Integer by using the default value 0 and addition as the append operation, or by using default value 1 and multiplication as the append operation. In such a case, we can wrap the data type in another data type and provide an alternative Monoid instance.

4
Working with Functors, Applicatives, and Monads

In this chapter, we will look at the following recipes:

- Working with Functors
- Binary tree as Functor
- Working with Applicatives
- Binary tree as Applicative
- Working with monad
- List as monad
- Working with IO monad
- Writing INI Parser:
  - Parser as Functor
  - Parser as Applicative
  - Parser as monad
- Errors and exception handling

Introduction

We have worked on functions, higher order functions, and also worked with data types in Haskell. We have looked at functions such as map and filter in the context of the data type list. In many of these examples, we have taken a function that operates on data of type a and applied them in the context of the list of type a. Look at the following definition of map:

```
map :: (a -> b ) -> [a] -> [b]
```

You can clearly see that we have taken a function that operates on data type a and produces b, and we converted it to a function that takes a list of a and produces a list of b (map :: (a -> b) -> ([a] -> [b])). Instead of the list of a, we can think of some parametric data type T a. Now, we can rewrite the declaration of map as follows:

```
map :: (a -> b) -> T a -> T b
```

In short, the preceding definition of map applies to any data type T a, given a function that operates on a. But how do we define map? How does it know what to do to data type T a so that it produces T b?

In this chapter, we will seek answers to such questions. Through these questions, you will discover that not only do such definitions create a generic concept, but, at the same time, they abstract the inherent property of a data type such as T a to adapt a function, such as a -> b to itself.

Creation of such abstract structures inherently makes Haskell program easy to express and comprehend. The preceding map-like operation is a property of Functor. In this chapter, we will also see Applicatives and monads, which are few of the most used, important, and talked-about type classes in Haskell.

Working with Functors

In this recipe, we will use the Functor type class to perform some easy tasks. We will see how Functor resembles a map of a list by applying it to a variety of data structures.

How to do it...

1. Use Stack to create a new project `working-with-functors` with the `simple` template:

   ```
   stack new working-with-functors simple
   ```

2. Open `src/Main.hs` in the editor. We will use this file to demonstrate the usage of `Functors`.

3. After initial module definition for `Main`, import the module that includes the `Functor` type class:

   ```
   import Data.Functor
   ```

4. Define a function to square a number. We will use it to demonstrate application of this function over several data structures:

   ```
   -- Square a number
   square :: Num a => a -> a
   square x = x * x
   ```

5. `Functor f` is a type class that needs `fmap :: (a -> b) -> f a -> f a`. `Data.Functor` defines a `function <$>` synonymous to `fmap`. **List** defines an instance for `Functor`. We will use a square function to apply over a list. Add the following code to get a square of all the elements in the list:

   ```
   -- Mapping a list
   squareList :: Num a => [a] -> [a]
   squareList xs = square <$> xs
   ```

6. Similarly, we can use `<$>` to apply over `Maybe` and `Either` data types. `Maybe` allows a function to be applied if the data is represented with `Just`. Otherwise, a function is not applied. The `Either` instance for `Functor` allows a function to be applied only when the `Right` constructor is used:

   ```
   -- Mapping a Maybe
   squareMaybe :: Num a => Maybe a -> Maybe a
   squareMaybe x = square <$> x

   -- Mapping an Either
   squareEither :: Num a => Either c a -> Either c a
   squareEither x = square <$> x
   ```

7. Now, define a data type `Function a b` to represent a function `a -> b`. We will define this to be an instance of `Functor`. The `Functor` instance for this data type will create a composition by using the composition function `(.)`:

```
data Function a b = Function (a -> b)

instance Functor (Function a) where
f `fmap` (Function g) = Function (f . g)
```

8. Define another utility function `double` to double a given value. We will use it in the `main` function to demonstrate the function's composition:

```
double :: Num a => a -> a
double x = x + x
```

9. Now, add the `main` function where we will put to test all the preceding definitions:

```
main :: IO ()
main = do
 putStrLn "Mapping a list"
 putStrLn $ show $ squareList [1..10]

 putStrLn ""
 putStrLn "Mapping Maybe"
 putStrLn "Just 10 -> Just 100"
 putStrLn $ show $ squareMaybe (Just 10)

 putStrLn ""
 putStrLn "Nothing -> Nothing"
 putStrLn $ show $ squareMaybe Nothing

 putStrLn ""
 putStrLn "Mapping Either"
 putStrLn "Right 10 -> Right 100"
 putStrLn $ show $ squareEither (Right 10 :: Either String Int)
 putStrLn "Left String -> Left String"
 putStrLn $ show $ squareEither (Left "Left Value" ::
  Either String Int)

 let squareF = Function square
     doubleSquare = double <$> squareF

 -- Take the resultant function out of doubleSquare
 let Function dsq = doubleSquare
 putStrLn "Double the Square of X"
 print $ dsq 10
```

10. Build and run the project:

```
stack build
stack exec -- working-with-functors
```

11. The output should look like this:

```
working-with-functors — -bash — 120×20
working-with-functors $stack exec -- working-with-functors
Mapping a list
[1,4,9,16,25,36,49,64,81,100]

Mapping Maybe
Just 10 -> Just 100
Just 100

Nothing -> Nothing
Nothing

Mapping Either
Right 10 -> Right 100
Right 100
Left String -> Left String
Left "Left Value"
working-with-functors $
```

How it works...

The Data.Functor module defines the type class Functor. The Functor class is available from Prelude, but defined in Data.Functor. The Functor type class is defined as follows:

```
class Functor (f :: * -> *) where
   fmap :: (a -> b) -> f a -> f b
   (<$) :: a -> f b -> f a
   {-# MINIMAL fmap #-}
```

Minimal definition of Functor requires fmap to be defined.

The function fmap takes a function a -> b and takes a data type f parameterised by a. It then applies the function to the content (of the type a) to produce b, thus producing f b.

Working with Functors, Applicatives, and Monads

For example, we can take `Maybe a`, which is defined as `Just a | Nothing`. When we apply a function `a -> b` to `Maybe a` through `fmap`, we would like to apply only for the data in the constructor `Just a`, producing `Just b`. The data constructor `Nothing` need not be operated upon.

Definition of `Functor` for `Maybe` and `Either` is defined in the following diagram:

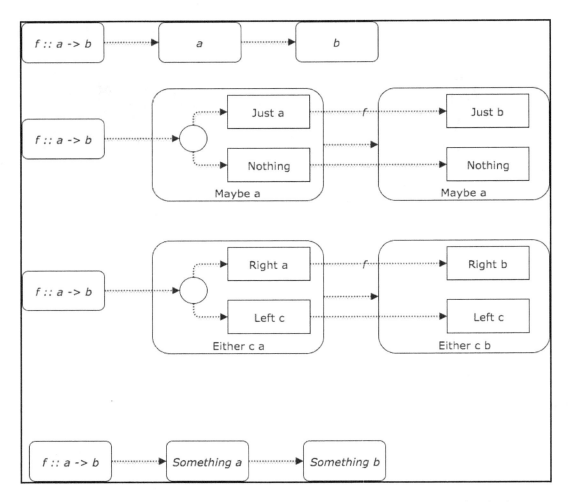

Note how `fmap` is defined for `Either c a`. The function `a -> b` is applied only for `Right a` constructor; the `Left c` constructor is left as it is. In the case of `List [a]`, `fmap` is the same as the function `map`, that is, the function is applied to each element of the list.

[112]

Thus, when we apply the `square` function to the `Maybe` and `Either` data types, the `square` function will apply only when the data types are defined with data constructors `Just` and `Right`, respectively.

Similarly, we defined the `Functor` definition for our data type as `Function a b`. The `fmap` definition takes in a function and composes it with the function pointed to by the data constructor `Function (a -> b)`.

The type class `Functor` also defines the function `(<$)`. This takes a value of type `a` and simply replaces `b` in `f b`. No definition is required for this function as it can be defined using the `const` function:

```
(<$) :: a -> f b -> f a
(<$)  a  fb = fmap  (const a) fb
```

Binary tree as Functor

In the last recipe, we have `Functor` instances defined for `Maybe`, `Either`, and `List`. We even defined the `Functor` instance. In this recipe, we will create a data type `Binary Tree` and define a `Functor` instance for it.

How to do it...

1. Create a new Haskell project `binary-tree-functor` using the `simple` Stack template:

   ```
   stack new binary-tree-functor simple
   ```

2. Open `src/Main.hs`. This is the file that will be used for our purposes.

3. After adding module definition for `Main`, add the following import:

   ```
   module Main where
   import Data.Functor
   ```

4. Define the `binary tree` and `utility` functions to create the `tree`:

   ```
   -- The tree can be empty (Leaf) or a node with a
   -- value, left and right trees.
   data Tree a = Leaf
       | Node (Tree a) a (Tree a)
       deriving (Show, Eq)
   ```

```
-- Create a tree given a value, left tree and a right tree
node :: Tree a -> a -> Tree a -> Tree a
node l x r = Node l x r

-- Induct a value into a new tree (node with empty left and
right trees)
singleton :: a -> Tree a
singleton x = Node Leaf x Leaf
```

5. Define an instance of a `Functor` for this `binary tree`. We have to consider two cases. The first one is what to do when the tree is empty. It is obvious that for an empty tree, the function application is vacuous and would return an empty tree. In the second case, we have a node with a value and two subtrees, that is, left tree and right tree. The function application for `Functor` will transform the value, and then we can use the definition of `fmap` recursively to transform the left and right subtrees as well:

```
instance Functor Tree where
fmap _ Leaf = Leaf
fmap f (Node left value right) =
Node (fmap f left) (f value) (fmap f right)
```

6. Write sample code to test our instance. First, we will create a sample integer tree:

```
sampleTree :: Tree Int
sampleTree = node l 1 r
where
    l = node ll 2 rl      -- l means left, and r means right tree
    r = node lr 3 rr
    ll = node lll 4 rll   -- ll means left subtree of a left node
    rl = node lrl 5 rrl   -- rl means right subtree of a left
    node.
    lr = node llr 6 rlr   -- and this naming convention continues
    rr = node lrr 7 rrr
    lll = singleton 8     -- we stop at lll. So lll is a
    singleton.
    rll = singleton 9     -- all subtrees from this level are
    empty
    lrl = singleton 10
    rrl = singleton 11
    llr = singleton 12
    rlr = singleton 13
    lrr = singleton 14
    rrr = singleton 15
```

7. In the `main` function, we will use the `show` function through `Functor` to convert a binary tree of integers to a binary tree of strings. We will then use the `read` function to convert this tree back to a tree of integers. To check that our function implementation is correct, we will check that the original integer tree is the same as the one that we get back after converting from strings:

```
main :: IO ()
main = do
let intTree = sampleTree
-- Convert tree of int to tree of strings
stringTree = fmap show intTree
-- We use read to convert it back to tree of ints
intTree1 = fmap (read :: String -> Int) stringTree
putStrLn "Original Tree"
print intTree
putStrLn "Tree of integers to Tree of strings"
print stringTree
putStrLn "Tree of strings converted back to Tree of integers is
same as original tree?"
print $ intTree == intTree1
```

8. Build and run the project:

```
stack build
stack exec -- binary-tree-functor
```

9. You will see the following output:

How it works...

In this recipe, we created an instance of Functor for the binary tree that we defined. When we create an instance of a Functor, we have to follow these laws of Functor:

Laws of Functor

An application of an identity function id should get the same data back:

fmap id == id

Applying two functions to the same data type in a sequence should be the same as the application of a composition of two functions:

fmap (p . q) == fmap p . fmap q

For the binary tree that we have defined, these laws are followed. If we apply the identity function id, then we apply it to the value in the node and subtrees. Since id does not change the value and we *preserve* the structure of the tree, an application of an identity function to our binary tree through fmap should get back the same tree. For the second law, we verified it through our sample code in the main function. The composition read . show is an identity function (since we are converting a data type to string and back). By successive application of fmap with show and read with tree we convert a tree of integers to tree of strings, and back again to a tree of integers. We check correctness of our implementation by checking that the original tree of integers and final tree of integers are indeed equal.

Working with Applicatives

An Applicative is a type class that is somewhere between a Functor and a Monad. An Applicative takes a Functor one step further. A Functor talks about application of a function a -> b to a data type f a, whereas an Applicative talks about application of a data type of a function f (a -> b) to a data type f a.

In this recipe, we will work with Maybe and Either data types, and see how we can work with Applicative instances in the context of these data types.

How to do it...

1. Create a new project `working-with-applicative` with the `simple` Stack template:

```
stack new working-with-applicative simple
```

2. Open `src/Main.hs` and add the following imports after the initial module definition. The `Applicative` type class is defined in the module `Control.Applicative`:

```
import Data.Functor
import Control.Applicative
```

3. We will use two operators, `Functor` application `<$>` (synonym for `fmap`) and `Applicative` application `<*>`. The `Applicative` function `<*>` is defined as `<*>` `:: f (a -> b) -> f a -> f b`. It takes a data type where values are functions of type `(a -> b)` and applies to a data type with values of type `a`, and gets back the data type with values of type `b`. In the first example, we will use a list:

```
-- Mapping a list
multiplyLists :: Num a => [a] -> [a] -> [a]
multiplyLists xs ys = (*) <$> xs <*> ys
```

In the next application of `Applicative`, we will use `Maybe`:

```
-- Mapping a Maybe
tupleMaybe :: Maybe a -> Maybe b -> Maybe (a,b)
tupleMaybe x y = (,) <$> x <*> y
```

We will now use `Either` in the context of `Applicative`. Here, instead of using `Functor`, we will use `pure` to induct a function into an `Applicative`:

```
-- Mapping an Either
addEither :: Num a => Either c a -> Either c a -> Either c a
addEither x y = pure (+) <*> x <*> y
```

4. We will now use the preceding functions in `main` with sample data:

```
main :: IO ()
main = do
  putStrLn "multiply lists"
  putStrLn $ show $ multiplyLists [1..3] [11..13]
  putStrLn ""
```

```
putStrLn "Tuple of maybes"
putStrLn "Just 10 -> Just \"String\" -> Just (10,\"String\")"
putStrLn $ show $ tupleMaybe (pure 10) (Just "String")
putStrLn ""
putStrLn "Just 10 -> Nothing -> Nothing"
putStrLn $ (show :: Maybe (Int,String) -> String) $
tupleMaybe (Just 10) Nothing
putStrLn ""
putStrLn "Adding Either"
putStrLn "Right 10 -> Right 100 -> Right 110"
putStrLn $ (show :: Either String Int -> String) $ addEither
(Right 10) (Right 100)

putStrLn "Left String -> Right 10 -> Left String"
putStrLn $ (show :: Either String Int -> String) $ addEither
(Left "String") (Right 10)
```

5. Build and run the project:

```
stack build
stack exec -- working-with-applicative
```

6. You should see the following output:

```
● ● ●                    working-with-applicaive — -bash — 96×18

working-with-applicaive $ stack exec -- working-with-applicaive
multiply lists
[11,12,13,22,24,26,33,36,39]

Tuple of maybes
Just 10 -> Just "String" -> Just (10,"String")
Just (10,"String")

Just 10 -> Nothing -> Nothing
Nothing

Adding Either
Right 10 -> Right 100 -> Right 110
Right 110
Left String -> Right 10 -> Left String
Left "String"
working-with-applicaive $
```

How it works...

The Applicative type class is defined as follows:

```
class Functor f => Applicative (f :: * -> *) where
  pure :: a -> f a
  (<*>) :: f (a -> b) -> f a -> f b
  (*>) :: f a -> f b -> f b
  (<*) :: f a -> f b -> f a
  {-# MINIMAL pure, (<*>) #-}
```

The minimal definition of an Applicative instance requires at least pure and <*> to be defined. The definition also implies that we can define an instance of an Applicative for f only if f is also an instance of a Functor.

The pure function takes a value and creates a data type. For example, in the context of List, Maybe, and Either, the pure function will fetch the following values:

```
pure 10 :: [Int] = [10]  -- in the context of List
pure 10 :: Maybe Int = Just 10 -- in the context of Maybe
pure 10 :: Either String Int = Right 10 -- in the context of Either
```

You can try the preceding code in the GHCi console for the project by running stack ghci in the project directory and trying out the preceding expressions.

Now we will look at the core of an Applicative, that is, the function <*>. As explained earlier, this function has the form as described:

```
<*> :: Applicative f => f (a -> b) -> f a -> f b
```

Remember the definition of a Functor and fmap:

```
fmap :: (a -> b) -> f a -> f b
```

If we take a function (a -> b -> c) and call fmap on a Functor instance, we will get the following code:

```
fmap :: (a -> b -> c) -> f a -> f (b -> c)
```

This is interesting because the application of `fmap` resulted in `f (b -> c)`. Now, we can take `f (b->c)` and apply it to `f b` using `<*>` and get `f c`. Thus, we can use a function such as `(*) :: a -> a -> a` and use it in the conjunction of `<$>` and `<*>` to apply more complex things such as multiplication on a couple of `Maybe`s:

```
(*) <$> Just 10 <*> Just 2 -- Will produce Just 20
(*) <$> Nothing <*> Just 2 -- Will produce Nothing
```

This way, one can see that the `Applicative` extends `Functor` by adding more expressiveness to it.

An `Applicative` does much more than just applying a function with multiple arguments to a data type. In the `Applicative`, we will encapsulate the function in the data type `f (a -> b)` and apply it to the data type with `f a`. This way, it is possible to carry more information in the structure `f` and apply it during the evaluation and application of the encapsulated function.

For example, one can consider `f a` as an operation carried out in parallel; `f (a -> b)` denotes that it needs to wait for the value to be produced by `f a` and then apply the function. Furthermore, we can create an `Applicative` type that represents a thread pool and schedules `f a` on each one of them, retaining the composing power of functions.

Binary tree as Applicative

In this example, we will define `binary tree` and define it as an instance of an `Applicative` type class.

How to do it...

1. Create a new project `binary-tree-applicative` using the `simple` Stack template.
2. Open `src/Main.hs`; we will add our recipe to this file.
3. After the initial module definition, add the following imports:

```
module Main where

import Data.Functor
import Control.Applicative
```

4. Define the `binary tree` and add the `Functor` instance too:

```
data Tree a = Leaf
    | Node (Tree a) a (Tree a)
    deriving (Show, Eq)

instance Functor Tree where
fmap _ Leaf = Leaf
fmap f (Node left value right) = Node (fmap f left) (f value)
(fmap f right)
```

5. Now, define the `Applicative` instance for the `binary tree`. Note the recursive definition for `pure`, producing an infinite tree:

```
instance Applicative Tree where
pure x = let t = Node t x t
    in t

(<*>) Leaf _ = Leaf
(<*>) _ Leaf = Leaf
(<*>) (Node lf f rf) (Node la a ra) = Node (lf <*> la) (f a)
(rf <*> ra)
```

The `pure` function creates an infinite tree, whereas for the `<*>` definition, we always return the empty tree if one of the arguments is empty. If the value is of the type `Node left v right`, then we apply function to the value and recursively apply the left encapsulated function `lf` to `la` and `rf` to `ra`.

6. Add a function to create a sample tree and the `main` function testing our instance of `Applicative` and laws of `Applicative`:

```
singleton :: a -> Tree a
singleton x = Node Leaf x Leaf

node :: Tree a -> a -> Tree a -> Tree a
node l x r = Node l x r

sampleTree :: Int -> Tree Int
sampleTree b = node l b r
where
    l = node ll (b+1) rl
    r = node lr (b+2) rr
    ll = node lll (b+3) rll
    rl = node lrl (b+4) rrl
    lr = node llr (b+5) rlr
    rr = node lrr (b+6) rrr
```

```
        lll = singleton (b+7)
        rll = singleton (b+8)
        lrl = singleton (b+9)
        rrl = singleton (b+10)
        llr = singleton (b+11)
        rlr = singleton (b+12)
        lrr = singleton (b+13)
        rrr = singleton (b+14)


 main :: IO ()
 main = do
  let intTree1 = sampleTree 1
    intTree2 = sampleTree 15
    finalTree = (+) <$> intTree1 <*> intTree2
 putStrLn "First Tree"
 print intTree1
 putStrLn "Second Tree"
 print intTree2
 putStrLn "Final Tree"
 print finalTree
 putStrLn "Checking Applicatives Laws"
 putStrLn "Identity Law: pure id <*> v == v"
 putStrLn "pure id <*> intTree1 == intTree1"
 print $ (pure id <*> intTree1) == intTree1
 putStrLn "Homomorphism: pure f <*> pure x == pure (f x)"
 putStrLn "This property is not possible to test here, as pure
 produces infinite tree"
 putStrLn "Interchange: u <*> pure y == pure ($ y) <*> u"
 putStrLn "This property is not possible to test here, as pure
 produces infinite tree"
 putStrLn "Composition: pure (.) <*> u <*> v <*> w == u <*> (v
 <*> w)"
 let square x = x * x
   double x = x + x
 putStrLn "(pure (.) <*> pure square <*> pure double <*>
 intTree1) == (pure square <*> (pure double
   <*> intTree1))"
 print $ (pure (.) <*> pure square <*> pure double <*> intTree1)
 == (pure square <*> (pure double
   <*> intTree1))
```

7. Build and run the project:

```
stack build
stack exec -- binary-tree-applicative
```

8. You should see the following output:

```
binary-tree-applicative $ stack exec -- binary-tree-applicative
First Tree
Node (Node (Node (Node Leaf 8 Leaf) 4 (Node Leaf 9 Leaf)) 2 (Node (Node Leaf 10 Leaf) 5 (Node Leaf 11 Leaf))) 1 (Node (Node (Node Leaf 1
2 Leaf) 6 (Node Leaf 13 Leaf)) 3 (Node (Node Leaf 14 Leaf) 7 (Node Leaf 15 Leaf)))
Second Tree
Node (Node (Node (Node Leaf 22 Leaf) 18 (Node Leaf 23 Leaf)) 16 (Node (Node Leaf 24 Leaf) 19 (Node Leaf 25 Leaf))) 15 (Node (Node (Node
Leaf 26 Leaf) 20 (Node Leaf 27 Leaf)) 17 (Node (Node Leaf 28 Leaf) 21 (Node Leaf 29 Leaf)))
Final Tree
Node (Node (Node (Node Leaf 30 Leaf) 22 (Node Leaf 32 Leaf)) 18 (Node (Node Leaf 34 Leaf) 24 (Node Leaf 36 Leaf))) 16 (Node (Node (Node
Leaf 38 Leaf) 26 (Node Leaf 40 Leaf)) 20 (Node (Node Leaf 42 Leaf) 28 (Node Leaf 44 Leaf)))
Checking Applicatives Laws
Identity Law: pure id <*> v == v
pure id <*> intTree1 == intTree1
True
Homomorphism: pure f <*> pure x == pure (f x)
This property is not possible to test here, as pure produces infinite tree
Interchange: u <*> pure y == pure ($ y) <*> u
This property is not possible to test here, as pure produces infinite tree
Composition: pure (.) <*> u <*> v <*> w == u <*> (v <*> w)
(pure (.) <*> pure square <*> pure double <*> intTree1) == (pure square <*> (pure double <*> intTree1))
True
binary-tree-applicative $
```

How it works...

The `Applicative` must follow these laws:

- **Identity Law**: An application of identity should not change the data:

  ```
  pure id <*> v == v
  ```

- **Homomorphism**: An application of a function to a data (`f x`) is equivalent to the application of `Applicative` of the function applied to `pure` data (data inducted in `Applicative`):

  ```
  pure f <*> pure x == pure (f x)
  ```

- **Interchange**: This is equivalent to saying that

  `f (a -> b) -> f a == f b`, which should be equivalent to `f ((a -> b) -> b) -> f (a -> b) == f b`:

  ```
  u <*> pure y = pure ($ y) <*> u
  ```

- **Composition**: Stipulates that an `Applicative` compose operator is similar to the function composition `(.)`:

```
pure (.) <*> u <*> v <*> w = u <*> (v <*> w)
```

Here, the application of the composition `pure (.) <*> u <*> v` on `w` is the same as application of `u` on `(v <*> w)`.

These are not just laws; they give a way to cross-check whether our implementation is correct. They also allow us to reason about an `Applicative` instance. These laws allow an `Applicative` to embed a computation and move it freely.

In the case of a binary tree, the first law `pure id <*> v == v` should hold. To be able to satisfy this law, we have to make the `pure x` instance of a binary tree an infinite recursively defined tree. In this, we will take the element and construct an infinite tree where all nodes have a value x and both left and right subtrees are the same as the root node. Hence, `pure` is defined as follows:

```
pure x = let tree = Node tree x tree
    in tree
```

The definition of `<*>` is quite straight forward. It extracts the function from the first argument `f (a -> b)` and applies it to the value contained within the node. Then, it takes the left subtree of the first argument and applies it to the left subtree of the second argument. This is repeated with the right subtree. The process is continued recursively until `Leaf` is found in either subtree. Whenever `Leaf` is found, we need not take any action, and the result is `Leaf`:

```
(<*>) Leaf _ = Leaf
(<*>) _ Leaf = Leaf
(<*>) (Node lf f rf) (Node la a ra) = Node (lf <*> la) (f a)
(rf <*> ra)
```

The recipe has an example to prove that our `Applicative` instance follows the first and fourth laws. However, since the definition of `pure` results in an infinite tree, we cannot execute it in a program. However, we can show that by equational reasoning, the homomorphism states the following:

```
pure f <*> pure x == pure (f x)
```

Consider the binary tree definition in the recipe; we can write the preceding statement by substituting the definition of `pure`:

```
tf <*> tx == tfx -- Note : this is not a Haskell code
where
 tf = Node tf f tf
 tx = Node tx x tx
 tfx = Node tfx (f x) tfx

-- The above expression becomes
Node tf f tf <*> Node tx x tx
= Node (tf <*> tx) (f x) (tf <*> tx) -- Recursive definition
evaluates to tfx
= Node tfx (f x) tfx
= tfx
```

Similarly, the interchange law can also be proved.

The important thing to note is that an Applicative allows sequencing, without needing to know about intermediate results. Hence, an Applicative is stronger than a Functor, but weaker than a monad.

Working with monad

In this recipe, we will define our own `Maybe` type. We will define the `Functor` and `Applicative` instances for our `Maybe`, which are prerequisites for creating a `Monad` instance. Then, we will continue to create an instance of `Monad`, and, finally, we will use them in an example.

`Maybe` is a simple type and its `monad` instance is simple to implement and understand. Hence, when we work with the `Maybe` monad, it becomes clearer why and how the monad works.

How to do it...

1. Create a new project `working-with-monad` using the `simple` Stack template:

   ```
   stack new working-with-monad simple
   ```

2. Open `src/Main.hs` and edit it.

3. After the initial module definition, add the following imports:

```
import Prelude hiding(Maybe(..))
```

 Note that we are importing otherwise implicitly imported module `Prelude` explicitly by hiding `Maybe`. This is because we are defining our own `Maybe` data type.

4. Import other required headers now. The header for monad is `Control.Monad`:

```
import Data.Functor
import Control.Applicative
import Control.Monad
```

5. Now, define the `Maybe` data type. Also, define the instance for `Functor` and `Applicative` for it:

```
data Maybe a = Nothing | Just a deriving Show

instance Functor Maybe where

fmap f (Just x) = Just (f x)
fmap f Nothing  = Nothing

instance Applicative Maybe where

pure x = Just x

(<*>) Nothing _ = Nothing
(<*>) _ Nothing = Nothing
(<*>) (Just f) (Just x) = Just (f x)
```

6. Now, define the instance of `Monad` for `Maybe`. We need to implement two functions, `return` and `>>=` or the `binding` function:

```
instance Monad Maybe where
return = Just

Nothing  >>= _ = Nothing
(Just x) >>= f = f x
```

7. Add the following function `add` to demonstrate the `do` notation for `monad`:

```
add :: Num a => Maybe a -> Maybe a -> Maybe a
add x y = do
i <- x
j <- y
return (i + j)
```

8. The function `liftM2` lifts a function to a `monad` and applies it to two arguments. The following example code shows that. Add it to `src/Main.hs`:

```
multiply :: Num a => Maybe a -> Maybe a -> Maybe a
multiply x y = liftM2 (*) x y
```

9. Now, add some utility functions along with `main` and complete the recipe:

```
fromOdd :: Integral a => a -> Maybe a
fromOdd x | odd x = Just x
fromOdd _ = Nothing

isJust :: Maybe a -> Maybe Bool
isJust (Just _) = Just True
isJust Nothing  = Just False

main :: IO ()
main = do
  print $ multiply (Just 10) (Just 2)
  print $ multiply (Just 10) Nothing
  print $ add (Just 10) (Just 2)
  print $ add Nothing (Just 2)
  print $ forM [1..10] Just
  print $ forM [1..10] fromOdd
  print $ filterM (isJust . fromOdd) [1..10]
  print $ (pure 10 :: Maybe Int) >>= \x -> return (x * x)
```

10. Build and run the project:

```
stack build
stack exec -- working-with-monad
```

11. You should see the following output:

```
● ● ●                          working-with-monad — -bash — 136×13
working-with-monad $ stack exec — working-with-monad
Just 20
Nothing
Just 12
Nothing
Just [1,2,3,4,5,6,7,8,9,10]
Nothing
Just [1,3,5,7,9]
Just 100
working-with-monad $
```

How it works...

One can look at `Monad` as a logical extension of `Applicative`, but with stronger implications. The `monad` type class is defined as follows:

```
class Applicative m => Monad (m :: * -> *) where
 (>>=) :: m a -> (a -> m b) -> m b
 (>>) :: m a -> m b -> m b
 return :: a -> m a
 fail :: String -> m a
 {-# MINIMAL (>>=) #-}
```

To define the `monad` instance, one needs to define the binding function `(>>=)`. In fact, the `return` function is equivalent to the `Applicative pure` function.

The `binding` function is interesting, with the following signature:

```
(>>=) :: m a -> (a -> m b) -> m b
```

To interpret the preceding function in the context of `Maybe`, consider the following illustration:

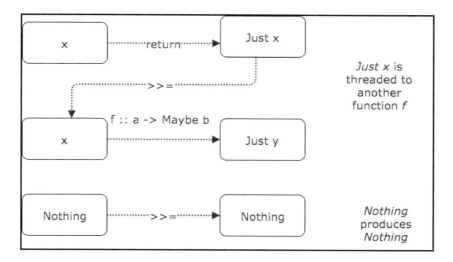

The `return` function that is equivalent to `pure` takes in a value and inserts the `monad` instance. In the context of `Maybe`, it means that we take some value `x` and create `Just x`.

The binding function (`>>=`) takes the `Just x`, extracts the value `x` out of it, and feeds it to a function `f :: a -> Maybe b`. This function `f` takes the value `x` and may produce `Just y` or `Nothing`. If instead we use `Nothing` and then bind it using (`>>=`) to the function `f`, the `monad` instance definition of (`>>=`) kicks in and produces `Nothing` without even considering `f`. This is apparent from our earlier implementation:

```
Nothing  >>= _ = Nothing
(Just x) >>= f = f x
```

Suppose now we want to use a function (`+`) to add contents in two `Maybes`, say `Just 10` and `Just 2` as we have used in our example. Using (`>>=`), we can write it as follows:

```
(Just 10) >>= ( \x -> Just 2 >>= \y -> return x + y )
-- x will get value from Just 10 i.e. 10 and
-- y will get value from Just 2 i.e. 2
-- expanding further
(Just 10) >>= ( \10 -> Just 2 >>= \2 -> return (10 + 2))
-- return will create Just ... Hence we expand above we will get
Just 12
```

This can be graphically shown as follows:

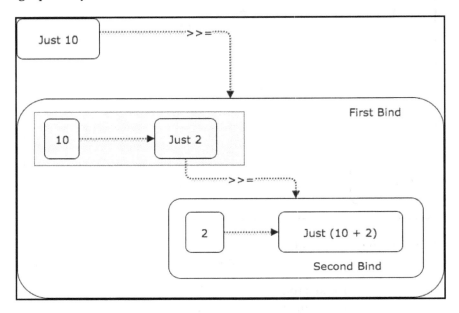

The first bind will associate Just 10 with a function that produces Just 2. The second bind will associate Just 2 with a function that adds ten from the first bind and two from the second bind. Note how the scope of the first bind is available to the second bind as well. Finally, the return (10 + 2) statement simply creates Just 2 back. If at any stage the binding results in a value Nothing, then all the remaining binding will not get called and will simply produce Nothing.

However, the syntax (Just 10) >>= (\x -> Just 2 >>= \y -> return x + y) is hard to understand and write; hence, the do... notation. The do notation makes it easier to work with monad and calls >>= internally. This is called **syntactic sugar**. The same expression now can be written as follows, with each line creating a binding:

```
add :: Maybe a -> Maybe a -> Maybe a
add m1 m2 = do
  x <- m1
  y <- m2
  return (x + y)
```

Note how the binding ensures that the previous computation has evaluated its result (for example, from `Just 10` extracting ten) before moving to next binding (that is, `Just 2` or addition as in the preceding example). This ensures that the steps in a monadic computation are evaluated in a sequence. The binding creates stronger implications for a monad.

There's more...

Once we understand how monad works and where the `do` notation originates, we can look at other functions in `Control.Monad` in conjunction with the monad that we have used in our recipe:

- **liftM2**: The `liftM2` function takes a function with two arguments (like `*`) and two values of a data type for which the `monad` instance is defined. It lifts the function and applies to the monad. In this regard, it is similar to the `add` function that we have defined here:

  ```
  liftM2 (*) (Just 10) (Just 2)
  ```

- **forM**: The `forM` function takes a traversable (like a list that can traverse through its elements) and applies a function (`a -> m b`) to each of those elements to produce a traversable of `b` in the monad `m`. Here is an example:

  ```
  forM [1..10] Just == Just [1..10]
  forM [1..10] fromOdd == Nothing -- as fromOdd returns Nothing
  for 2,4,6..
  ```

- **filterM**: The `filterM` function is similar to filter, except that it applies to monad. It takes a function (`a -> m Bool`) that produces a boolean value in the `monad` instance. It then filters out the elements in the list that do not return `True`:

  ```
  filterM (isJust . fromOdd) [1..10] == [1,3,5,7,9]
  ```

List as monad

In this recipe, we will revisit `list` and look at it as a `monad`. List is a monad, and we will work with a few examples of how to work with a list with monadic syntax and functions.

How to do it...

1. Create a new project `list-as-monad` using the `simple` Stack template.

2. Open `src/Main.hs` and edit it.

3. Add the following import for monad:

   ```
   import Control.Monad
   ```

4. Write a function that takes an integer `x` and returns a list of all integers starting with *x ([x, x+1, x+2,...])*:

   ```
   nexts :: Num a => a -> [a]
   nexts x = do
   x : nexts (x+1)
   ```

5. Write a function that takes two lists and returns all ordered pairs from this list:

   ```
   pairs :: [a] -> [b] -> [(a,b)]
   pairs xs ys = do
   x <- xs
   y <- ys
   return (x,y)
   ```

6. Write a partitioning function using `list` comprehension. The same function is also written using the monadic syntax:

   ```
   partition :: (a -> b -> Bool) -> [a] -> [b] -> [(a,b)]
   partition f xs ys = [ (x, y) | x <- xs, y <- ys, f x y]

   partition1 :: (a -> b -> Bool) -> [a] -> [b] -> [(a,b)]
   partition1 f xs ys = do
   x <- xs
   y <- ys
   if f x y then
     return (x,y)
   else
   []
   ```

7. Use the preceding functions along with `forM` and `filterM` with `list`:

   ```
   main :: IO ()
   main = do
   putStrLn "Next 10 elements from 11"
   print $ take 10 (nexts 11)
   putStrLn "Filtering out even elements from [1..1]"
   ```

```
print $ filterM (\x -> if odd x then [True] else [False])
[1..10]
putStrLn "Applying forM over a list and Maybe and embedding
them in a list"
print $ forM [1..10] (:[])
print $ forM (Just 10) (:[])
putStrLn "All pairs between [1..5] and ['a'..'c']"
print $ pairs [1..5] ['a'..'c']
putStrLn "Partition the ordered pairs between [i] and [j] such
that i > j"
print $ partition (>) [1..10] [1..10]
putStrLn "Partition the ordered pairs between [i] and [j] such
that i < j"
print $ partition1 (<) [1..10] [1..10]
```

8. Build and run the project:

```
stack build
stack exec -- list-as-monad
```

9. You should see the following output:

How it works...

The first function `nexts` shows that `list` is a monad. It uses the `do` notation and uses recursion to infinitely define the list.

The `pairs` function shows how the `list` monad works. The function is defined as follows:

```
pairs :: [a] -> [b] -> [(a,b)]
pairs xs ys = do
x <- xs
y <- ys
return (x,y)
```

It should read as follows:

```
for each x in xs
for each y in ys
create list of (x,y)
concatenate lists to return a single list
```

The `list` monad binds each element of a `list` to the function, creating another `list`, and concatenates them back together. The `return` function creates a singleton list.

The partition function is implemented in two ways. The list comprehension for partition is *[(x,y) | x <- xs, y <- ys, f x y]*, which is a short form for the monadic syntax implemented in the function `partition1`. Both functions are equivalent. The `partition1` function uses the `if .. else` block, whereas `list` comprehension simply specifies the boolean condition with `f x y`.

Working with IO monad

In the recipes that we saw earlier, we all worked with IO, and used functions such as `putStrLn :: String -> IO ()` or `print :: Show a => a -> IO ()`. We already know that these functions print the string or a value to standard output.

In this recipe, we will open a file, read it line by line, and output it on the `stdout` along with the line number. We will also understand how IO works as a monad and how IO allows a Haskell program to interact with the outside world.

How to do it...

1. Create a new project `io-monad` with the `simple` Stack template:

   ```
   stack new io-monad simple
   ```

2. Open `src/Main.hs`; we will be editing this file.

3. After initial module definition, add the following imports. Only those functions that are used in the program are imported from the corresponding module:

```
import System.IO (hGetLine, hIsEOF, withFile, Handle,
IOMode(..))
import System.Environment (getArgs)
import Control.Monad
import Data.List (intercalate)
```

4. Write the function `getLineSeq`, which returns a list of lines when given a `file handle`:

```
-- From the file handle, check if we have reached end of file,
-- otherwise read the file line by line
getLinesSeq :: Handle -> IO [String]
getLinesSeq h = do
eof <- hIsEOF h
-- Use (:) to get the line and append remaining ...
if eof then return [] else (:) <$> hGetLine h <*> getLinesSeq h
```

5. Write the function `printLine` to print the line number and line in the format `line number : line`. It uses the `intercalate` function, which separates the items in the `list` by a given element:

```
-- Print line number and string separated by :
printLine :: (Int, String) -> IO ()
printLine (lineno, line) = putStrLn $ intercalate " : " [show
lineno, line]
```

6. Write the `withLineNumbers` function, which takes any monad that emits a list of strings and returns a list of tuple. Each tuple contains the line number and line itself:

```
-- Given a monad that gives us list of strings, return the
list of
-- (int,string) where int is the line number, and string
represents
-- the corresponding line.
withLineNumbers :: Monad m => m [String] -> m [(Int,String)]
withLineNumbers m = zip <$> pure [1..] <*> m
```

7. Now, write the `main` function to open a file and print the contents along with the line number:

```
main :: IC ()
main = do
-- Throw an error if number of arguments is not 1
args <- getArgs
when (length args /= 1) $ do
putStrLn $ "Incorrect arguments " ++ (show args)
error "Provide file name"
-- Open the file and print the lines with line number
withFile (head args) ReadMode (\h -> do
    -- Each line is zipped with line number
    lines <- withLineNumbers (getLinesSeq h)
    -- Print line
    forM_ lines printLine
    )
```

8. Build and run the project. Note that we give the argument `Setup.hs` to the command prompt:

```
stack build
stack exec -- io-monad Setup.hs
```

9. Upon running the project, you should see the following output--contents of `Setup.hs` along with the line number:

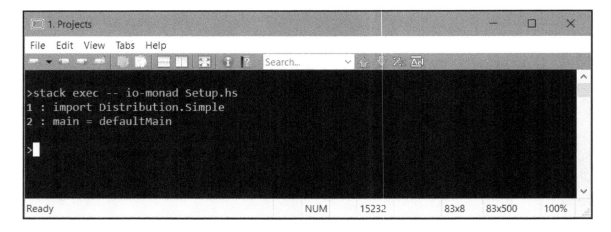

How it works...

We have been using IO and functions related to IO in a limited way in our previous recipes. The usage was limited to printing the output using either putStrLn or print. We should spend some time to understand what IO is and how it is inevitable for a Haskell program.

Haskell works with pure functions without side effects. It means that the evaluation of pure functions does not affect the outside world in any way. To be able to interact with the outside world, the outside world would need to contain memory, a console, file I/O, networking, and so on. The IO monad enables a Haskell program to interact with the outside world. IO monad is the gateway for pure Haskell functions to the outside world.

By interacting with IO, Haskell functions enforce side effects such as printing to a standard output, opening a file, or doing network operations. This is effectively shown here:

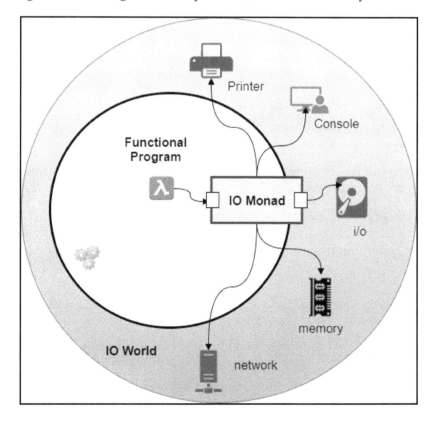

Since the IO operations are imperative, the first step is executed before the following ones. For example, we cannot write to a file without opening it first. It is, hence, logical that IO is an instance of a monad and implicitly Applicative and Functor.

Moving to the recipe, to open the file and print the lines along with the line numbers, the following points are to be noted. The function (getLinesSeq :: Handle -> IO [String]) takes a handle to the file and produces a list of strings in IO monad. We will first check whether we have reached the end of the file using the hIsEOF function. If we have reached the end of the file, we will just return []. Otherwise, we will use Applicative in a very interesting way:

```
(:) <$> hGetLine h <*> getLinesSeq h
```

This is a very interesting pattern, and Applicative fits perfectly in this. We used hGetLine :: Handle -> IO String to get a single line from the file. The rest of the lines can be retrieved using the getLinesSeq function recursively. Now, we need to put the single line ahead of the rest of the lines returned by getLinesSeq. For the pure list, we can achieve it by the (:) function. Using the Functor <$> and Applicative <*> functions, we can easily represent this pattern. If we use the monadic do notation, this can be written as follows:

```
do
  line <- hGetLine h
  lines <- getLinesSeq h
  return (line : lines)
```

Using the Functor and Applicative patterns, the preceding code can be represented in a very succinct and expressive way.

The function withLineNumbers takes in a monad (any) that represents a list of strings. It again lifts the function zip :: [a] -> [b] -> [(a,b)] to the monad to add the line number to each input line. It again uses the Functor/Applicative pattern:

```
-- In fact Monad m is not necessary here.. Applicative m should
 suffice.
withLineNumbers :: Monad m => m [String] -> m [(Int,String)]
withLineNumbers m = zip <$> pure [1..] <*> m
```

The preceding code can also be written in a monadic notation as follows:

```
withLineNumbers m = do
  let linenumbers = [1..] -- infinite list [1,2,...]
  lines <- m -- Input monad represents a list of lines
  return (zip linenumbers lines)
```

In the `main` function, we used `getArgs` to get the arguments to the function. The `when` function checks if the number of arguments is correct. When it is not correct, we raise an error `Provide file name`. If we run the program without an argument (or more than one argument), then the error causes an exception to be raised, and the program will terminate. You should see the following output:

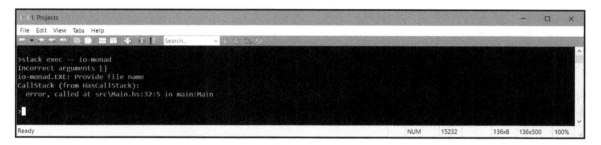

We use the `withFile :: FilePath -> IOMode -> (Handle -> IO a) -> IO a` function. This function takes three arguments:

- The first argument is the path of the file, which we would like to open.
- The second is `IOMode` (`ReadMode, WriteMode, ReadWriteMode ...`), where we use `ReadMode` as we want to open the file only for reading.
- The third argument is the function that actually works with the opened handle. Once this function evaluates, the file handle is closed by `withFile`.

We use an anonymous function (`\h -> ...`) to work with the opened file. We call `withLineNumbers` along with `getLinesSeq` to get a list of lines with line numbers. We then use `Control.Monad.forM_` to print each line using `printLine`.

Writing INI parser

In this recipe, we will further build on the concepts of Functor, Applicative, and monad, and build a parser for the `INI` file from scratch. We will write a simple parser, and define its `Functor`, `Applicative`, and `monad` instances. Then, we will slowly build upon the concept to finally build an INI parser.

The INI file is usually used as a configuration file. A typical INI file contains the number of sections, each section representing a set of name-value assignments. A sample INI file may look like this:

```
[Section]
name1 = value1
name2 = value2

[Section2]
name1 = value1
name3 = value3
```

How to do it...

1. Create a new project `ini-parser` using the `simple` Stack template:

   ```
   stack new ini-parser simple
   ```

2. Open the file `src/Main.hs` for editing.

3. After the initial module header, add the following imports:

   ```
   import Data.Functor
   import Control.Applicative
   import Control.Monad
   import Data.Map hiding (empty)
   import Data.Char
   ```

4. Define the INI file data structure. Represent name-value pairs in each section (variables) as a `map` of name to values. Both name and values are represented by strings. The sections inside an INI file are a `map` between the section name and variables for each section:

   ```
   type Variables = Map String String
   type Sections = Map String Variables
   newtype INI = INI Sections
   ```

5. Start defining the parser. A parser is defined as follows:

   ```
   data Parser a = Parser { runParser :: String -> Maybe (a,
   String) }
   ```

The parser is represented as a data type around a function `runParser` that takes a string as input and generates a tuple (a String) where a is the type of the value parsed by the parser. The second member of the `tuple`, a `string`, represents the remaining input after parsing the value of type a. Since we can fail during parsing, we use `Maybe` so that we can represent either `tuple` or nothing.

6. If we have a parser of type a, then we can define a `Functor` instance. If we apply a function of type a `->` b, we can convert `Parser` a into `Parser` b. Define the `Functor` instance as follows:

```
instance Functor Parser where
fmap f (Parser p) =
let parserfunc input = do
  (x, remaining) <- p input -- run supplied parser against
  input
  return (f x, remaining)    -- apply function on parsed value
in Parser parserfunc
```

7. Similarly, we can define the `Applicative` instance for our parser as follows:

```
instance Applicative Parser where
pure x = let parserfunc input = Just (x, input)
in Parser parserfunc

(Parser pf) <*> (Parser pa) =
let parserfunc input = do
  (f, remaining) <- pf input
  (a, remaining2) <- pa remaining
  return (f a, remaining2)
  in Parser parserfunc
```

 Do note how we create a `parser` function on the fly that takes input and produces certain output.

8. Now, we can go ahead with the monad instance for our parser:

```
instance Monad Parser where
return = pure
(Parser pa) >>= fab =
let parsefunc input = do
(a, remaining) <- pa input
runParser (fab a) remaining
in Parser parsefunc
```

It runs a parser on input, producing certain output. Then, it feeds this output to another parser, with the remaining input to continue parsing.

9. We will now implement an `Alternative` instance for our parser. The `Alternative` is a logical extension of Applicative, where it allows us to define an empty (or complementary to pure) case for our data type, and if we have two values of data types, we can go with the second one if the first one is empty. Define the `Alternative` instance for our parser now:

```
instance Alternative Parser where
empty = Parser (\_ -> Nothing )

(Parser pa) <|> (Parser pb) =
let parsefunc input = case pa input of
                  Nothing -> pb input
                  Just (x, remaining) -> Just (x, remaining)
in Parser parsefunc

-- return a list of v for which v satisfies. The list should
satisfy at least one v.
some v =
let parsefunc input = do
  (x, remaining) <- runParser v input
  (xs, remaining2) <- runParser (many v) remaining
  return (x:xs, remaining2)
  in Parser parsefunc

-- return a list of v for which v satisfies, the list can
satisfy zero or more v.
many v =
let parsefunc input = case runParser (some v) input of
                  Just (xs, remaining) -> Just (xs,
                  remaining)
                  Nothing -> Just ([], input)
                  in Parser parsefunc
```

The definition of some and many is interesting. In the parsing context, some matches at least one value, whereas many matches zero or more values parsed by the supplied parser.

10. The basic machinery for parsing is now done. Now, start writing concrete parsing functions. If the parser fails, the parser function should return `Nothing`; otherwise, it should return value successfully parsed and the remaining input.

11. The first function to be used is a conditional character parser. If the character meets certain criteria, we will return the character as a successfully parsed value:

```
conditional :: (Char -> Bool) -> Parser Char
conditional f =
let parsefunc [] = Nothing  -- Input is empty, nothing to
produce
parsefunc (x:xs) | f x = Just (x, xs)  -- We got a match,
produce output
parsefunc _ = Nothing  -- No match, just fail.
in Parser parsefunc
```

Use the `conditional` parser to implement a parser to match the given character:

```
char :: Char -> Parser Char
char c = conditional (== c)
```

12. We will implement the `bracketed` parser. We are interested in the enclosed value (such as within open and closed parenthesis and without parenthesis):

```
bracketed :: Parser a -> Parser b -> Parser c -> Parser b
bracketed pa pb pc = do
pa  -- match first parser, but ignore value
b <- pb  -- interested in value parsed by pb
pc  -- match end parser, again ignoring value
return b -- return second value
```

13. Now, implement a bunch of parsers to match square bracket characters, alpha-numeric characters, and white spaces. We use `many` with white space to match one or more white spaces:

```
bracketOpen :: Parser Char
bracketOpen = char '['

bracketClose :: Parser Char
bracketClose = char ']'

alphanum :: Parser Char
alphanum = conditional isAlphaNum

isWhiteSpace :: Char -> Bool
isWhiteSpace ' ' = True
```

```
isWhiteSpace '\t' = True
isWhiteSpace _ = False

whitespace :: Parser Char
whitespace = conditional isWhiteSpace

whitespaces :: Parser String
whitespaces = many whitespace
```

14. `SectionHeader` is the section name enclosed in brackets:

```
sectionName :: Parser String
sectionName = bracketed whitespaces (some alphanum) whitespaces

sectionHeader :: Parser String
sectionHeader = bracketed bracketOpen sectionName bracketClose
```

15. A name is some alpha-numeric identifier. The value can either be alpha numeric or may be a quoted value (which can have spaces):

```
name :: Parser String
name = (some alphanum)

quote :: Parser Char
quote = char '\"'

-- allow alpha numeric and white space characters
quotedchar :: Parser Char
quotedchar = conditional (\c -> isAlphaNum c || isWhiteSpace c)

quotedvalue :: Parser String
quotedvalue = bracketed quote (many quotedchar) quote

value :: Parser String
value = name <|> quotedvalue
```

An assignment is a name-value pair separated by the = character. We ignore the white spaces around these:

```
assignment :: Parser (String,String)
assignment = do
 whitespaces
 name <- name
 whitespaces
 char '='
 whitespaces
 value <- value
 return (name, value)
```

16. Finally, write a parser for a section. A section has a section header and name-value pairs separated by `newline`:

```
newline :: Parser Char
newline = conditional (\c -> c == '\r' || c == '\n' )

newlines :: Parser ()
newlines = many newline >> return ()

blank :: Parser ()
blank = whitespaces >> newline >> return ()

blanks :: Parser ()
blanks = many blank >> return ()

assignments :: Parser Variables
assignments = fromList <$> many (blanks >> assignment)

section :: Parser (String, Variables)
section = do
 blanks
 whitespaces
 name <- sectionHeader
 blanks
 variables <- assignments
 return (name, variables)
```

17. The `INI` file is a list of many sections. Use Functor `fmap` to do the job of converting many sections into the `INI` data type:

```
ini :: Parser INI
ini = (INI . fromList) <$> many section
```

18. Finally, write the `main` function to parse an `INI` file:

```
main :: IO ()·
main = do
args <- getArgs
contents <- readFile (head args)
case runParser ini contents of
Just inicontents -> print inicontents
Nothing -> putStrLn "Could not parse INI file"
```

19. Build the project. Then, create a `sample.ini` file with the following contents and run it against the project:

```
stack build
stack exec -- ini-parser sample.ini
```

20. The sample file is shown here:

```
[section]
name = value
name2 = "quoted value"
[ section2]
name = value
name2 = "quoted value 2"
```

21. The output should look like this:

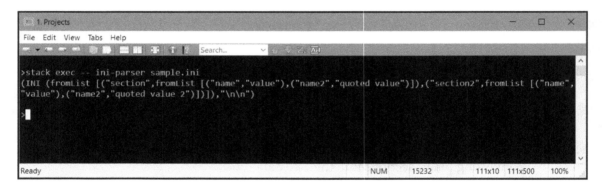

How it works...

The `INI` parser is a combinatorial top-down recursive-descent parser. Its `monad` instance creates a `composable` function that can be run later with `runParser` with input. We used monad/Applicative and Functor to combine the parser combinatorially from smaller units such as `char`, `quotedchar`, `quotedvalue`, and so on until we build the whole `INI` file parser.

Every time we compose two parsers, we create a function that first runs one parser, evaluates its value and remaining input, and then invokes the second parser to again evaluate its value. Such nesting and sequencing of parsers gives rise to a composition of parsing functions. The resultant `parser` function can be run on input to get the desirable value.

The parser is diagrammatically explained here:

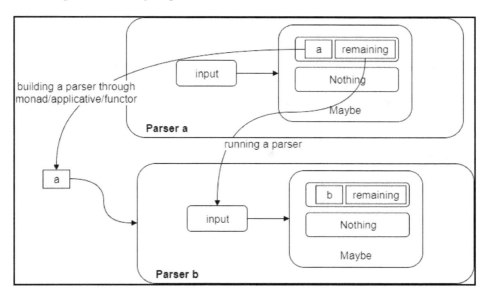

Errors and exception handling

We have been looking at `Maybe` and `Either` in earlier recipes and used them for conveying error. For example, `Nothing :: Maybe a` conveys that the evaluation has resulted in an error, and that is how we now have `Nothing`. Either is more informative than `Maybe` and conveys more information through its `Left` constructor.

In this recipe, we will work with three situations:

- Working with error and catching it later
- Working with IO exception and catching it
- Creating a custom exception, raising it, and catching it

How to do it...

1. Create a new project exceptions with the simple Stack template.

2. Open src/Main.hs and edit it.

3. After the module declaration, add the following imports for Exception and for doing IO:

```
import qualified Control.Exception as E
import System.IO
```

4. We will write a function div1 to divide one integer by another. However, when we encounter the division by zero situation, we use the error :: String -> a function to raise an error. This function takes and raises SomeException:

```
div1 :: Int -> Int -> Int
div1 x 0 = error "Division by zero"
div1 x y = x `div` y
```

5. Now, we will write safeDiv1 and safeDiv2 , which will catch the exception and will safely show the result of the division:

```
safeDiv1 :: Int -> Int -> IO ()
safeDiv1 x y = E.catch (putStrLn $ show $ div1 x y) (\e ->
putStrLn (show $ (e ::
  E.SomeException)))

safeDiv2 :: Int -> Int -> IO ()
safeDiv2 x y = do
result <- E.try (putStrLn $ show $ div1 x y)
case result of
  Left e -> putStrLn $ show (e :: E.SomeException)
  Right r -> putStrLn $ show r
```

6. Now, we will write a function, safeReadFile, which reads the contents of the file and returns it. If the file does not exist, it catches the error and returns it. In this case, it catches exceptions of type IOException:

```
safeReadFile :: FilePath -> IO String
safeReadFile filepath = do
E.catch (readFile filepath)
(\e -> do
putStrLn $ "ERROR " ++ (show (e :: E.IOException))
return "" )
```

7. Now, we will a create custom exception. We will create a data type for representing Point and Line. We will also add a function to get the square of the distance between two points:

```
data Point = Point Float Float deriving Show
data Line = Line Point Point deriving Show

distanceSq :: Point -> Point -> Float
distanceSq (Point x1 y1) (Point x2 y2) = xx + yy
where
  square t = t * t
  xx = square (x1 - x2)
  yy = square (y1 - y2)

-- Minimum valid distance allowed between two points
tolerance :: Float
tolerance = 1e-6
```

We also added a function tolerance, which represents the minimum allowed length for a line.

8. Now, define the custom exception GeometryException. It needs to be an instance of Show and Exception type class:

```
data GeometryException = ZeroLengthLine

instance Show GeometryException where

show ZeroLengthLine = "Line with zero or less than tolerance
length"

  instance E.Exception GeometryException
```

9. Now, create a function safeLine to create a line. This function throws ZeroLengthLine whenever it encounters two points too close to each other. The function showLine catches the error and shows it, or it shows the contents of the line:

```
safeLine :: Point -> Point -> Line
safeLine p1 p2 | distanceSq p1 p2 < tolerance = E.throw
ZeroLengthLine
safeLine p1 p2 = Line p1 p2

showLine :: Line -> IO ()
showLine line =
E.catch (putStrLn $ show line)
```

```
(\e -> do
  putStrLn $ "ERROR " ++ (show (e :: GeometryException))
  return ()
)
```

10. Now, use all the functions used earlier to test different situations, normal division, `division by zero`, opening a file that does not exist, and trying to create a line of zero length:

```
main :: IO ()
main = do
-- Catch all exceptions
safeDiv1 4 2
safeDiv1 7 0
-- Using try just
safeDiv1 12 2
safeDiv1 7 0

-- Safe file read
contents <- safeReadFile "some-arbitrary-name"
putStrLn "The contents should be blank"
putStr contents

let p1 = Point 10 10
   p2 = Point 0 0

putStrLn "Line with zero length"
showLine (safeLine p1 p1)
putStrLn "Valid line"
showLine (safeLine p1 p2)
```

11. Build and run the project:

stack build
stack exec -- exceptions

12. You should see the following output:

```
exceptions — -bash — 136×19
exceptions $ stack exec — exceptions
2
Division by zero
CallStack (from HasCallStack):
  error, called at src/Main.hs:7:12 in main:Main
6
Division by zero
CallStack (from HasCallStack):
  error, called at src/Main.hs:7:12 in main:Main
ERROR some-arbitrary-name: openFile: does not exist (No such file or directory)
The contents should be blank
Line with zero length
ERROR Line with zero or less than tolerance length
Valid line
Line (Point 10.0 10.0) (Point 0.0 0.0)
exceptions $
```

How it works...

- The `error` function takes a string, and creates an exception. However, this exception is realizable only in the IO monad. Hence, we catch it while we are printing the result of `div1`.

- The function `catch` runs an IO action and takes a handler to catch the exception. It is possible to catch all exceptions by specifying the type of exception as `SomeException`.

- The `try` function also runs an IO action. However, it returns the result in `Either e a` where `e` is the exception and `a` is the result of the IO action. Thus, we can check using `Either` that we have a valid result.

- Typically, IO functions such as `readFile` raise an exception of type `IOException`.

- We can create custom exceptions by creating an instance of `Show` and `Exception`. The `Show` instance is required to show the exception in a user-friendly string. We can throw custom exceptions using the `throw :: e -> a` function. This is better than just `error`.

One must differentiate between an error and an exception. An error is a programming error and must be handled by a programmer. It represents certain assumptions or a case that is not handled. Exceptions, on the other hand, should be extremely rare and raised because of external factors rather than the program.

5
More about Monads

In this chapter, we will cover the following recipes:

- Writing a State Monad
- Computing a fibonacci number with State Monad
- Writing a State Monad transformer
- Working with the Reader monad transformer
- Working with the Writer monad transformer
- Combining monad transformers

Introduction

In the previous chapter, we looked at Functor, Applicative, and monads. In this chapter, we will look at State Monad, a monad where we can store a state and modify it. Once we understand monad, we will understand that we can implement a monad (or an Applicative) for a specific purpose.

It is very likely that a situation will arise where we would like to combine two monads to make a single monad. For example, consider a parser monad, `Parser a` and a State Monad `State s a` (where `s` is the state and `a` is the output of the parser). If we also would like to maintain a state along with the parsing output, then we can combine them together with `Parser (State s a)`. With this, now, we can either operate in the outer `Parser` monad or internal `State s a` monad.

Let's take an example of IO monad with Maybe:

```
foo :: IO (Maybe Int)
foo = Just 10

bar :: IO (Maybe Int)
bar = Nothing

add :: IO (Maybe Int) -> IO (Maybe Int) -> IO (Maybe Int)
add xfoo ybar = do  -- We are in IO Monad
 x <- xfoo -- This will get us Maybe Int from xbar
 y <- ybar -- This will get us Maybe Int from ybar
 let z = do    -- Now we are in Maybe monad
   inx <- x     -- We will get data stored in x
   iny <- y     -- Data stored in y
   return $ x + y   -- Add if both x and y contained data, Nothing
   otherwise.
   return z

main :: IO ()
main = do
print $ add foo bar   -- Should print Nothing
print $ add foo foo   -- Should print "Just 20"
```

You can see that we need to switch context from IO monad to the Maybe monad to be able to do the computation in the monad that we are interested in.

In this chapter, we will look at a particular class of monads called **monad transformers**. These work by combining one monad with a base monad and providing the ability to transparently work with either of the monads. We will start with State Monad and convert the State Monad into a monad transformer. Then, we will look at mtl package (https://hackage.haskell.org/package/mtl), a monad transformer library. This is a very popular library that provides an array of useful monads and their transformers. We will look at reader and writer monads in particular.

Writing a State Monad

In this recipe, we will write our own State Monad. We will use the state monad to store the effect of cursor movements.

How to do it...

1. Create a new project `state-monad` using the `stack` command with the `simple` template:

   ```
   stack new state-monad simple
   ```

2. Open the file `src/Main.hs`; we will add our code here after the initial `module` declaration.

3. Import the following modules:

   ```
   import Prelude hiding (Either(..))
   import Data.Functor
   import Control.Applicative
   import Control.Monad
   ```

4. Now, add the definition for the State Monad. A State Monad will store state `s` with the monad:

   ```
   data State s a = State { runState :: s -> (a, s) }
   ```

5. Now, we will write the `Functor` instance for the state. Writing the `Functor` instance is easy; we need to transform output `a` with the function `f :: a -> b` and produce `b`:

   ```
   instance Functor (State s) where
   fmap f (State stateFunc) =
   let nextStateFunction s =
   let (xa, s1) = stateFunc s
   in (f xa, s1)
     in State nextStateFunction
   ```

6. Now, we will write the `Applicative` instance for the `state` type:

   ```
   instance Applicative (State s) where
   ```

7. Write the `pure` instance for the Applicative. This involves introducing the given input and introduces it in the `state` data type. The pure implementation involves grabbing input `a` to `pure` function and returning the `state` function, which returns state `s` along with input `a`:

   ```
   pure x = let pureState s = (x, s) in State pureState
   ```

8. The `Applicative` function `<*>` involves taking in `State s (a -> b)` and applying it on `State s a` to produce `State s b`:

```
sf <*> sa =
let stateFunc s =
let (f, s1) = runState sf s
  (a, s2) = runState sa s1
in (f a, s2)
in State stateFunc
```

Apply the `state` function with input `s` on `sf`, that is, `State s (a-> b)` first. We will retrieve state `s1` in this step, along with the function `f :: a -> b` in this step.

Then, apply the `state` function on `State s a`. Use state `s1` and then apply it to get a with state *s2*. Apply `f` to a to produce b and use `s2` as the resultant state.

9. Now, we will define the `monad` instance for the state:

```
instance Monad (State s) where
return = pure

sa >>= fsb = let stateFunc s =
  let (a, s1) = runState sa s
  in runState (fsb a) s1
  in State stateFunc
```

10. Implement a function to get the state. Note how we implement it in the same monad:

```
get :: State s s
get = let stateFunc s = (s, s)
in State stateFunc
```

11. Now, implement a function to change the existing state:

```
put :: s -> State s ()
put s = let stateFunc _ = ((), s)
in State stateFunc
```

12. Define a data type to define a cursor. A cursor is a position from the top-left point on the screen:

```
data Cursor = Cursor Int Int deriving Show
```

13. Now, define the movement of the cursor in four directions, *right*, *left*, *up*, and *down*:

```
data Move = Up Int | Down Int | Left Int | Right Int deriving
Show
```

14. Define the function `apply` to apply a move on the current cursor. This will change the cursor position according to the move:

```
apply :: Cursor -> Move -> Cursor
apply (Cursor x y) (Up i) = Cursor x (y-i)
apply (Cursor x y) (Down i) = Cursor x (y+i)
apply (Cursor x y) (Right i) = Cursor (x + i) y
apply (Cursor x y) (Left i) = Cursor (x -i) y
```

15. Suppose we have many moves that need to be applied to the cursor position. Use State Monad, in which state the current position of the cursor is. Whenever we wish to apply a move to the cursor, we will get the current cursor in the current state, apply the move, and then put the changed cursor back into the state:

```
applyMoves :: [Move] -> State Cursor ()
applyMoves [] = return ()   - No moves are left
applyMoves (x:xs) = do
  cursor <- get   -- Get the current cursor position
  let newcursor = apply cursor x
  put newcursor   -- set the new cursor
  applyMoves xs   -- apply remaining move
```

16. Define a list of `moves`. We will move the cursor in a square of `100` units and bring it back to the same position:

```
moves :: [Move]
moves = [Down 100, Right 100, Up 100, Left 100]
```

17. Apply the `moves` to the function `applyMoves` to get a State Monad. Experiment with different initial states. Here, we have two initial cursor positions, which are cursor at the top-left position `Cursor 0 0` and cursor at position `Cursor 12 12`. In both cases, the movement should result in the same position:

```
resultCursor :: ((), Cursor)
resultCursor = runState (applyMoves moves) (Cursor 0 0)

resultCursor1 :: ((), Cursor)
resultCursor1 = runState (applyMoves moves) (Cursor 12 12)
```

18. Write the `main` function to test the State Monad:

```
main :: IO ()
main = do
print (snd $ resultCursor)
print (snd $ resultCursor1)
```

19. Build and execute the project:

```
stack build
stack exec -- state-monad
```

20. You should see the following output:

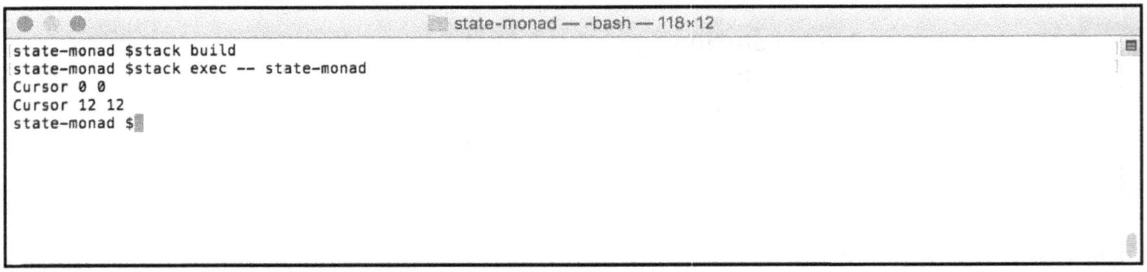

```
                                state-monad — -bash — 118×12
state-monad $stack build
state-monad $stack exec -- state-monad
Cursor 0 0
Cursor 12 12
state-monad $
```

How it works...

A State Monad is a function that takes a state **s** and produces an output (**a**, **s**). Here, **a** is the result of monadic computation, and in all monad steps, the state **s** is threaded through each step. This is illustrated in the following diagram:

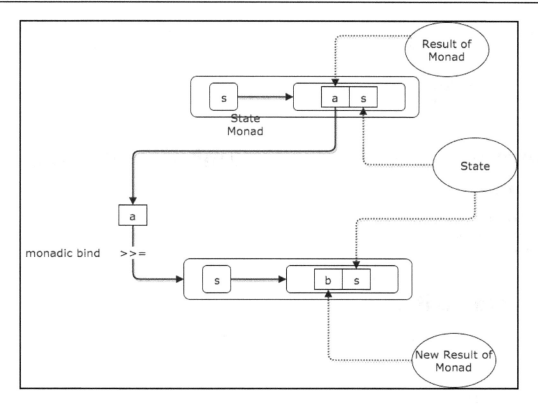

During the **monadic bind** operations, the result of the previous operation is taken and is fed into a function that produces the next output, as shown in the preceding diagram.

It is important to note two specific operations that are defined in the context of the State Monad. These operations are `get` and `put`, used for getting the current state and saving a new state, respectively.

In the `get` operation, we will create the State Monad function in such a way that state is the result of the monad:

```
get :: State s s
get = let stateFunc \s -> (s, s)
   in State stateFunc
```

Similarly, in the `put` operation, we will create a State Monad function in such a way that the given input replaces the current state. In this case, we will produce the `void()` output:

```
put :: s -> State s ()
put newstate = let stateFunc \_ -> ((), newstate)
   in State stateFunc
```

Computing a fibonacci number with State Monad

In this recipe, we will use the State Monad as defined by the `mtl` library. The `mtl` library defines many useful, well-articulated monads. We will use the State Monad to calculate a fibonacci number.

How to do it...

1. Create a new project using the `simple` Stack template:

   ```
   stack new fibonacci-state simple
   ```

2. Open `fibonacci-state.cabal` and add packages `mtl` and `containers` to the `build-depends` subsection of the `executable` section:

   ```
   executable fibonacci-state
   hs-source-dirs: src
   main-is: Main.hs
   default-language: Haskell2010
   build-depends: base >= 4.7 && < 5
           , mtl
           , containers
   ```

3. Build the project so that the dependent packages will be pulled by `stack`:

   ```
   stack build
   ```

4. Open `src/Main.hs`. We will be editing this file.
5. Import the following modules after initial module declaration:

   ```
   import Control.Applicative
   import Control.Monad.State
   import Data.Map.Strict as M
   ```

The module `Control.Monad.State` defines the state, `monad.Data.Map.Strict` defines the strict version of an associative container. We will use `Map` for storing fibonacci numbers against their indices.

6. Add type synonym for the fibonacci map. It is a map of the fibonacci index against the fibonacci number at the index:

   ```
   type FibMap a = Map a a
   ```

7. Add type synonym for state where state is the fibonacci map:

   ```
   type FibState a b = State (FibMap a) b
   ```

8. Now, define the function to get the fibonacci number stored in the state at the given index. If the number is found, we will get `Just v` (where `v` is the fibonacci number) or `Nothing` if the number was not previously found:

   ```
   getFib :: Integral a => a -> FibState a (Maybe a)
   getFib i = M.lookup i <$> get
   ```

   We get the `state` and `lookup` to see if something is placed at the given index.

9. Now, define a function to add fibonacci number `v` at the index `i` and store it in the current `map`. We will fetch the `map` using `get` and then `insert` the new values in the `map` and return the value `v`:

   ```
   putFib :: Integral a => a -> a -> FibState a a
   putFib i v = do
   -- get the map, and insert given number into it.
   mp <- (pure $ M.insert i v) <*> get
   -- Put the map back into the state
   put mp
   -- Return the value
   return v
   ```

10. Now, define the function to calculate the fibonacci number. We will use state (`map` between index and fibonacci number) as a cache. We will first try to retrieve the number out of the cache; if we do not find the number, we will calculate it. We will insert a new number into the cache immediately:

    ```
    fibWithState :: Integral a => a -> FibState a a
    ```

11. The first case is base case where the index can be 0 or 1. In this case, we will check if the map contains these values; otherwise, we will insert it into the map:

```
fibWithState i | i == 0 || i == 1 = do
            f <- getFib i
            case f of
              Just v -> return v
              Nothing -> putFib i i
```

12. The second and generic case is where we calculate the fibonacci number only if it is not in the cache:

```
-- Handle generic case
fibWithState n = do
n_1 <- getFibOr (n-1)
n_2 <- getFibOr (n-2)
putFib n (n_1 + n_2)

where
  getFibOr m = do
  fm <- getFib m
  case fm of
  Just fv -> return fv
  Nothing -> fibWithState m
```

13. Now, we will use the preceding lines of code to calculate few fibonacci numbers in the `main` function:

```
main :: IO ()
main = do
let mp = execState (fibWithState 30) M.empty
putStrLn "Calling fibWithState 30, would sore fibonacci number
till 30 in the map"
print mp
putStrLn "Calling any fibonacci number till 30 is memoized, and
will be only looked up"
print $ evalState (fibWithState 15) mp
```

14. Run and execute the program:

```
stack build
stack exec -- fibonacci state
```

15. You should see the following output:

```
●  ●  ●                          ▦ fibonacci-state — -bash — 118×20
fibonacci-state $stack exec -- fibonacci-state
Calling fibWithState 30, would sore fibonacci number till 30 in the map
fromList [(0,0),(1,1),(2,1),(3,2),(4,3),(5,5),(6,8),(7,13),(8,21),(9,34),(10,55),(11,89),(12,144),(13,233),(14,377),(1
5,610),(16,987),(17,1597),(18,2584),(19,4181),(20,6765),(21,10946),(22,17711),(23,28657),(24,46368),(25,75025),(26,121
393),(27,196418),(28,317811),(29,514229),(30,832040)]
Calling any fibonacci number till 30 is memoized, and will be only looked up
610
fibonacci-state $
```

How it works...

We have revisited fibonacci numbers in this recipe. Here, we used the State Monad to store the intermediate results while calculating the fibonacci number. We defined a map between the fibonacci index and its number as a state. Two functions getFib and putFib are defined. The getFib function uses State Monad function GET to get the map and checks if the result was previously cached. If the result was not cached before, then it proceeds by calculating the $n-1^{th}$ and $n-2^{th}$ fibonacci numbers and caching all intermediate results. In fact, since the $n-1^{th}$ number calculation will involve the $n-2^{th}$ number as well, the calculation will be quickly done *(O(n) complexity)*.

We used the function execState to run our fibonacci number calculation with state. The function execState does not return the result of the computation, but it results the last state.

In our example, we calculated the 30th fibonacci number. The state should include all fibonacci numbers between 1 to 30. Next time, when we calculate the 15th fibonacci number using the preceding state, the calculation would involve only looking up the index in the map.

We used the `evalState` function to get the result of the computation (state will be thrown away). We can also use `runState`, which returns both the last state and the result of the computation.

Writing a State Monad transformer

In this recipe, we will write our own State Monad transformer from scratch. In the state transformer, we embed another monad into a State Monad. Hence, all actions are performed in the embedded monad, whereas the state transformer is responsible for keeping state.

How to do it...

1. Create new project `state-monad-trans` using the `simple` Stack template:

   ```
   stack new state-monad-trans simple
   ```

2. Open `src/Main.hs`. We will be adding our state transformer here.

3. Add the following imports after the initial module declaration:

   ```
   import Data.Functor
   import Control.Applicative
   import Control.Monad
   ```

4. Define the State Monad transformer. Note how we embed `middle m (monad)` in the type:

   ```
   newtype StateT s m a = StateT { runStateT :: s -> m (a, s) }
   ```

5. Define the `Functor` instance for our state transformer:

   ```
   instance Functor m => Functor (StateT s m) where
   fmap f (StateT func) =
   let stateFunc s = (\(xa,xs) -> (f xa, xs)) <$> func s
   in StateT stateFunc
   ```

6. Now, define an `Applicative` instance for our state transformer. We make use of the fact that the embedded monad is also an instance of Applicative and use it to lift the embedded `Applicative` instance, that is, m (a -> b) -> m a -> m b to our state related m ((a, s) -> (b, s)) -> m (a, s) -> m (b, s):

```
instance Applicative m => Applicative (StateT s m) where

-- Use the applicative instance of the embedded applicative to
-- induce both x as well as state s into it.
pure x = let stateFunc s = pure (x, s)
   in StateT stateFunc

-- Get a function from State s m (a -> b) and apply it to
-- State s m a to produce State s m b

f <*> fa =
let stateFunc s =
let sf = runStateT f s -- m (f :: a -> b, s)
    sa = runStateT fa s -- m (a, s)
    -- Convert m (f :: a -> b, s) to
    -- m (f :: (a, s) -> (b, s) )
    func (fab, _) = (\(xa, st) -> (fab xa, st))
    in (func <$> sf) <*> sa
    in StateT stateFunc
```

7. Now, implement the monad instance for our transformer:

```
instance Monad m => Monad (StateT s m) where

return = pure

sma >>= smab =
let stateFunc s =
  let ma = runStateT sma s -- m (a, s)
  in do
    (a, s1) <- ma
    runStateT (smab a) s1
    in StateT stateFunc
```

8. Now, define get (to get the current state) and put (to put a new state) for our transformer:

```
get :: Monad m => StateT s m s
get = let stateFunc s = pure (s, s)
in StateT stateFunc

put :: Monad m => s -> StateT s m ()
put s = let stateFunc _ = pure ((), s)
in StateT stateFunc
```

9. We should allow an operation in the embedded monad in the context of our state transformer. Write the function lift to embed the action into our State Monad:

```
lift :: Monad m => m a -> StateT s m a
lift ma = let stateFunc s = do
  a <- ma
  return (a, s)
  in StateT stateFunc
```

10. Now, write an example in which we embed IO monad in our state transformer. To demonstrate, we simply get the current state and modify it with the supplied argument:

```
example :: Int -> StateT Int IO ()
example j = do
i <- get
lift $ putStrLn $ "Current state is " ++ (show i)
put j
i' <- get
lift $ putStrLn $ "Current state is " ++ (show i')
```

11. Then, use the example function in our main function:

```
main :: IO ()
main = do
(_, state) <- runStateT (example 10) 100
putStrLn $ "Result state is " ++ (show state)
(_, state1) <- runStateT (example 1234) 12
putStrLn $ "Result state is " ++ (show state1)
```

12. Build and execute the program:

```
stack build
stack exec -- state-monad-trans
```

13. You should see the following output:

```
state-monad-trans — -bash — 118×20
state-monad-trans $stack exec -- state-monad-trans
Current state is 100
Current state is 10
Result state is 10
Current state is 12
Current state is 1234
Result state is 1234
state-monad-trans $
```

How it works...

The state transformer that we defined is a pretty powerful construct. It lets us use another monad in the context of State Monad. Implementation may look a little hard to get the first time. However, if you remember that all the actions are performed in the internal monad (whatever it might be). To do this, we took advantage of the `do..` syntax for the monad (and that it is a `Functor` and an `Applicative` instance). All the internal monadic actions are modified from `m a` to `m (a, s)` and that is how we are able to achieve embedding of a monad inside a state transformer. All monad transformers follow a similar strategy.

In the `mtl` implementation of state transformer, you will see two implementations, lazy and strict. In the strict version, the state actions are sequenced using `seq`.

Working with the Reader monad transformer

In the previous recipe, we implemented our own State Monad transformer. In this recipe, we will revisit the `mtl` library and use the Reader monad transformer. The Reader monad transformer is a restricted version of the State Monad transformer in which we are allowed only to get the state (but not modify it).

How to do it...

1. Create a new project read-trans using the simple Stack template.

2. Open read-trans.cabal and add the following dependencies in the build-depends subsection of the executable section:

```
executable read-trans
hs-source-dirs: src
main-is: Main.hs
default-language: Haskell2010
build-depends: base >= 4.7 && < 5
         , mtl
```

3. Open src/Main.hs. We will add our example over here. Import the following module after the initial module declaration:

```
import Control.Monad.Reader
```

4. Write an example in which we keep read from an integer state, and check if our state meets certain criteria:

```
example :: ReaderT Int IO ()
example = do
s <- ask
lift $ putStrLn $ "Current env state is " ++ (show s)

s_is_10 <- asks (== 10)
lift $ putStrLn $ "Current state is 10? " ++ (show s_is_10)
```

5. Write another function where we will call the preceding example and call it again in a locally modified environment:

```
cover :: ReaderT Int IO ()
cover = do
example
local (const 10) example
```

6. Now, call the preceding function in main function:

```
main :: IO ()
main = runReaderT cover 100
```

7. Build and run the program:

```
stack build
stack exec -- read-trans
```

8. You should see the following output:

```
read-trans — -bash — 118×20

read-trans $stack exec -- read-trans
Current env state is 100
Current state is 10? False
Current env state is 10
Current state is 10? True
read-trans $
```

How it works...

The Reader monad is a monad transformer with the purpose of providing an environment. We use the monad transformer ReaderT :: r m a, which is defined in the Control.Monad.Reader module. In the mtl library, usually, each transformer has an associated type class. The transformer ReaderT is an instance of MonadReader type class:

```
class Monad m => MonadReader r (m :: * -> *) | m -> r where
  ask :: m r
  local :: (r -> r) -> m a -> m a
  reader :: (r -> a) -> m a
```

A special monad called `Identity` exists in `Data.Functor.Identity`, which is the simplest monad. Its only purpose is to embed a pure value into a monad. The `Reader` monad is defined as `ReaderT` with `Identity` as an embedded monad:

```
type Reader r = ReaderT r Identity
```

`MonadReader` provides three functions. The `ask :: MonadReader r m => m r` function gets the current environment. The function `asks :: MonadReader r m => (r -> a) -> m a` can be used to use a function that takes the current environment and produces some value that can be used in the context of the monad.

The function `local` is special, as shown here:

```
local :: MonadReader r m => (r -> r) -> m a -> m a
```

It takes a function that produces another environment. The supplied computation is executed under the modified environment. However, the current environment is unaffected.

Working with the Writer monad transformer

In the previous recipe, we worked with the Reader monad transformer. In this recipe, we will work with the Writer monad transformer. Like the Reader monad transformer, the Writer monad transformer is also a restricted version of a state transformer, in which we can only write (but cannot read).

Getting ready

In this example, we will use the Writer monad transformer to keep updating a balance sheet with transactions. We will keep pushing transactions to the Writer monad, finally yielding the balance after all transactions are processed.

We will work with the `mtl` library in this recipe.

How to do it...

1. Create a new project `write-trans` using the `simple` Stack template.

2. Open `write-trans.cabal` and add the `mtl` dependency in the `build-depends` subsection of the `executable` section:

```
executable write-trans
hs-source-dirs: src
main-is: Main.hs
default-language: Haskell2010
build-depends: base >= 4.7 && < 5
        , mtl
```

3. Open `src/Main.hs`. We will edit this file for our purpose.

4. Add the following imports after initial module declaration for the `WriterT` monad transformer:

```
import Data.Monoid
import Control.Monad.Writer
```

5. Add the data type `Transaction`. We will also add a `monoid` instance for the `Transaction`:

```
newtype Transaction = Transaction Double deriving Show
```

Add the `monoid` instance. We will define an empty transaction as a transaction with 0 amount. Appending two transactions involves summing up the transaction values. A positive transaction indicates a credit, whereas a negative transaction indicates a debit:

```
instance Monoid Transaction where

mempty = Transaction 0

(Transaction x) `mappend` (Transaction y) = Transaction (x + y)
```

6. Add a utility to classify the transaction as either a credit or a debit:

```
printTransaction :: Transaction -> IO ()
printTransaction (Transaction x) | x < 0 = putStrLn $ "Debiting
" ++ (show x)
printTransaction (Transaction x) | x > 0 = putStrLn $
"Crediting " ++ (show x)
printTransaction (Transaction x) = putStrLn "No Change"
```

7. Given a list of transactions, write a function to keep balancing using the Writer transformer:

```
balanceSheet :: [Transaction] -> WriterT Transaction IO ()
balanceSheet [] = lift $ putStrLn "Finished balancing"
balanceSheet (b:bs) = do
tell b
lift $ printTransaction b
balanceSheet bs
```

8. Create some random transactions:

```
transactions = [ Transaction (-10.0)
               , Transaction 5
               , Transaction 17
               , Transaction (-29)
               , Transaction 10]
```

9. Write `main` to calculate these transactions, and print balance:

```
main :: IO ()
main = do
(_, Transaction b) <- runWriterT (balanceSheet transactions)
putStrLn $ "Balance is " ++ (show b)
```

10. Build and execute the program:

```
stack build
stack exec -- write-trans
```

11. You should see the following output:

```
write-trans — -bash — 118×20
write-trans $stack exec write-trans
Debiting -10.0
Crediting 5.0
Crediting 17.0
Debiting -29.0
Crediting 10.0
Finished balancing
Balance is -7.0
write-trans $
```

How it works...

A Writer monad works with an assumption that the write state is an instance of a monoid. As a monoid, you will get two properties:

- mempty: This is a scratch value
- mappend: This is a way to combine two values

A Writer monad hence starts with an empty (or scratch) value. As we use the function tell in the context of Writer monad, the Writer monad keeps combining the existing value with a new value and updates the writer state.

In our recipe, we used Transaction and its monoid instance to keep our balance sheet automatically updated.

Combining monad transformers

So far, we have seen different monad transformers dedicated to specific causes. What if we would like to work with more than one transformer at the same time? In this recipe, we will be doing exactly that! We will work with Reader and Writer transformers with IO monad.

We will revisit the cursor example that we wrote earlier and then transform it to use it with multiple monad transformers.

How to do it...

1. Create a new project `combine-trans` with the `simple` Stack template.

2. Add `mtl` to the `build-depends` subsection of the `executable` section:

```
executable combine-trans
  hs-source-dirs: src
  main-is: Main.hs
  default-language: Haskell2010
  build-depends: base >= 4.7 && < 5
          , mtl
```

3. Open `src/Main.hs` and add the following imports after the initial module declaration. Import `Prelude` as well to avoid a clash with some names:

```
import Prelude hiding (Either(..))
import Control.Monad.Reader
import Control.Monad.Writer
import Data.Monoid
```

4. Define `Cursor` data type to show `Cursor` position from top-left position of the screen:

```
data Cursor = Cursor Int Int deriving Show
```

5. Define monoid instance for `Cursor`. When we combine two cursors, we simply sum their positions:

```
instance Monoid Cursor where

mempty = Cursor 0 0

(Cursor p q) `mappend` (Cursor r s) = Cursor (p + r) (q + s)
```

6. Define data type `Move` to define the movement of the cursor:

```
data Move = Up Int | Down Int | Left Int | Right Int deriving
Show
```

7. Define the function `toCursor` to `convertMove` to the cursor movement. For example, we will convert the `Up` movement to result in a cursor with a negative second component to indicate that we will be moving up the screen:

```
toCursor :: Move -> Cursor
toCursor (Up p) = Cursor 0 (-p)
toCursor (Down q) = Cursor 0 q
toCursor (Left p) = Cursor (-p) 0
toCursor (Right q) = Cursor q 0
```

8. Write the function `updateCursor`. It uses `tell` to update the state. A composition `tell . toCursor` converts `Move` to `Cursor` and updates the state as well:

```
updateCursor :: Monad m => Move -> WriterT Cursor m ()
updateCursor = tell . toCursor
```

9. Now, write the function `moveCursor`, which reads the current state from the `Reader` monad and uses `IO` and `Writer` actions to move the cursor according to the supplied moves:

```
moveCursor :: [Move] -> ReaderT Cursor (WriterT Cursor IO) ()
moveCursor ms = do
c <- ask      -- Get the position from the environment
lift $ tell c  -- Update the position
lift $ moveCursor' ms -- Keep moving cursor

where
moveCursor' [] = lift $ return ()
moveCursor' (m:ms) = do
lift $ putStrLn $ "Applying move " ++ (show m)
updateCursor m
moveCursor' ms
```

Note how we use `lift` for moving from the outer monad to the inner monad.

10. Create some random moves and write the `main` function to combine moves with Reader and Writer monad transformers:

```
moves = [Up 10, Right 10, Down 20, Left 5]

main :: IO ()
main = do
(_, cursor) <- runWriterT (runReaderT (moveCursor moves)
(Cursor 10 10))
putStrLn "Final cursor position"
print cursor
```

11. Build and execute the program:

```
stack build
stack exec -- combine-trans
```

12. You should see the following output:

```
● ● ●                        combine-trans — -bash — 118×20
combine-trans $stack exec -- combine-trans
Applying move Up 10
Applying move Right 10
Applying move Down 20
Applying move Left 5
Final cursor position
Cursor 15 20
combine-trans $
```

How it works...

When we combine monad transformers, we embed one type into another. For example, for our current recipe, the type is shown here:

```
ReaderT Cursor (WriterT Cursor IO) ()
```

It can be read as follows:

- The innermost monad is IO.
- WriterT embeds IO into it. The writer state is the Cursor.
- ReaderT embeds WriterT (and IO) monads. The ReaderT has the environment Cursor.
- Essentially, we start from the innermost monad and keep wrapping it with another monad.

To run the preceding monad, we have unwrapped the outer most monad first. Here, is our example:

- Outermost monad is ReaderT. We will unwrap it with runReaderT.
- Then next monad is WriterT. We will unwrap it with runWriterT.
- The IO monad actions are embedded innermost. When we unwrap everything, we are left with IO monad, which we executed in the main function, which is IO monad itself.

Hence, for our recipe to be able to run the composition of monads, we need to run the outer most monad (Reader Monad) first and then run the inner the monad (Writer Monad).

```
runWriterT (runReaderT (combined_monad) reader_state)
```

We can freely call actions from any monad. We need to remember to lift the actions. lift is a function which takes an action meant for one of the inner monads, and converts it into action in outer monad. For example, we need to lift $ putStrLn ... so that we can call the inner monad from the outer monad.

Also, note that the IO monad always remains the innermost monad. This is obvious as the IO monad reflects the outside world, which we are going to affect, and should be the very first monad to embed (so that it becomes the innermost monad).

6
Working with Common Containers and Strings

In this chapter, we will cover the following recipes:

- Working with sets
- Shopping cart as a set
- Working with maps
- Log analysis with map
- Working with vector
- Working with text and bytestring
- Creating and testing a priority queue
- Working with Foldable and Traversable

Introduction

We have looked at the basics of Haskell data types, functions, higher order functions, and other abstractions such as type classes. We have also looked at important type classes and concepts such as Functors, Applicatives, and monads.

In this chapter, we will look at common container data types and will work with them. We will visit strings again in this chapter, but with the intention of working in an efficient way. The `text` and `bytestring` packages provide us with an opportunity to work with efficient string types. Furthermore, the containers being a collection such as `list` also provides a way to fold and traverse in a similar way. We will look at two type classes, `Traversable` and `Foldable`, which give a unified way of folding and traversing over a data type.

A **set** is an ordered collection of unique items. If we insert an item which is already present in the set, then we get the same set back. One important difference between collections in Haskell and other languages is that the collections in Haskell (as other data types) are immutable. The set is implemented as a binary tree.

Working with sets

In this recipe, we will work with a set and its APIs. A `set` is a container that stores unique ordered values.

How to do it...

1. Create a new project `working-with-set` using the `simple` Stack template:

   ```
   stack new working-with-set simple
   ```

2. In the project folder, open the `working-with-set.cabal` file. Add the new dependency `containers` in the subsection `build-depends` of section `executable`:

   ```
   executable working-with-set
     hs-source-dirs:     src
     main-is:            Main.lhs
     default-language:   Haskell2010
     build-depends:      base >= 4.7 && < 5
                       , Containers
   ```

   The `containers` library is a commonly used library that implements containers such as `set`, `map`, and so on.

3. Open `src/Main.hs` for editing. We will work with `set`s in this file:

   ```
   module Main where
   ```

4. Import `Data.Set` for using `set` and related functions:

   ```
   import Data.Set as S
   ```

5. Write `main`; we will write `set` examples in the `main` function:

```
main :: IO ()
main = do
```

6. Create an empty `set`:

```
let emptyS = S.empty :: S.Set String
putStrLn "Empty String Set"
print emptyS
```

7. Create a singleton `set`:

```
let singleS = S.singleton "Single"
putStrLn "Singleton Set"
print singleS
```

8. Insert a string into a `set`:

```
let insS = S.insert "Another" singleS
putStrLn "Singleton with insertion"
print insS
```

9. Get the size of the `set`:

```
putStrLn "Size of the set"
print $ S.size insS
```

10. Create a `set` from a `list`:

```
let fromL = S.fromList [0..9] :: S.Set Int
putStrLn "Set from list"
print fromL
```

11. Create the `list` from the `set`:

```
let toL = S.toList fromL
putStrLn "List from set"
print toL
```

12. Create the ascending and descending lists from the `set`:

```
let toAscL = S.toAscList fromL
let toDscL = S.toDescList fromL
putStrLn "Set to ascending and descending lists"
print toAscL
print toDscL
```

13. Remove the minimum and maximum elements:

```
let removeMinS = S.deleteMin fromL
let removeMaxS = S.deleteMax fromL
putStrLn "Removing minimum and maximum elements"
print removeMinS
print removeMaxS
```

14. Union and intersection of two `set`s:

```
putStrLn "Take two sets [0..9] and [5..15]"
let fS = S.fromList [0..9]
let sS = S.fromList [5..15]
let intS = S.intersection fS sS
let uniS = S.union fS sS
putStrLn "Printing intersection and union respectively"
print intS
print uniS
```

15. Look up an element greater than and equal to an element:

```
putStrLn "Construct set from list [1, 2, 4]"
let exS = S.fromList [1,2,4] :: S.Set Int
putStrLn "Find element greater than 2"
print $ S.lookupGT 2 exS
putStrLn "Find element greater than or equal to 2"
print $ S.lookupGE 2 exS
```

16. Check whether it is an item element of `set`:

```
putStrLn "Find if 4 is part of the set from [0..9]"
print $ S.member 4 fromL
```

17. Fold over the set. In this case, we will use both foldr and foldl to fold over elements in the set.

```
putStrLn "Fold over the set using foldr and foldl"
print $ S.foldr (:) [] fromL
print $ S.foldl (flip (:)) [] fromL
```

18. Build and run the project:

```
stack build
stack exec -- working-with-set
```

19. You should see the following output:

```
working-with-set $ stack exec -- working-with-set
Empty String Set
fromList []
Singleton Set
fromList ["Single"]
Singleton with insertion
fromList ["Another","Single"]
Size of the set
2
Set from list
fromList [0,1,2,3,4,5,6,7,8,9]
List from set
[0,1,2,3,4,5,6,7,8,9]
Set to ascending and descending lists
[0,1,2,3,4,5,6,7,8,9]
[9,8,7,6,5,4,3,2,1,0]
Removing minimum and maximum elements
fromList [1,2,3,4,5,6,7,8,9]
fromList [0,1,2,3,4,5,6,7,8]
Take two sets [0..9] and [5..15]
Printing intersection and union respectively
fromList [5,6,7,8,9]
fromList [0,1,2,3,4,5,6,7,8,9,10,11,12,13,14,15]
Construct set from list [1, 2, 4]
Find element greater than 2
Just 4
Find element greater than or equal to 2
Just 2
Find if 4 is part of the set from [0..9]
True
Fold over the set using foldr and foldl
[0,1,2,3,4,5,6,7,8,9]
[9,8,7,6,5,4,3,2,1,0]
working-with-set $
```

How it works...

A `set` is an ordered collection of unique items. If we insert an item which is already present in the `set`, then we will get the same `set` back. The `set` is implemented as a binary tree.

Shopping cart as a set

In this recipe, we will create a shopping cart for books. The books are uniquely identified by ISBN numbers. If we add the same item in the shopping cart, we should be able to update the existing item or insert a new item in the shopping cart. We will use set as a container for shopping items.

How to do it...

1. Create a new project `shopping-cart` using the `simple` Stack template:

   ```
   stack new shopping-cart simple
   ```

2. Open `shopping-cart.cabal` and add a dependency on the `containers` library in the `build-depends` subsection of the `executable` subsection:

   ```
   executable shopping-cart
     hs-source-dirs:      src
     main-is:             Main.lhs
     default-language:    Haskell2010
     build-depends:       base >= 4.7 && < 5
                        , containers
   ```

3. Open `src/Main.hs`; we will add our code here. Import the module `Data.Set`:

   ```
   module Main where

   import Data.Set as Set
   ```

4. Create a type to represent a book. The book contains the ISBN number, title of the book, and name of the author:

```
data Book = Book { isbn :: String
          , title :: String
          , author :: String }
            deriving Show
```

5. Create the equality and ordering of the book solely by looking at the ISBN. We cannot use the default order instance, as it will also use other fields to create an order between two books. For our purpose, we will only consider ISBN as the primary key for creating an order:

```
instance Eq Book where

book1 == book2 = isbn book1 == isbn book2

instance Ord Book where

book1 `compare` book2 = isbn book1 `compare` isbn book2
```

6. Now, create an item for the shopping cart. Each item contains a book and the quantity ordered for it. Also, define instances of `Eq` and `Ord` for the item, as we do not want the number of books to be considered during the ordering of the items:

```
data Item = Item Book Int deriving Show

instance Eq Item where
(Item b1 _) == (Item b2 _) = b1 == b2

instance Ord Item where
(Item b1 _) `compare` (Item b2 _) = b1 `compare` b2
```

7. The shopping cart is represented by a set of items:

```
type ShoppingCart  = Set Item
```

8. Create an empty shopping cart:

```
emptyCart :: ShoppingCart
emptyCart = Set.empty
```

9. Add a book to the cart. We will create an item with `1` as the default quantity. We will add a new entry if the book is not present in the cart. If the book is already entered into the cart, we will increase the quantity by one:

```
addBook :: Book -> ShoppingCart -> ShoppingCart
addBook book cart =
let item = Item book 1
search = Set.lookupGE item cart
in case search of
 Nothing -> Set.insert item cart
 Just (Item b i) -> if isbn b == isbn book then
     Set.insert (Item b (i+1)) cart
     else
     Set.insert (Item book 1) cart
```

10. Similarly, remove a book from the cart; we will reduce the count of the book if it is already present in the cart. If the count goes down to zero, then we will remove the book from the cart. If the book is not present in the cart, then obviously, we do not need to do anything:

```
removeBook book cart =
let item = Item book 1
search = Set.lookupGE item cart
in case search of
Nothing -> cart
Just (Item b i) -> if isbn b == isbn book then
   if 0 >= (i -1) then
    Set.delete item cart
   else
    Set.insert (Item b (i-1)) cart
   else
    cart
```

11. Now, create some books and add them to the cart. We will add few books and remove few books:

```
main :: IO ()
main = do
let book1 = Book { isbn = "0262162091"
            , author = "Pierce, Benjamin C."
            , title = "Types and Programming Languages" }

book2 = Book { isbn = "8173715270"
            , author = "Abelson, Herold et. al."
            , title = "Structure and Interpretation of Computer
Programs" }
```

```
let cart = emptyCart
    cart1 = addBook book1 cart
    cart2 = addBook book2 cart1
    cart3 = addBook book1 cart2
    cart4 = addBook book1 cart3
    cart5 = removeBook book1 cart4
    cart6 = removeBook book2 cart5

putStrLn "Empty Cart"
print cart

putStrLn "Add book 1 to cart"
print cart1

putStrLn "Add book 2 to cart"
print cart2

putStrLn "Add book 1 again"
print cart3

putStrLn "And add book 1 once more"
print cart4

putStrLn "Remove book 1 from cart"
print cart5

putStrLn "Remvoe book 2, this should delete the book from the
cart"
print cart6
```

12. Build and execute the project:

```
stack build
stack exec -- shopping-cart
```

13. You should see the following output:

```
shopping-cart $ stack exec — shopping-cart
Empty Cart
fromList []
Add book 1 to cart
fromList [Item (Book {isbn = "0262162091", title = "Types and Programming Languages", author = "Pierce, Benjamin C."}) 1]
Add book 2 to cart
fromList [Item (Book {isbn = "0262162091", title = "Types and Programming Languages", author = "Pierce, Benjamin C."}) 1,Item (Book {i
sbn = "8173715270", title = "Structure and Interpretation of Computer Programs", author = "Abelson, Herold et. al."}) 1]
Add book 1 again
fromList [Item (Book {isbn = "0262162091", title = "Types and Programming Languages", author = "Pierce, Benjamin C."}) 2,Item (Book {i
sbn = "8173715270", title = "Structure and Interpretation of Computer Programs", author = "Abelson, Herold et. al."}) 1]
And add book 1 once more
fromList [Item (Book {isbn = "0262162091", title = "Types and Programming Languages", author = "Pierce, Benjamin C."}) 3,Item (Book {i
sbn = "8173715270", title = "Structure and Interpretation of Computer Programs", author = "Abelson, Herold et. al."}) 1]
Remove book 1 from cart
fromList [Item (Book {isbn = "0262162091", title = "Types and Programming Languages", author = "Pierce, Benjamin C."}) 2,Item (Book {i
sbn = "8173715270", title = "Structure and Interpretation of Computer Programs", author = "Abelson, Herold et. al."}) 1]
Remvoe book 2, this should delete the book from the cart
fromList [Item (Book {isbn = "0262162091", title = "Types and Programming Languages", author = "Pierce, Benjamin C."}) 2]
shopping-cart $
```

How it works...

The item in a `set` needs to be ordered, and being ordered also forces a definition of equality. Hence, we have defined `Eq` and `Ord` instances for our data type. Depending on the situation, we might want to create the order differently. For example, if you would like, you can make the search based on the book title or author.

 In a case where a different type class behavior is expected than the implementation, a typical trick is to wrap the existing data type, for which type class instance is already defined, in another type, and then define the type class instance for it instead.

Working with maps

In this recipe, we will look at `Data.Map`. A `map` keeps an association between the key and the corresponding value. The map stores the ordered keys and their values (dictionaries). There are two variants of `Map` in the container library, **strict** and **lazy**. In this recipe, we will look at the strict variant. The lazy variant has the same interface, except that the implementation is lazy.

How to do it...

1. Create a new project `work-with-map` using the `simple` stack template.

2. Add the `containers` library to the `build-depends` subsection of the executable subsection:

```
executable working-with-map
  hs-source-dirs:     src
  main-is:            Main.hs
  default-language:   Haskell2010
  build-depends:      base >= 4.7 && < 5
                  , containers
```

3. Open `src/Main.hs`; we will use this as our playground for dealing with map:

```
module Main where
```

4. Import `Data.Map` to use the `map` functions. We will use the strict version of map:

```
import Data.Map.Strict as M
```

5. We will use the `main` function directly to work with map functions:

```
main :: IO ()
main = do
```

6. **Map Construction**--Create an empty map or a map with a single entry:

```
let e = M.empty :: Map Int Int
let s = M.singleton 1 "Haskell Curry" :: Map Int String
putStrLn "Empty and singleton maps"
print e
print s
```

7. It is also possible to create a map from the list of keys and values:

```
let ml = M.fromList [(1, "Alphonso Church"), (2, "Haskell
Curry")] :: Map Int String
putStrLn "Map from list"
print ml
```

8. Insert into `Map`.

   While inserting, we have to deal with the fact that the key might be already there in the map. Map implementation deals with this fact by providing variants to manage different needs:

   ```
   let ml1 = M.insert 3 "Alan Turing" ml
   putStrLn "Inserting into map"
   print ml1
      -- [(1,"Alphonso Church"),(2, "Haskell Curry"), (3, "Alan
   Turing")]
   ```

9. Replace a value in a map:

   ```
   print $ M.insert 2 "Haskell Curry, Haskell inspiration" ml1
   -- [(1,"Alphonso Church"),(2, "Haskell Curry, Haskell
   inspiration"), (3, "Alan Turing")]
   ```

10. Use `insertWith` for insertion. It gives the ability to look at the old value in the map, and gives the chance to use the new value to construct the new value. In word count, we add the new value, equal to the addition of the old value and word count found since the last update:

    ```
    -- Word count in a para
    let iml = M.fromList [("a",10), ("an",2), ("the", 8)] :: Map
    String Int
    print (M.insertWith (+) "a" 2 iml)
    -- [("a",12),("an",2),("the",8)]
    ```

11. Delete from the map.

    Remove the article `"the"` from the preceding map. We will provide a key to delete a key-value pair from the container.

    ```
    print (M.delete "the" iml)
    -- [("a",10),("an",2)]
    ```

12. Update the map.

Use the variant `updateWithKey`. It takes a function that looks at a key, and the value, and possibly produces another value. This can result in either replacing a value or deleting the key-value pair in the map. Define the `updater` function. It changes value of `"an"` in the article map we created earlier. It also deletes the key `the` from the map. Everything else is kept the same:

```
let updater "an" _ = Just 5
    updater "the" 8 = Nothing
    updater _  v   = Just v
print $ M.updateWithKey updater "an" im1
-- [("a",10),("an",5),("the",8)]
print $ M.updateWithKey updater "the" im1
-- [("a",10),("an",2)]
```

13. Union and difference of maps.

Two maps can be combined to create a single map. We will use the `unionWith` variant here. We will create another word count map and combine it here. We will add the counts if duplicate entries are found. This is done by supplying the `(+)` function to `unionWith`:

```
let im11 = M.fromList [("a",3),("and",6)]
print $ M.unionWith (+) im1 im11
-- [("a",13),("an",2),("and",6),("the",8)]
```

14. Similarly, we can find the difference between two maps. We use `differenceWith` where we can select whether to keep the value in the first map or not. Use `differenceWith` if you'd like to remove the duplicate keys. Note that the second map that the difference function takes does not have the same value type. The key type should be same, though:

```
let im12 = M.fromList [("an",False),("the",True)]
let diff v False = Nothing
    diff v _     = Just v
print $ M.differenceWith diff im1 im12
-- [("a",10),("the",8)]
```

15. Find the intersection of two maps by finding common keys. The `intersection` function prefers the value int the first map. If the key is present in both the maps, then the intersection function will keep the value in the first map.
    The `intersectionWith` function lets you decide what to do with the values. Here, we will use the `intersection` function:

    ```
    print $ M.intersection im1 im11
    -- [("a",10)]
    ```

16. Build and execute the project:

    ```
    stack build
    stack exec -- working-with-map
    ```

17. The program output should agree with our expected answers:

```
working-with-map $ stack exec -- working-with-map
Empty and singleton maps
fromList []
fromList [(1,"Haskell Curry")]
Map from list
fromList [(1,"Alphonso Church"),(2,"Haskell Curry")]
Inserting into map
fromList [(1,"Alphonso Church"),(2,"Haskell Curry"),(3,"Alan Turing")]
fromList [(1,"Alphonso Church"),(2,"Haskell Curry, Haskell inspiration"),(3,"Alan Turing")]
fromList [("a",12),("an",2),("the",8)]
fromList [("a",10),("an",2)]
fromList [("a",10),("an",5),("the",8)]
fromList [("a",10),("an",2)]
fromList [("a",13),("an",2),("and",6),("the",8)]
fromList [("a",10),("the",8)]
fromList [("a",10)]
working-with-map $
```

How it works...

We have seen common functions for dealing with `map`. Typically, the function without the suffix `With` or `WithKey` has default behavior. For example, in insert, the default behavior is to replace the existing value. The suffix `With` takes two values to produce a new value. The suffix `WithKey` also takes into consideration the key for which we are combining values.

There are two variants of map, `Data.Map.Strict` and `Data.Map.Lazy`. Both the modules export the same function names. These functions vary in their strictness. The `strict` map will immediately evaluate the resulting map, whereas the `lazy` map will do so lazily by storing the expressions and reducing them only when asked for.

However, the `functor` and `Applicative` instances of both the maps are lazy. Hence, it is wiser to use functions in the `strict` map module (and not `Functor` or `Applicative` class functions) if efficiency is of importance.

Log analysis with map

In this recipe, we will use `map` to analyze the access log for the Apache web server. The log contains access parameters for each host accessing the web server per line. The log looks like this:

```
64.242.88.10 - - [07/Mar/2004:16:10:02 -0800] "GET
/mailman/listinfo/hsdivision HTTP/1.1" 200 6291
64.242.88.10 - - [07/Mar/2004:16:11:58 -0800] "GET
/twiki/bin/view/TWiki/WikiSyntax HTTP/1.1" 200 7352
64.242.88.10 - - [07/Mar/2004:16:20:55 -0800] "GET
/twiki/bin/view/Main/DCCAndPostFix HTTP/1.1" 200
5253
```

The line starts with `hostname` or `IP` that is accessing the web server. The remaining part of the line includes date and time, method of access (`GET`, `PUT`, `POST`, and so on), and the path of the web server being accessed. The server also prints status information.

How to do it...

1. Create a new project `log-parser` with the `simple` Stack template:

```
stack new log-parser simple
```

2. Open `log-parser.cabal` and add the library `containers` as a dependent library in the subsection `build-depends` of the section `executable`:

```
executable log-parser
hs-source-dirs:      src
main-is:             Main.hs
default-language:    Haskell2010
build-depends:       base >= 4.7 && < 5
                   , containers
```

3. Open `src/Main.hs` and edit it. We will add log parsing and analysis here:

```
module Main where
```

4. Import modules for `file IO` and the `strict` map:

```
import System.IO
import qualified Data.Map.Strict as M
import System.Environment
import Control.Monad
```

5. Read the file line by line:

```
hLines :: Handle -> IO [String]
hLines h = do
isEOF <- hIsEOF h
if isEOF then
  return []
else
  (:) <$> hGetLine h <*> hLines h
```

6. We are only interested in the `host` or `IP`. Grab it. Return an empty string if you are presented with an empty list:

```
host :: [String] -> String
host (h:_) = h
host _     = ""
```

7. Convert the list of lines into a list of host names using the functions `words` (to convert a line into words) and `host` (to take only the first of those words):

```
hosts :: Handle -> IO [String]
hosts h = fmap (host . words) <$> hLines h
```

8. Given a `hostname` and a `map`, add the `hostname` to the `map` with access count one. If the host is already present in the `map`, then add the counts:

```
updateAccessCount :: String -> M.Map String Int -> M.Map String
   Int
updateAccessCount h mp = M.insertWith (+) h 1 mp
```

9. Fold over the list of hosts, starting with an empty map and adding the hostname with the access count. Use the function `updateAccessCount` to combine the `hostname` (or `IP`) with the access count map:

```
foldHosts :: [String] -> M.Map String Int
foldHosts = foldr updateAccessCount M.empty
```

10. Get the data from `http://www.monitorware.com/en/logsamples/apache.php`. The data is free to be used. We will give the relative path of the log file as an argument. Then, proceed to get a `map`. We will then convert the `map` to the `list` and then print the names of the hosts and their access count:

```
main :: IO ()
main = do
(log:_) <- getArgs
accessMap <- withFile log ReadMode (fmap foldHosts . hosts)
let accesses = M.toAscList accessMap
forM_ accesses $ \(host, count) -> do
putStrLn $ host ++ "\t" ++ show count
```

11. Build and run the project:

```
stack build
stack exec -- log-parser access_log/access_log
```

12. The output should print the statistics of `hostname` or `IP` against its accesses:

```
● ● ●                          log-parser — -bash — 106×37
log-parser $ stack exec -- log-parser access_log/access_log
0x503e4fce.virnxx2.adsl-dhcp.tele.dk    3
1-320.cnc.bc.ca 4
1-729.cnc.bc.ca 7
10.0.0.153      270
12.22.207.235   1
128.227.88.79   14
142.27.64.35    7
145.253.208.9   7
1513.cps.virtua.com.br  1
194.151.73.43   4
195.11.231.210  1
195.230.181.122 1
195.246.13.119  12
2-110.cnc.bc.ca 11
2-238.cnc.bc.ca 1
200-55-104-193.dsl.prima.net.ar 13
200.160.249.68.bmf.com.br       2
200.222.33.33   1
203.147.138.233 13
206-15-133-153.dialup.ziplink.net       1
206-15-133-154.dialup.ziplink.net       1
206-15-133-181.dialup.ziplink.net       1
207.195.59.160  20
208-186-146-13.nrp3.brv.mn.frontiernet.net      2
208-38-57-205.ip.cal.radiant.net        11
208.247.148.12  4
212.21.228.26   1
212.92.37.62    14
213.181.81.4    1
216-160-111-121.tukw.qwest.net  12
216.139.185.45  1
219.95.17.51    1
3_343_lt_someone        10
4.37.97.186     1
61.165.64.6     4
61.9.4.61       3
```

How it works...

The recipe reads the file line by line. Each line is split into words using the function `words`. Since we are interested in only the `host` or its `IP`, we will take only the first word. Each host name / IP is considered as a tuple (`hostname`, 1), where 1 denotes that each entry corresponds to single access. We used the `insertWith` function to insert the preceding entry. If the entry already exists in the map, then we would use combining function to add 1 to the existing access count. We got hosts in the ascending order using the function `toAscList`. We used `Control.Monad.forM_` to iterate over the list of accesses and print them to the console.

Working with vector

In this recipe, we will look at `Data.Vector` from the `vector` package. So far, we have been extensively using lists. Though lists are ubiquitous in Haskell, they are not efficient where array-like access and operations are required. A vector supports arrays such as *O(1)* access to elements, as well as list-like incremental access. The vectors come in two flavors—immutable and mutable. We will look at both in this recipe.

How to do it...

1. Create a new project `working-with-vector` with the `simple` Stack template:

   ```
   stack new working-with-vector simple
   ```

2. Add the dependency on the `vector` package in the `build-depends` subsection of the executable section:

   ```
   executable working-with-vector
     hs-source-dirs:      src
     main-is:             Main.hs
     default-language:    Haskell2010
     build-depends:       base >= 4.7 && < 5
                        , vector
   ```

3. Open `src/Main.hs` and start coding there. We will experiment with vector in this file:

   ```
   module Main where
   ```

4. Import both immutable and mutable vector modules:

   ```
   import qualified Data.Vector as V
   import qualified Data.Vector.Mutable as MV
   import Data.Vector ((//),(!),(!?))
   ```

5. We will use smaller functions to demonstrate the vector and its abilities.

6. **Construction**: We can construct immutable vectors either as empty, singleton, replicated, generated over input index, or combined with the previous value:

   ```
   constructVectors :: IO ()
   constructVectors = do
   let e = V.empty :: V.Vector Int
     s = V.singleton "one" :: V.Vector String
   ```

```
      r = V.replicate 10 "same" :: V.Vector String
      g = V.generate 10 (const "generated")  :: V.Vector String
      i = V.iterateN 10 ('x':) "o"
      putStrLn $ "Empty vector " ++ show e
      putStrLn $ "Singleton vector " ++ show s
      putStrLn $ "Replicated vector " ++ show r
      putStrLn $ "Generated vector " ++ show g
      putStrLn $ "Iterated vector " ++ show i
```

7. Construct vectors through enumeration. The function `enumFromTo` can also be used, but it is slower than `enumFromN`:

```
enumeratedVectors :: IO ()
enumeratedVectors = do
  putStrLn "Create a list of 10 floats, 1.1, 2.1 ... etc"
  print $ (V.enumFromN 1.1 10 :: V.Vector Float)
  putStrLn "Create a list of 10 floats, incremented by 0.5"
  print $ (V.enumFromStepN 1.1 0.5 10 :: V.Vector Float)
```

8. **Vector as list**: Vector supports many functions similar to `list`. Note that all operations are *O(1)*:

```
vectorAsList :: IO ()
vectorAsList = do
let vec = V.enumFromStepN 1 3 30 :: V.Vector Int
putStrLn "All elements but the last"
print $ V.init vec
putStrLn "Head of the vector"
print $ V.head vec
putStrLn "Tail of the vector"
print $ V.tail vec
putStrLn "Take first five elements"
print $ V.take 5 vec
putStrLn "Drop first five elements"
print $ V.drop 5 vec
putStrLn "Prepend and Append an element"
print $ V.cons 99 vec
print $ V.snoc vec 99
putStrLn "Concatenate two vectors"
print $ vec V.++ (V.fromList [101,102,103])
```

9. Bulk update of vectors:

```
bulkOperations :: IO ()
bulkOperations = do
putStrLn "Replace elements by list of index and value."
print $ (V.fromList [2,5,8]) // [(0,3),(1,6),(2,9)]
```

```
putStrLn "Update with another vector with index and value"
print $ (V.fromList [2,5,8]) `V.update` (V.fromList [(0,3),
(1,6),(2,9)])
```

10. Indexing operations—access elements in vector randomly:

```
indexing :: IO ()
indexing = do
  let vec = V.enumFromStepN 1.1 0.5 20
  putStrLn "Input Vector"
  print vec
  putStrLn "Accessing 10 th element"
  print $ vec ! 9
  putStrLn "Safely accessing 10th element, and 100th one"
  print $ vec !? 9
  print $ vec !? 99
```

11. Create a mutable vector. Mutable vectors are created either in IO or ST monad. Here, we will create it with `IOVector`:

```
mutableVec :: IO (MV.IOVector Int)
mutableVec = do
v <- MV.new 2  -- Create a vector of size 2
MV.write v 0 1 -- Assign all values
MV.write v 1 2
return v
```

12. Use the mutable vector and `freeze` it to convert to immutable vector:

```
useMutable :: IO ()
useMutable = do
mv <- mutableVec
vec <- V.freeze mv
putStrLn "Mutable to vector conversion"
print vec
```

13. Put all of the preceding code snippets together:

```
main :: IO ()
main = do
putStrLn "Constructing Vectors"
constructVectors
putStrLn "Enumerating Vectors"
enumeratedVectors
putStrLn "Vector as fast lists"
vectorAsList
putStrLn "Bulk operations on vector"
```

```
bulkOperations
putStrLn "Accessing elements of vector"
indexing
putStrLn "Working with mutable, and converting it to vector"
useMutable
```

14. Build and run the project:

```
stack build
stack exec -- working-with-vector
```

15. You should see following output:

How it works...

When compared to list, map, and set, vector proposes a very different approach. It is a very efficient collection and most access operations are done with *O(1)* access. The vector is used in many efficient libraries such as *aeson (a popular library for dealing with JSON)*, where efficiency and random access is required. The vector itself is immutable and provides effective subsetting through list-like operations.

The mutable vector, on the other hand ,works through monad, by allowing us to programmatically construct the vector and then freeze it to convert it to an immutable vector.

Working with text and bytestring

In this recipe, we will look at alternative representations of *string*. The *string* is a list of *Char* and is not an efficient implementation. The text and bytestring packages are the most popular packages for alternative and efficient string implementations. While text implements *unicode* characters, bytestring is good for binary data. In this recipe, we will work with these data types and convert them into each other, and also explore a GHC extension for strings.

How to do it...

1. Create a new project working-with-text-and-bytestring with the simple Stack template:

   ```
   stack new working-with-text-and-bytestring simple
   ```

2. Add dependency on the text and bytestring libraries in the build-depends subsection of the executable section:

   ```
   executable working-with-text-and-bytestring
   hs-source-dirs:      src
   main-is:             Main.hs
   default-language:    Haskell2010
   build-depends:       base >= 4.7 && < 5
                      , text
                      , bytestring
   ```

3. Open src/Main.hs. We will add our source here.

4. At the top of the file, add the following `pragma` for using overloaded strings before the `Main` module definition:

```
{-# LANGUAGE OverloadedStrings #-}
module Main where
```

This is the way an extension is enabled for the GHC. This particular extension allows us to use string of types `string`, `text`, and `ByteString`. In fact, you will notice that all these data types are instances of the class `IsString`. If a data type is an instance of `IsString`, then the extension `OverloadedStrings` can be applied in the context of that data type. One of the advantages of using the `OverloadedStrings` extension is that we can use a quoted string without having to explicitly convert it from the built-in `string` data type. We will see this in action when we are dealing with `Text` and `ByteString`.

5. Add the following modules for working with `Text` and `ByteString`:

```
import qualified Data.Text as T
import qualified Data.Text.IO as TIO
import qualified Data.ByteString.Char8 as B
import qualified Data.Text.Encoding as TE
import System.IO
```

6. Create `ByteString` and `Text`:

```
bString :: B.ByteString
bString = "This is a bytestring"
```

7. Create `Text`:

```
tString :: T.Text
tString = "This is a text string"
```

8. Convert from `string` to `Text` and `ByteString`:

```
stringToByteString :: B.ByteString
stringToByteString = B.pack "Converted from string to
bytestring"

stringToText :: T.Text
stringToText = T.pack "Converted from string to text"
```

9. Convert from `ByteString` and `Text` to `String`:

```
bytestringToString :: String
bytestringToString = B.unpack "From bytestring to string"

textToString :: String
textToString = T.unpack "From text to string"
```

10. Convert between `bytestring` and `text`:

```
bytestringToText :: T.Text
bytestringToText = TE.decodeUtf8 "From bytestring to text"

textToBytestring :: B.ByteString
textToBytestring = TE.encodeUtf8 "From text to bytestring"
```

11. List like operations on `text` and `bytestring`, most of the operations on string work on `text` and `bytestring`:

```
textHead :: Char
textHead = T.head "First" -- returns 'F'

textTail :: T.Text
textTail = T.tail "First" -- returns 'F'

byteHead :: Char
byteHead = B.head "First" -- should get "irst"

byteTail :: B.ByteString
byteTail = B.tail "First" -- should get "irst"
```

12. Write the `main` function. In this recipe, we will not use all the preceding functions in `main`. Instead, we will only print `bytestring` and `text` using `putStrLn`. The `text` and `bytestring` modules define their own versions of the `System.IO` functions. In the following function, we will print `ByteString` and `Text`, respectively:

```
main :: IO ()
main = do
TIO.putStrLn tString
B.putStrLn bString
-- Open a file and write both the strings into the same file.
withFile "text-out.txt" WriteMode $ \h -> do
TIO.hPutStrLn h tString
B.hPutStrLn h bString
```

13. Build and execute the project:

```
stack build
stack exec -- working-with-text-and-bytestring
```

14. You should see the following output:

```
● ● ●                    working-with-text-and-bytestring — -bash — 107×16
working-with-text-and-bytestring $ stack exec -- working-with-text-and-bytestring
This is a text string
This is a bytestring
working-with-text-and-bytestring $
```

The program should also write an output to text-out.txt by writing the same lines.

How it works...

Text and ByteString are very efficient implementations of String. We have already
used ByteString in the recipe where we used Attoparsec to parse the INI files. We will
use these types in many recipes to come.

Creating and testing a priority queue

In this recipe, we will create and test our own collection **priority queue** based on a
binary tree, and at the same time, we will test it based on its invariant. Many collections and
data structures require binary tree as a basic ingredient.

A priority queue that we will consider is a `leftist` heap. A `leftist` heap is implemented as a `heap-ordered` binary tree. In a `heap-ordered` binary tree, the value at the node is less than or equal to the values of children. A priority queue is used where we are always interested in the *minimum* element in the collection and would like to extract or remove it from the collection. The `leftist` priority queue obeys `leftist` property.

 The `leftist` property says that the **rank** of a *left child* is greater than or equal to the **rank** of a *right child*. The **rank** of a node is the length of the rightmost path from the node to an empty node. This path is called the **right spine** of the node. As a result of the `leftist` property, we get a tree where the right spine of any node is always the shortest path to an empty node.

Getting ready

We will be using `QuickCheck` as our testing infrastructure to help write tests for priority queue.

How to do it...

1. Create a new project `priority-queue` with the `default` Stack template:

   ```
   stack new priority-queue
   ```

2. Delete the `src/Lib.hs` file. Create a directory `src/Data/` and create a new file `src/Data/PriorityQueue.hs`. We will add implementation of priority queue here.

3. Open `priority-queue.cabal`. Remove `Lib` from the `exposed-modules` subsection from the `library` section. Replace it with our new `Data.PriorityQueue` module:

   ```
   library
     hs-source-dirs:      src
     exposed-modules:     Data.PriorityQueue
     build-depends:       base >= 4.7 && < 5
     default-language:    Haskell2010
   ```

4. Open `src/Data/PriorityQueue.hs`. We will implement the priority queue here.

5. Add the module definition for `Data.PriorityQueue`:

```
module Data.PriorityQueue where
```

6. Let's define the `Queue` as a sum type. The `Queue` can either be empty or it can have two subqueues. We will also keep the `rank` information with the queue:

```
data Queue a = Empty
     | Queue Int a (Queue a) (Queue a)
     deriving Show
```

Note that the queue is defined as heap-ordered. Automatically, it also follows that the values on the right spine are heap-ordered, as well. Since the priority queue that we are implementing obeys the leftist property, we will look at a problem where this property gets disturbed. There are two instances when the leftist property will be violated:

1) When we are inserting a value
2) When we are deleting a value (that is, extracting the minimum)

In both cases, we will have to find a subtree where we are inserting a value (or removing a value). This would result in a possible violation of the leftist property. Here, we have to take the violated path (where the rank of the left child is less than the rank of the right child) and readjust the elements. We will do this by merging two trees.

7. Write a function to merge two trees, adjusting the `rank` along the way:

```
mergeQs :: Ord a => Queue a -> Queue a -> Queue a
mergeQs Empty q = q
mergeQs q Empty = q
mergeQs left@(Queue _ lv ll lr) right@(Queue _ rv rl rr) =
if lv <= rv then
  swipe lv ll (mergeQs lr right)
else
  swipe rv rl (mergeQs left rr)
```

Here, the `swipe` function checks the ranks for two trees being merged, and swaps them if they violate the `leftist` property. We will implement `swipe` later.

8. Write the function to find the `rank` of the queue:

```
rank :: Queue a -> Int
rank Empty = 0
rank (Queue r _ _ _) = r
```

9. Write the `swipe` function to check the rank and `swipe` `left` and `right` branches to obey the `leftist` property:

```
swipe :: a -> Queue a -> Queue a -> Queue a
swipe v left right =
if rank left >= rank right then
  Queue (rank right + 1) v left right
else
  Queue (rank left + 1) v right left
```

10. Now, write the interface functions for our `Queue` implementation. We need three functions `insert`, `minimum`, and `deleteMin` to manipulate the `Queue`. However, before that, we need to have helper functions to construct a `Queue`.

11. Create an empty queue:

```
emptyQ :: Queue a
emptyQ = Empty
```

12. Create a singleton queue from a value. The singleton node will have a rank `1`:

```
singletonQ :: a -> Queue a
singletonQ v = Queue 1 v Empty Empty
```

13. Implement the `insert` function. The `insert` operation is equivalent to merging a singleton into an existing queue:

```
insert :: Ord a => a -> Queue a -> Queue a
insert v q = mergeQs (singletonQ v) q
```

14. Implement the `minimum` function. The `minimum` function returns `Nothing` if the queue is empty; otherwise, it returns the root value in the tree, which is guaranteed to be minimum:

```
minimum :: Queue a -> Maybe a
minimum Empty = Nothing
minimum (Queue _ v _ _) = Just v
```

15. Implement the `deleteMin` function. We will take out the root value and merge the two remaining trees:

```
deleteMin :: Ord a => Queue a -> Queue a
deleteMin Empty = Empty
deleteMin (Queue _ _ l r) = mergeQs l r
```

16. We are now done with implementation of the priority queue.
    Open `app/Main.hs`. Import the `Data.PriorityQueue` module:

    ```
    import Data.PriorityQueue as Q
    ```

17. Open `src/Main.hs`. We will add our source here. In the `main` function, create an
    empty queue and keep adding a few integers:

    ```
    main :: IO ()
    main = do
    let e = emptyQ :: Queue Int
    q1 = insert 10 e
    q2 = insert 20 q1
    q3 = insert 15 q2
    q4 = insert 2 q3
    -- This should print 2 (minimum value)
    print (Q.minimum q4)
    -- This should remove minimum
    let q5 = deleteMin q4
    -- This should now print 10
    print (Q.minimum q5)
    ```

18. Build and execute the project:

    ```
    stack build
    stack exec -- priority-queue-exe
    ```

19. You should see the following output:

20. We will add the tests to verify our claims about invariants in the priority queue. We will use the `QuickCheck` library to verify our claims. Open `priority-queue.cabal` and add the `QuickCheck` dependency to the `build-depends` subsection of the `test-suite` section. Note that the `stack` has already added the dependency on our library `priority-queue` here:

```
test-suite priority-queue-test
type:              exitcode-stdio-1.0
hs-source-dirs:    test
main-is:           Spec.hs
build-depends:     base
                 , priority-queue
                 , QuickCheck
ghc-options:       -threaded -rtsopts -with-rtsopts=-N
default-language:  Haskell2010
```

21. Import the `QuickCheck` module:

```
import Test.QuickCheck
 import qualified Data.PriorityQueue as Q
```

22. The `QuickCheck` library, contrary to other unit test libraries, generates tests. Here, we write `properties` that should be verified by `QuickCheck`. This saves us from a developer's bias, and at the same time, we get a minimum input (or steps) that would fail the property. We need to generate arbitrary instances of queue. Let's use the `Arbitrary` class to do that. We will take a list of values and generate a queue out of it using the `Gen` monad. The `Arbitrary` instance of `Queue` first generates the list of values and then *inserts* these values into a queue through `foldr`:

```
qFromList :: Ord a => [a] -> Gen (Q.Queue a)
qFromList xs = return (foldr Q.insert Q.emptyQ xs)

instance (Arbitrary a, Ord a) => Arbitrary (Q.Queue a) where
arbitrary = listOf arbitrary >>= qFromList
```

23. We will first verify the claim about the `leftist` property of the tree. To be able to do this, we will write a function that takes a tree and verifies that each node follows the `leftist` property. We will also verify `rankstored` in the queue in the process:

```
qrank :: Q.Queue a -> Int
qrank Q.Empty = 0
qrank (Q.Queue _ _ l r) = 1 + minimum [qrank l, qrank r]
```

```
verifyLeftist :: Q.Queue a -> Bool
verifyLeftist Q.Empty = True
verifyLeftist q@(Q.Queue rnk v l r) =
and [ qrank q == rnk
    , qrank l >= qrank r
    , verifyLeftist l
    , verifyLeftist r ]
```

24. Now, test the `heapOrdered` property of the queue:

```
heapOrdered :: Ord a => Q.Queue a -> Bool
heapOrdered Q.Empty = True
heapOrdered (Q.Queue _ _ Q.Empty Q.Empty) = True
heapOrdered (Q.Queue _ v Q.Empty r@(Q.Queue _ rv _ _)) =
  and [ v <= rv, heapOrdered r ]
heapOrdered (Q.Queue _ v l@(Q.Queue _ lv _ _) Q.Empty) =
  and [ v <= lv, heapOrdered l ]
heapOrdered (Q.Queue _ v l@(Q.Queue _ lv _ _) r@(Q.Queue _ rv _
_)) =
  and [ v <= lv, v <= rv, heapOrdered l, heapOrdered r]
```

25. Now, we have two properties, `verifyLeftist` and `heapOrdered`, which take a queue and return a boolean. We will use these properties in conjunction with `quickCheck` to run the tests:

```
main :: IO ()
main = do
putStrLn ""
putStrLn "Verifying Leftist Property"
quickCheck (verifyLeftist :: Q.Queue Int -> Bool)
putStrLn "Verifying Heap Ordered Property"
quickCheck (heapOrdered :: Q.Queue Int -> Bool)
```

26. Build and execute the test. Run the `stack build` command with the `--test` argument:

`stack build --test`

27. You should be able to see the following output:

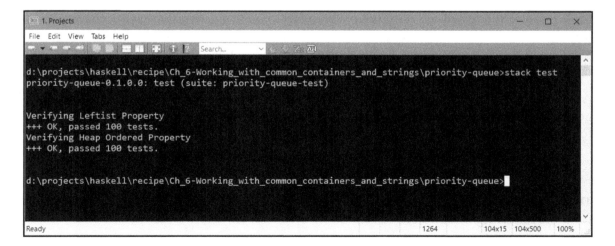

The preceding test result shows that it ran `100` tests with each property. We can introduce a bug (this time, in our testing code by modifying the `qrank` function not to add `1` to the children ranks). Define `qrank` as follows:

```
qrank (Q.Queue _ _ l r) = minimum [qrank l, qrank r]
```

28. If you now run the test by executing `stack test`, you should see following output! In case of failure, you should also see the input queue for which the test failed. This is really helpful and shows the strength of `QuickCheck`:

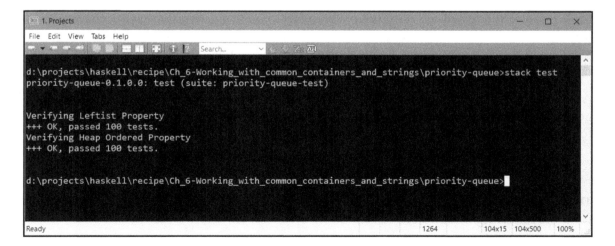

How it works...

We implemented a **Leftist Tree** here. This is a very good example of immutability, data persistence, and in general, how to implement a data structure in Haskell. We started with a representation for a `queue`, `heap`, and an invariant `Leftist` property. A typical leftist tree looks like the one shown in this diagram:

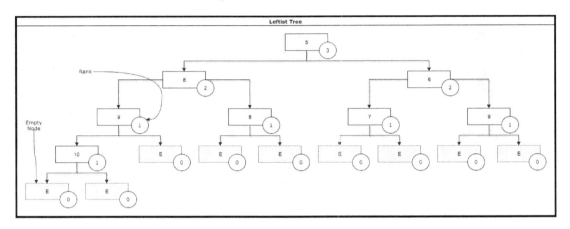

Then, we proceeded to implement a `mergeQs` function, which is at the heart of the implementation. The operations `insert` and `deleteMin` both result in an operation that changes the structure of the tree. This change can violate the leftist property or the heap order. The `mergeQs` function merges two trees and restores these invariants.

Most importantly, we tested our queue with `QuickCheck`, a generative approach towards testing. The `QuickCheck` works by generating random data and tries to zoom in to a problem in the case of a failure, by generating a smaller set of data. This is very helpful, and it is possible to catch *subtle* bugs with this approach. It also removes developer bias.

At the heart of `QuickCheck` is the class `Arbitrary`, which has an `arbitrary` function to generate random instances of data types. The core of `QuickCheck` comes from the following definition of `Testable`:

```
class Testable prop where
property :: prop -> Property
```

The data type `Property` is the result of testing `prop`. The real genius of `QuickCheck` comes from the following instance of `Testable`:

```
instance [safe] (Arbitrary a, Show a, Testable prop) =>
            Testable (a -> prop)
```

The preceding instance tells us that if we have a `Testable` property and an `Arbitrary` instance of `a`, then we can test a function `a -> prop`. This fantastic definition helps us test our functions such as `verifyLeftist :: Queue a -> Bool`. The `Bool` is a `testable` property. Thus, our function also becomes testable. The `QuickCheck` library will generate arbitrary instances of `Queue a` and run the tests!

Working with Foldable and Traversable

In this recipe, we will work with two type classes, `Traversable`, and `Foldable`. Both these classes are the generalization of the functions that we have seen when working with `Lists`. `Traversable`, as the name suggests, allows us to browse a data structure to traverse from left to right. Similarly, the `Foldable` type class allows us to *fold* the elements of a data type.

In fact, in previous versions of GHC, traversals and folding were defined for lists. In recent versions, those functions are generalized to include `Traversable` and `Foldable`, making them applicable to a wide range of data structures.

We will also define `Traversable` and `Foldable` instances for a tree.

How to do it...

1. Create a new project `working-with-traversable-foldable-map` with the `simple` Stack template:

   ```
   stack new working-with-traversable-foldable-map simple
   ```

2. Add dependency on the containers library in the `build-depends` subsection of the `executable` section:

   ```
   executable working-with-traversable-foldable-map
   hs-source-dirs:     src
   main-is:            Main.hs
   default-language:   Haskell2010
   build-depends:      base >= 4.7 && < 5
                     , containers
   ```

3. Open `src/Main.hs`. We will add our source here. Import the `Map` module:

   ```
   import Data.Map.Strict as M hiding (foldr)
   ```

4. Create a list of tuple of `Int` and `String`:

```
a2z :: [(Int,String)]
a2z = zipWith (\i c -> (i,c:[])) [1..] ['a'..'z']
```

5. Create a map from the preceding list:

```
imap :: M.Map Int String
imap = M.fromList a2z
```

6. `Map` is an instance of `Foldable`. Use `foldMap` and `foldr` to concatenate and combine all the values. Use the `id` function in `foldMap` to just concatenate the strings:

```
ifold :: M.Map Int String -> String
ifold = foldMap id

ifoldr :: M.Map Int String -> String
ifoldr = foldr (\s t -> s ++ ", " ++ t) ""
```

7. Use the `Traversable` instance to traverse over the map:

```
itraverse :: M.Map Int String -> [Map Int String]
itraverse = traverse (\x -> [x ++ "-travsered" ])
```

8. Implement the `Foldable` and `Traversable` instances for a tree. Define the binary tree:

```
data Tree a = Empty
    | Tree (Tree a) a (Tree a)
      deriving Show
```

9. Implement the `Foldable` instance:

```
instance Foldable Tree where

foldMap f Empty = mempty
foldMap f (Tree left v right) = (foldMap f left) `mappend` f v
`mappend` (foldMap f right)

foldr f x Empty = x
foldr f x (Tree left v right) = foldr_left
where
 foldr_right = foldr f x right
 foldr_value = f v foldr_right
 foldr_left = foldr f foldr_value left
```

10. Implement the `Traversable` instance for the `Tree`. For `Travesable`, a `Functor` instance is also required:

```
instance Functor Tree where
fmap f Empty = Empty
fmap f (Tree left v right) = Tree (fmap f left) (f v) (fmap f
right)
instance Traversable Tree where

traverse f Empty = pure Empty
traverse f (Tree left v right) = Tree <$> traverse f left <*> f
v <*> traverse f right
```

11. Create `sampleTree`:

```
sampleTree :: Tree Int
sampleTree = Tree l 10 r
where
  l = Tree ll 8 lr
  ll = Tree Empty 7 Empty
  lr = Tree Empty 9 Empty
  r = Tree rl 12 rr
  rl = Tree Empty 11 Empty
  rr = Tree Empty 13 Empty
```

12. Fold the tree to find the sum of values of all the nodes:

```
sampleSum :: Tree Int -> Int
sampleSum = foldr (+) 0
```

13. Traverse the tree to create a list of all the values in the node:

```
sampleTraverse :: Tree Int -> [Tree String]
sampleTraverse = traverse (\x -> [show x])
```

14. Use the map examples and tree to fold and traverse:

```
main :: IO ()
main = do
putStrLn "Given the map"
print imap

putStrLn "Fold the map"
print $ ifold imap
print $ ifoldr imap

putStrLn "Traverse the map"
```

```
print $ itraverse imap

putStrLn "Given a tree"
print sampleTree

putStrLn "Folding the tree (Find the sum)"
print $ sampleSum sampleTree

putStrLn "Traverse the tree (create a list)"
print $ sampleTraverse sampleTree
```

15. Build and execute the project:

stack build
stack exec -- working-with-traversable-foldable-map

16. You should see the following output:

```
● ● ●                working-with-traversable-foldable-map — -bash — 107×28
working-with-traversable-foldable-map $ stack exec — working-with-traversable-foldable-map
Given the map
fromList [(1,"a"),(2,"b"),(3,"c"),(4,"d"),(5,"e"),(6,"f"),(7,"g"),(8,"h"),(9,"i"),(10,"j"),(11,"k"),(12,"l"
),(13,"m"),(14,"n"),(15,"o"),(16,"p"),(17,"q"),(18,"r"),(19,"s"),(20,"t"),(21,"u"),(22,"v"),(23,"w"),(24,"x
"),(25,"y"),(26,"z")]
Fold the map
"abcdefghijklmnopqrstuvwxyz"
"a, b, c, d, e, f, g, h, i, j, k, l, m, n, o, p, q, r, s, t, u, v, w, x, y, z, "
Traverse the map
[fromList [(1,"a-travsered"),(2,"b-travsered"),(3,"c-travsered"),(4,"d-travsered"),(5,"e-travsered"),(6,"f-
travsered"),(7,"g-travsered"),(8,"h-travsered"),(9,"i-travsered"),(10,"j-travsered"),(11,"k-travsered"),(12
,"l-travsered"),(13,"m-travsered"),(14,"n-travsered"),(15,"o-travsered"),(16,"p-travsered"),(17,"q-travsere
d"),(18,"r-travsered"),(19,"s-travsered"),(20,"t-travsered"),(21,"u-travsered"),(22,"v-travsered"),(23,"w-t
ravsered"),(24,"x-travsered"),(25,"y-travsered"),(26,"z-travsered")]]
Given a tree
Tree (Tree (Tree Empty 7 Empty) 8 (Tree Empty 9 Empty)) 10 (Tree (Tree Empty 11 Empty) 12 (Tree Empty 13 Em
pty))
Folding the tree (Find the sum)
70
Traverse the tree (create a list)
[Tree (Tree (Tree Empty "7" Empty) "8" (Tree Empty "9" Empty)) "10" (Tree (Tree Empty "11" Empty) "12" (Tre
e Empty "13" Empty))]
working-with-traversable-foldable-map $
```

How it works...

`Foldable` and `Traversable` are very generic and can be defined for a variety of data types. Instances of these type classes allow us to define traversal and foldable, and use common functions such as `foldr`, `foldl`, and so on, for a variety of data structures.

7
Working with Relational and NoSQL Databases

In this chapter, we will work with the following recipes:

- Working with Persistent
- Managing migrations
- Creating custom data types
- Using Esqueleto to do advanced SQL queries
- Using hedis to work with redis (key-value, list, and hash)
- Using hashsets and sorted sets in redis to create a Trie

Introduction

So far, we have looked at Haskell language features, type classes, and collections and worked with various examples. But all of those constructs were purely Haskell features. In this chapter, we will be interfacing with the outside world (apart from the console), by interacting with databases.

To be able to write a backend, or a storage service, it is imperative that we will at some time think about storing the data in a relational database, or a binary serializable format or a file such as JSON or YAML. In this chapter, we will use the *persistent* library to work with relational databases. Using the *persistent* model, we will define the relations, do a query, insert, update, and a deletion of the stored data. We will move on to *Esqueleto* for advanced queries. *Esqueleto* defines a **DSL** (**Domain Specific Language**) so that enables us to do advanced queries.

We will then move to *hedis,* a backend for the *redis* database. We will work with *hedis* queries, and work our way towards key-value pairs, sorted sets, and hashsets.

Working with Persistent

In this recipe, we will work with the *persistent* library, which has been designed to abstract the concept of defining the schema (the data models and the relationships between them), and working with a storage backend (such as SQL*ite,* and PostgreSQL).

In this recipe, we will create a model to store the following data:

- User details (u*sername, email*)
- Stock that the user is interested in (e*xchange, symbol*)

We will use SQL*ite* as the backend, as it does not require any installation. But the model defined here can be worked out with any *persistent* backend, such as PostgreSQL. The model definition in the *persistent* library is created through *Template Haskell*. Template Haskell enables programmers to generate code at compile time. This involves writing macros and generating code.

How to do it...

1. Create a new project called `working-with-persistent` with the `simple` stack template:

   ```
   stack new working-with-persistent simple
   ```

2. Add a dependency to `persistent` and `persistent-sqlite`, in the `build-depends` subsection of the `executable` section. Also add `persistent-template`, `text`, and `mtl` (monad transformers) in the same section:

   ```
   executable working-with-persistent
     hs-source-dirs:    src
     main-is:           Main.hs
     default-language:  Haskell2010
     build-depends:     base >= 4.7 && < 5
                      , persistent
                      , persistent-sqlite
                      , persistent-template
                      , text
                      , mtl
   ```

3. Open `src/Main.hs`. We will be adding our source here.

4. At the top, we need to enable many extensions that are required for the `persistent` backend:

```
{-# LANGUAGE EmptyDataDecls              #-}
{-# LANGUAGE FlexibleContexts            #-}
{-# LANGUAGE FlexibleInstances           #-}
{-# LANGUAGE GADTs                       #-}
{-# LANGUAGE GeneralizedNewtypeDeriving  #-}
{-# LANGUAGE MultiParamTypeClasses       #-}
{-# LANGUAGE OverloadedStrings           #-}
{-# LANGUAGE QuasiQuotes                 #-}
{-# LANGUAGE TemplateHaskell             #-}
{-# LANGUAGE TypeFamilies                #-}
{-# LANGUAGE DeriveGeneric               #-}
```

These are some features that can be enabled by putting them in the pragmas as is done here. We have already seen `OverloadedStrings` in the last chapter. These features enable specific extensions in GHC. We will be looking at some extensions in upcoming chapters. The extension that is most relevant for this recipe is `TemplateHaskell`.

5. Write the module declaration for the `Main` module:

```
module Main where
```

6. Import the modules that we will need for defining the entities and relations between them.

   `TH` usually indicates that Template Haskell is required to use it:

```
import Database.Persist.TH
import Data.Text as T
import Database.Persist.Sqlite
import Database.Persist.Sql as S
import Control.Monad.Reader
import Control.Monad.IO.Class
```

7. Define the model. We will define three tables, `Stock`, `User`, and `UserStock`. `Stock` stores information about stock, exchange, and symbol, whereas `User` stores information about the user's name and email ID. We will declare that the email ID should be unique. `UserStock` is an association between user and stock:

```
share [mkPersist sqlSettings, mkMigrate "migrateAll"]
[persistLowerCase|
Stock
  exchange Text
  symbol Text
  UniqueStockId exchange symbol
  deriving Show
User
  name Text
  email Text
  UniqueEmailId email
  deriving Show
UserStock
 userid UserId
 stockid StockId
 Primary userid stockid
 deriving Show
|]
```

Note the *Template Haskell* syntax, where we enclose the expressions in square brackets, define tables by simply indenting, and specify the type of the data. Also note how we have created the foreign key reference to `User` and `Stock` in the `UserStock` table, where a composite key is defined with fields (`userid`, `stockid`). Here, `userid` and `stockid` refer to *uid* in the `User` table, and *sid* in the `Stock` table respectively.

8. The preceding *Template Haskell* code will result in the following data types-- `User`, `Stock` and `UserStock`.

9. Create the tables and schema. The database operations run in a `Monad m`, which supports `IO` as well (as denoted by `MonadIO` type class). Note that we write the query generically, and are oblivious as to which backend database will be used:

```
createSchema :: (Monad m, MonadIO m) => ReaderT SqlBackend m ()
createSchema = runMigration migrateAll
```

10. Insert a few users and stocks. Associate the users and stocks:

```
insertData :: (Monad m, MonadIO m) => ReaderT SqlBackend m (Key
User, Key User, Key Stock, Key Stock)
insertData = do
johnid <- insert $ User "John Broker" "john@example.com"
liftIO $ putStrLn $ "Added user John" ++ show johnid
janeid <- insert $ User "Jane Investor" "jane@example.com"
liftIO $ putStrLn $ "Added user Jane" ++ show janeid

-- Insert few stocks
dbsid <- insert $ Stock "XSES" "D05"
liftIO $ putStrLn $ "Added Singapore Exchange DBS stock" ++
show dbsid
infyid <- insert $ Stock "XNSE" "INFY"
liftIO $ putStrLn $ "Added NSE India, Infosys stock" ++ show
infyid

-- Associate the user with stock
john_d05 <- insert $ UserStock johnid dbsid
liftIO $ putStrLn $ "John subscribed to DBS stock" ++ show
john_d05
john_infy <- insert $ UserStock johnid infyid
liftIO $ putStrLn $ "John subscribed to INFY stock" ++ show
john_infy
jane_d05 <- insert $ UserStock janeid dbsid
liftIO $ putStrLn $ "Jane subscribed to DBS stock" ++ show
jane_d05
 return (johnid, janeid, dbsid, infyid)
```

11. Run a query to get the stocks associated with the user:

```
queryUserStockCount :: MonadIO m => Key User -> ReaderT
SqlBackend m Int
queryUserStockCount user = do
  S.count [UserStockUserid ==. user]
```

12. Delete a `stock` from the user:

```
deleteUserStock :: MonadIO m => UserId -> StockId -> ReaderT
SqlBackend m ()
deleteUserStock user stock = do
  S.delete (UserStockKey user stock)
```

13. Update the name of a `user`:

```
updateUserName :: MonadIO m => UserId -> Text -> ReaderT
SqlBackend m ()
updateUserName user newname =
  S.update user [UserName =. newname]
```

14. Use the preceding functions to create the schema, add data to it, and manipulate it. We are running against an in-memory SQL*ite* database:

```
main :: IO ()
main = runSqlite ":memory:" $ do
  createSchema
  (johnid, janeid, dbsid, infyid) <- insertData
  count <- queryUserStockCount johnid
  liftIO $ putStrLn $ "John has " ++ show count ++ " stocks"
  liftIO $ putStrLn $ "Delete John's DBS stock"
  deleteUserStock johnid dbsid
  count1 <- queryUserStockCount johnid
  liftIO $ putStrLn $ "Now John has " ++ show count1 ++ "
  stocks"
  liftIO $ putStrLn $ "Change Jane's name"
  updateUserName janeid "Jane Quant"
  -- Retrieve new name
  jane <- get janeid
  liftIO $ putStrLn $ "Jane's name is now " ++ show jane
  return ()
```

15. Build and execute the project:

```
stack build
stack exec -- working-with-persistent
```

You should see the following output:

How it works...

In this recipe, we have touched upon many aspects of defining, storing, and querying the model. Let's us look at each aspect one by one.

The definition of the model starts with the following statement:

```
share [mkPersist sqlSettings, mkMigrate "migrateAll"]
```

This definition shows how we would like to persist the model. `sqlSettings` denotes that we would like to use a SQL backend for storing the model. `mkMigrate` takes a string argument. This should be name of the function (in this case, `migrateAll`) that represents the creation of all the schemata defined in the model.

The model itself is defined within *[persistLowerCase| ...]*. It persists the names of tables and fields using lowercase letters. The following definition of `Stock` is converted into two representations - Haskell and its corresponding SQL representation:

```
Stock
    exchange Text
    symbol Text
    UniqueStockId exchange symbol
    deriving Show
```

At the command prompt, run the following:

```
stack ghci
```

It should open up a GHCi interactive prompt, inspect the types of User, Stock, and UserStock by using commands such as :i User. Note that the generated data types are defined using **Generic Algebraic Data Types (GADTs)**. In the model definition, we use the following convention. The first unindented line specifies the name of the table (or data type). The next indented lines define the fields. For example, *exchange Text* defines an *exchange* field with the type Text. The *persistent* maps Haskell data types to compatible data types in the backend such as *SQLite or Postgresql*.

It is also possible to specify the constraints. In the definition of the *Stock* table, we have created unique constraints for two fields together, *exchange* and *symbol*. For the UserStock table, the primary key is a composite key comprising *userid* and *stockid*. In fact, both *userid* and *stockid* are foreign keys for the tables User and Stock:

```
data User = User {userName :: !Text, userEmail :: !Text}
data Stock = Stock {stockExchange :: !Text, stockSymbol :: !Text}
data UserStock
  = UserStock {userStockUserid :: !Key User,
        userStockStockid :: !Key Stock}
```

Also note that for the User and Stock, we did not specify the key. The key type is generated automatically by *Persistent* as follows:

```
newtype instance Key User = UserKey {...}
newtype instance Key Stock = StockKey {...}
data instance Key UserStock = UserStockKey {...}
```

You will notice that persistent also defines the key type for the user as *UserId*. This type is a synonym of Key User. In the definition of the UserStock *userid* field, we specify *UserId* as the type. This way, the foreign key constraint is automatically created. It is also possible to create a foreign key constraint by specifying *Foreign* in the model definition.

If the primary key is not given, then *Persistent* creates a default integer based, auto-incremented key.

For every field, a TableField type is created. For example, for the field name of User, a UserName type is created. This is used in the expressions for *query*, *update*, and *delete* functions. By using a specific type, we are indicating a specific field in a data structure. This way, we can do type -safe queries over the database.

For example, in the following update command, we specify the key User table and then specify the expression [UserName =. newname], where UserName is the entity field type, and in conjunction with newname (a string value), it creates a update statement:

```
update user [UserName =. newname]
```

At the command prompt, in GHCi, you can also run runSqlite with user.db as an argument. (use :set -XOverloadedStrings to enable the overloaded strings extension at the command prompt):

```
*Main> runSqlite "user.db" createSchema
```

This will create a SQLite database called user.db in the current directory, and create the schema. You can open the database file using the SQL*ite* executable. You can print the schema using the .schema command. It should print the following:

```
*Main> runSqlite "user.db" createSchema
Migrating: CREATE TABLE "stock"("id" INTEGER PRIMARY KEY,"exchange" VARCHAR NOT NULL,"symbol" VARCHAR NOT NULL,CONSTRAINT "unique_stock_id" UNIQUE ("exchange","symbol"))
Migrating: CREATE TABLE "user"("id" INTEGER PRIMARY KEY,"name" VARCHAR NOT NULL,"email" VARCHAR NOT NULL,CONSTRAINT "unique_email_id" UNIQUE ("email"))
Migrating: CREATE TABLE "user_stock"("userid" INTEGER NOT NULL REFERENCES "user","stockid" INTEGER NOT NULL REFERENCES "stock", PRIMARY KEY ("userid","stockid"))
*Main>
```

You can also run the main with this file, and later inspect the data created with SQL commands.

Managing migrations

When you are working on the databases, and trying to abstract the model on the backend at the same time, you already know that you will need a change in the model, database, or both at some point in time. Catering to changes in the requirements, performance criteria, database schema, or the data model on the backend is inevitable. Changing the database schema without breaking the backend becomes an important and time-consuming task.

In this recipe, we will look at migrations and see how *Persistent* approaches this issue. We will create a simple model and make a change to the model and run migrations again. We will be using SQL*ite* as the backend.

How to do it...

1. Create a new project called `managing-migrations` with the `simple stack` template:

```
stack new managing-migrations simple
```

2. Add dependencies on the `persistent, persistent-template, persistent-sqlite, text,` and `mtl` libraries in the `build-depends` sub-section of the `executable` section:

```
executable manage-migrations
  hs-source-dirs:      src
  main-is:             Main.hs
  default-language:    Haskell2010
  build-depends:       base >= 4.7 && < 5
                     , persistent
                     , persistent-template
                     , persistent-sqlite
                     , text
                     , mtl
```

3. Open `src/Main.hs`. We will be adding our source here.

4. Add the extensions required for invoking *Persistent* and `persistent-template` functions:

```
{-# LANGUAGE EmptyDataDecls              #-}
{-# LANGUAGE FlexibleContexts            #-}
{-# LANGUAGE FlexibleInstances           #-}
{-# LANGUAGE GADTs                       #-}
{-# LANGUAGE GeneralizedNewtypeDeriving  #-}
{-# LANGUAGE MultiParamTypeClasses       #-}
{-# LANGUAGE OverloadedStrings           #-}
{-# LANGUAGE QuasiQuotes                 #-}
{-# LANGUAGE TemplateHaskell             #-}
{-# LANGUAGE TypeFamilies                #-}
{-# LANGUAGE DeriveGeneric               #-}
```

5. Add the declaration for the `Main` module:

```
module Main where
```

6. Add the required imports:

```
import Database.Persist.TH
import Data.Text as T
import Database.Persist.Sqlite
import Database.Persist.Sql as S
import Control.Monad.Reader
import Control.Monad.IO.Class
```

7. Create the model for the database. The following model represents a marine vessel that has structures and compartments arranged hierarchically:

```
share [mkPersist sqlSettings, mkMigrate "migrateAll"]
[persistLowerCase|
Asset
    name Text
Structure
    name Text
    parent StructureId Maybe
    deriving Show
Compartment
    name Text
    parent CompartmentId Maybe
|]
```

8. The `mkMigrate "migrateAll"` function creates a `migrateAll` function that inspects the existing database for the tables, and emits the SQL statements required to change the existing schema to achieve the intended schema.

9. Write the `main` function to run the migration. Create a database file called `"ship.db"` and run the migration against the database:

```
main :: IO ()
main = runSqlite "ship.db" $ runMigration migrateAll
```

10. Build and execute the project:

```
stack build
stack exec -- managing-migrations
```

You should see the following output:

```
● ● ●                        manage-migrations — -bash — 139×18
manage-migrations $ stack exec -- manage-migrations
Migrating: CREATE TABLE "asset"("id" INTEGER PRIMARY KEY,"name" VARCHAR NOT NULL)
Migrating: CREATE TABLE "structure"("id" INTEGER PRIMARY KEY,"name" VARCHAR NOT NULL,"parent" INTEGER NULL REFERENCES "structure")
Migrating: CREATE TABLE "compartment"("id" INTEGER PRIMARY KEY,"name" VARCHAR NOT NULL,"parent" INTEGER NULL REFERENCES "compartment")
manage-migrations $ ls -l ship.db
-rw-r--r--  1 yogeshsajanikar  staff  16384 Jul 31 20:25 ship.db
manage-migrations $
```

11. However, we realize that we have to maintain multiple assets in the database, and structures and compartments always belong to one and only one asset at a time. So, we have to add a reference to the asset in the Structure as well as the Compartment. At the same time, it is not necessary to have a name for a structure. Sometimes, internal structures in a ship are just given a number (primary key, in our case), and not a name. So, we make the name of each structure optional. Make the changes in the definition of the model. Change the preceding model to the following:

```
share [mkPersist sqlSettings, mkMigrate "migrateAll"]
[persistLowerCase|
Asset
   name Text
Structure
   name Text Maybe
   parent StructureId Maybe
   owner AssetId
   deriving Show
Compartment
   name Text
   owner AssetId
   parent CompartmentId Maybe
|]
```

12. Now again run `main`, but this time, instead of calling `runMigration`, call `printMigration`. You should see the following output after building and executing:

```
CREATE TEMP TABLE "structure_backup"("id" INTEGER PRIMARY
KEY,"name" VARCHAR NULL,"parent" INTEGER NULL REFERENCES
"structure","owner" INTEGER NOT NULL REFERENCES "asset");
INSERT INTO "structure_backup"("id","name","parent") SELECT
"id","name","parent" FROM "structure";
DROP TABLE "structure";
CREATE TABLE "structure"("id" INTEGER PRIMARY KEY,"name"
VARCHAR
NULL,"parent" INTEGER NULL REFERENCES "structure","owner"
INTEGER NOT NULL REFERENCES "asset");
INSERT INTO "structure" SELECT "id","name","parent","owner"
FROM
"structure_backup";
DROP TABLE "structure_backup";
CREATE TEMP TABLE "compartment_backup"("id" INTEGER PRIMARY
KEY,"name" VARCHAR NOT NULL,"owner" INTEGER NOT NULL
REFERENCES
"asset","parent" INTEGER NULL REFERENCES "compartment");
INSERT INTO "compartment_backup"("id","name","parent") SELECT
"id","name","parent" FROM "compartment";
DROP TABLE "compartment";
CREATE TABLE "compartment"("id" INTEGER PRIMARY KEY,"name"
VARCHAR NOT NULL,"owner" INTEGER NOT NULL REFERENCES
"asset","parent" INTEGER NULL REFERENCES "compartment");
INSERT INTO "compartment" SELECT "id","name","owner","parent"
FROM "compartment_backup";
DROP TABLE "compartment_backup";
```

You can see that the migration has taken care to alter the schema by adding references to `Asset`. At the same time, it also creates the SQL statements to copy the data from the old tables to the modified ones.

How it works...

In this recipe, we ran the migration against an empty database, and the migration created the schema from the scratch. When we modified the model, and ran the migration against the existing `ship.db` database, the migration detected the change, and created the migration script. It is a better idea to *print* the migration than *run* the migration. It would give a chance to rectify any errors in the migration.

In fact, in the example that we have seen, we have added an extra reference to Asset as a foreign key in Structure and Compartment. This would create a problem during migration, as we will not have reference to an asset in the old data.

As the recipe is being written, using the runMigration function against the SQLite database produces an error.

Creating custom data types

In the model definition for *Persistent*, we can use data types such as Int, Text, and Int64. They are translated to proper SQL data types according to the SQL dialect that we are working with. Sometimes, the supported data types are not sufficient for our needs, and we might want to write a custom data type.

In this recipe, we will write a custom data type that represents email.

How to do it...

1. Create a new project called custom-datatype with the simple stack template:

```
stack new custom-datatype simple
```

2. Add dependencies on the persistent, persistent-template, persistent-sqlite, text, and mtl libraries in the build-depends sub-section of the executable section. Also add *email-validate* as a dependency. We will use it to store grammatically valid email addresses. Also add a Custom module to the other-modules subsection in the same section (you will have to add this subsection). Other-modules represents a set of modules that are part of the compilation but aren't exposed to the user. We will be adding the Custom module for defining a custom data type:

```
executable custom-datatype
  hs-source-dirs:    src
  main-is:           Main.hs
  other-modules:     Custom
  default-language:  Haskell2010
  build-depends:     base >= 4.7 && < 5
                   , persistent
                   , persistent-template
                   , persistent-sqlite
```

```
                    , text
                    , mtl
                    , email-validate
```

3. Open `src/Main.hs`. We will be adding our source here.

4. Add the extensions required for invoking `persistent` and `persistent-template` functions:

```
{-# LANGUAGE EmptyDataDecls               #-}
{-# LANGUAGE FlexibleContexts             #-}
{-# LANGUAGE FlexibleInstances            #-}
{-# LANGUAGE GADTs                        #-}
{-# LANGUAGE GeneralizedNewtypeDeriving   #-}
{-# LANGUAGE MultiParamTypeClasses        #-}
{-# LANGUAGE OverloadedStrings            #-}
{-# LANGUAGE QuasiQuotes                  #-}
{-# LANGUAGE TemplateHaskell              #-}
{-# LANGUAGE TypeFamilies                 #-}
{-# LANGUAGE DeriveGeneric                #-}
```

5. Add the declaration for the `Main` module:

```
module Main where
```

6. Add the required imports:

```
import Database.Persist.TH
import Data.Text as T
import Database.Persist.Sqlite
import Database.Persist.Sql as S
import Control.Monad.Reader
import Control.Monad.IO.Class
import Text.Email.Validate
import Custom
```

7. Open a new file in the same directory called `Custom.hs`. Add the customary extensions, module declarations, and so on to the file. Note that the custom file must be defined in a separate module, or the module definition produces an error:

```
{-# LANGUAGE TemplateHaskell #-}
module Custom where

import Database.Persist.TH
import Text.Email.Validate
```

8. Add the user statuses, `Active` and `Inactive`. Use `derivePersistField` to create a custom data type:

```
data Status = Active | Inactive
                deriving (Show, Eq, Read)

derivePersistField "Status"
```

9. Define the custom field for the email address:

```
derivePersistField "EmailAddress"
```

10. Close the file, and return to `src/Main.hs`. Write the model definition:

```
share [mkPersist sqlSettings, mkMigrate "migrateAll"]
[persistLowerCase|
User
  status Status
  email EmailAddress
|]
```

11. Add the data, and query it:

```
sampleData :: MonadIO m => ReaderT SqlBackend m ()
sampleData = do
  let Right jupitermail = validate "jupyter@planets.com"
      Right plutomail = validate "pluto@planets.com"
      Right earthmail = validate "earth@planets.com"
  insert $ User Custom.Active jupitermail
  insert $ User Custom.Active earthmail
  insert $ User Custom.Inactive plutomail
  return ()

main :: IO ()
main = runSqlite ":memory:" $ do
  runMigration migrateAll
  sampleData
  -- Get all users (provide empty filter for SQL *)
  all <- S.count ([] :: [Filter User])
  active <- S.count ([UserStatus ==. Custom.Active])
  liftIO $ putStrLn $ "There are " ++ show all ++ " users"
  liftIO $ putStrLn $ show active ++ " are active"
```

12. Build and execute the project:

```
stack build
stack exec -- custom-datatype
```

13. You should see the following output:

```
● ● ●                          custom-datatype — -bash — 139×18
custom-datatype $ stack exec — custom-datatype
Migrating: CREATE TABLE "user"("id" INTEGER PRIMARY KEY,"status" VARCHAR NOT NULL,"email" VARCHAR NOT NULL)
There are 3 users
2 are active
custom-datatype $
```

How it works...

Creating custom data types using *Persistent* is easy. You can make use of *template Haskell* to manufacture the custom data type. Template Haskell takes advantage of the `Show` and `Read` instances of the data to convert the data to and from the `String` representation.

Using Esqueleto to do advanced SQL queries

We have used the *Persistent* library and SQL expressions using the `Database.Persist.SQL` module. We have used the generated types for each field in the filter, insert, and update expressions. But the complexity of the query can increase rapidly. Of course, there is a way to do a plain SQL query with the *persistent* library. Here, in this recipe, we will be using the `Esqueleto` library to do complex queries such as joins.

In this recipe, we will write a complex SQL query that is type-safe and easy to write. Being type-safe is good, because we will catch any major issues earlier on!

How to do it...

1. Create a new project called `using-esqueleto` with a `simple` stack template:

```
stack new using-esqueleto simple
```

2. Add dependencies on the `persistent`, `persistent-template`, `persistent-sqlite`, `text`, and `mtl` libraries in the `build-depends` sub-section of the `executable` section. Also add `esqueleto` to the same sub-section:

```
executable using-esqueleto
  hs-source-dirs:     src
  main-is:            Main.hs
  default-language:   Haskell2010
  build-depends:      base >= 4.7 && < 5
                    , persistent
                    , persistent-template
                    , persistent-sqlite
                    , text
                    , mtl
                    , esqueleto
```

3. Open `src/Main.hs`. We will be adding our source here.

4. Add the extensions required for invoking *Persistent* and `persistent-template` functions:

```
{-# LANGUAGE EmptyDataDecls             #-}
{-# LANGUAGE FlexibleContexts           #-}
{-# LANGUAGE FlexibleInstances          #-}
{-# LANGUAGE GADTs                      #-}
{-# LANGUAGE GeneralizedNewtypeDeriving #-}
{-# LANGUAGE MultiParamTypeClasses      #-}
{-# LANGUAGE OverloadedStrings          #-}
{-# LANGUAGE QuasiQuotes                #-}
{-# LANGUAGE TemplateHaskell            #-}
{-# LANGUAGE TypeFamilies               #-}
{-# LANGUAGE DeriveGeneric              #-}
```

5. Add the declaration for the `Main` module:

```
module Main where
```

6. Add the required imports:

```
import Database.Persist.TH
import Data.Text as T hiding (count, groupBy)
import Database.Persist.Sqlite (runSqlite)
import Control.Monad.Reader
import Control.Monad.IO.Class
import Database.Esqueleto
```

7. Create the model for the database. The following model represents a referral system in which one user can refer other users. This is usually used to award a user who can help pull in more users:

```
share [mkPersist sqlSettings, mkMigrate "migrateAll"]
[persistLowerCase|
User
     email         Text
     UniqueEmail   email
     referredBy    UserId Maybe
     verified      Bool
     deriving Show
|]
```

The preceding model represents a user with a unique email address. Users can register themselves, or can be referred by other users. Merely registering does not help; the user also has to validate their address (usually by clicking on the link sent for verification).

8. Write a query to get users with referral greater than 0. Note that only verified users count:

```
getAllRefCounts :: MonadIO m => SqlPersistT m [(Value Text,
Value Int)]
getAllRefCounts =
   select $ from $ \(p `InnerJoin` r) -> do
      on (r ^. UserReferredBy ==. just (p ^. UserId))
      where_ (r ^. UserVerified ==. val True)
      groupBy (p ^. UserEmail, p ^. UserId)
      let cr = count (r ^. UserId )
      orderBy [ desc cr ]
      return (p ^. UserEmail, cr)
```

9. Add data to the referral system. Add users referred by others. One user hasn't verified their email yet:

```haskell
createData :: MonadIO m => SqlPersistT m ()
createData = do
  a <- insert $ User "a@example.com" Nothing True
  b <- insert $ User "b@example.com" (Just a) True
  insert $ User "c@example.com" (Just a) True
  insert $ User "d@example.com" (Just b) True
  insert $ User "e@example.com" Nothing True
  insert $ User "f@example.com" (Just a) False
  return ()

main :: IO ()
main = runSqlite ":memory:" $ do
  runMigration migrateAll
  createData
  referrals <- getAllRefCounts
  liftIO $ putStrLn "Referral counts"
  liftIO $ print referrals
```

10. Build and execute the project:

```
stack build
stack exec -- using-esqueleto
```

11. You should see the following output:

How it works...

In this recipe, we did a self-join to get the referral count for the users. The query using esqueleto is as follows:

```
select $ from $ \(p `InnerJoin` r) -> do
  on (r ^. UserReferredBy ==. just (p ^. UserId))
  where_ (r ^. UserVerified ==. val True)
  groupBy (p ^. UserEmail, p ^. UserId)
  let cr = count (r ^. UserId )
  orderBy [ desc cr ]
  return (p ^. UserEmail, cr)
```

The query looks very similar to SQL itself. E*squeleto* uses a monadic DSL for writing queries in the tune of SQL. For example a `select * from users` query will become the following in *Esqueleto*:

```
select (from $ \user -> return user)
```

If we are searching for a particular user, then we can write the following:

```
select (from $ \user -> do
  where_ (user ^. UserEmail ==. val "a@example.com")
  return user
)
```

In our example, we have used `InnerJoin` on two tables. We have specified this with p `InnerJoin` q. We then added the criteria using the on, where_, groupBy, orderBy and count functions, which translate to the corresponding SQL keywords (ON, GROUPBY, ORDERBY and COUNT).

Using hedis to work with redis (key-value, list and hash)

Redis (http://redis.io) is a key-value store and more. It offers facilities very different than relational databases. As a NoSQL database, one has to employ a different philosophy, such as duplicating keys across stores, maintaining reverse lookup, and so on.

In this recipe, we will be using redis to create key-value stores, sorted sets, and hash sets. We will be using the *hedis* library to connect to Redis and manipulate the data.

Getting ready...

1. Install *Redis* from `http://redis.io`. On Microsoft Windows, use the Windows port from the Microsoft Open Tech Group at `https://github.com/MicrosoftArchive/redis`.

2. Start *Redis* in a default mode by simply running *redis-server* from the command line. You should see the following messages on successful start. You might want to go with the Windows service on Microsoft Windows or a daemonized mode on Unix flavoured systems. Optionally, you can also supply the configuration file:

```
d:\Tools\redis>redis-server.exe --maxheap 1G
```

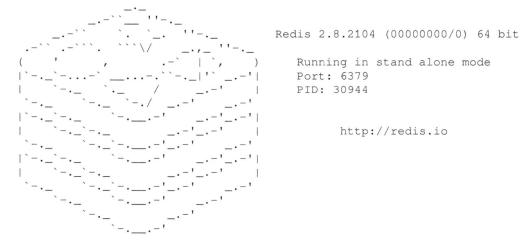

```
                                     Redis 2.8.2104 (00000000/0) 64 bit

                                     Running in stand alone mode
                                     Port: 6379
                                     PID: 30944


                                     http://redis.io
```

```
[30944] 01 Aug 09:21:07.275 # Server started, Redis version 2.8.2104
[30944] 01 Aug 09:21:07.275 * The server is now ready to accept connections
on port 6379
```

3. Usually, Redis starts on port `6379`.

How to do it...

1. Create a new project called `using-hedis` with a `simple` stack template:

```
stack new using-hedis simple
```

2. Add a dependency on the `hedis` library in the `build-depends` sub-section of the `executable` section. Also add a dependency on the `bytestring` package:

```
executable using-hedis
  hs-source-dirs:     src
  main-is:            Main.hs
  default-language:   Haskell2010
  build-depends:      base >= 4.7 && < 5
                    , hedis
                    , bytestring
```

3. Open `src/Main.hs`. We will be adding our source here.

4. Add an initial module declaration and import the required headers. Enable `OverloadedStrings` as we will be dealing with *ByteString* in this recipe:

```
{-# LANGUAGE OverloadedStrings #-}
module Main where

import Database.Redis
import Data.ByteString.Char8 as B
import Control.Monad
import Control.Monad.IO.Class
import Data.Maybe
```

5. Work with the key-value store. *hedis* implements a composite data type called `RedisCtx m f`, where m is the context, and f is some sort of container. This way, we can apply the same code to both redis transactions (multiple commands sent atomically to redis) outside transactions. For the commands sent to outside transactions, the preceding type becomes *Redis (Either Reply a)* and when we apply it in the transactional scenario, it becomes `RedisTx` *(Queued a)*. Here, we apply the commands to outside transactions.

6. Let's work out setting up keys and values. A key is a `ByteString` key:

```
createKV :: Redis ()
createKV = do
  -- Add exchange codes and their names
  liftIO $ B.putStrLn "Setting stock exchange code and their
  descriptions"
  set "XSES" "Singapore Stock Exchange"
  set "XBSE" "Bombay Stock Exchange"
  set "XNSE" "National Stock Exchange of India"
  -- Delete a key
  del ["XBSE"]
```

```
-- Get the values back
xses <- get "XSES"
xbse <- get "XBSE"
xnse <- get "XNSE"
-- Delete a key
let xchanges = (,,) <$> xses <*> xbse <*> xnse
liftIO $ print xchanges
```

7. Work with lists. You can create a list simply by pushing values to it. A list can have duplicate values. It is possible to retreive the list by specifying the range and you can also delete the elements:

```
createList :: Redis ()
createList = do
    -- Push symbols in a list of stocks
    liftIO $ B.putStrLn "Adding symbols to the stock list"
    lpush "STOCKS" ["AAPL"]
    lpush "STOCKS" ["GOOGL"]
    lpush "STOCKS" ["FB"]
    -- Get all symbols. (-1) indicates end of the range.
    symbols <- lrange "STOCKS" 0 (-1)
    liftIO $ print symbols
    liftIO $ B.putStrLn "Changing some stocks and removing some"
    -- Set a value to something else
    lset "STOCKS" 0 "GOOGLE"
    -- Remove all values for FB
    lrem "STOCKS" 0 "FB"
    symbols1 <- lrange "STOCKS" 0 3
    liftIO $ B.putStrLn "Printing new stock list"
    liftIO $ print symbols1
```

8. Work with hash sets. You can create a hashset with a key and set different fields:

```
createHash :: Redis ()
createHash = do
    liftIO $ B.putStrLn "Set hashes for AAPL and FB"
    hset "AAPL" "CATEGORY" "TECH"
    hset "FB" "CATEGORY" "SOCIAL"
    hmset "AAPL" [("HINT", "BUY"),("SENTIMENT","POSITIVE")]
    -- Get FB Category
    fbcat <- hget "FB" "CATEGORY"
    liftIO $ B.putStrLn "Print FB Category"
    liftIO $ print fbcat
    -- Get multiple fields
    aapls <- hmget "AAPL" ["HINT","SENTIMENT"]
    liftIO $ B.putStrLn "What is suggestion for AAPL"
    liftIO $ print aapls
```

9. Connect to the Redis server and run the preceding functions:

```
main :: IO ()
main = do
  -- Connect with default information
  conn <- checkedConnect defaultConnectInfo
  runRedis conn $ do
   createKV
   createList
   createHash
  return ()
```

10. Build and execute the project:

```
stack build
stack exec -- using-hedis
```

11. You should see the following output:

How it works...

Hedis wraps up the *Redis* commands in a monad called `RedisCtx m f`. At first, this seems complicated, but it helps us to run *Redis* commands individually or together in a transaction. In the transactions, however, it is not possible to use the result value of the command, as the commands are queued. The `hedis` library wraps *redis* commands with the functions with same names (but lowercase).

All the commands work with `ByteString`. Any serialization should be done to and from the `ByteString`.

Using hashsets and sorted sets in redis to create a Trie

In this recipe, we will be using *hedis* to create simple *trie* in R*edis*. We will a use *hashset* to store an object, and store its searchable *index* in the *sorted set* in redis. We will be using the prefix trie to create a searchable index. For example, if we are searching for "APPLE", we will index all prefixes ("A","AP","APP","APPL", and "APPLE") in the index. Whenever a user enters a string to search, we will be able to look up our index and get the result.

Getting ready

Start the Redis server, and note down the connection info. In this recipe, we will assume that Redis is working on the same machine at the port 6379. This is what *hedis* assumes to connect to the *Redis* server using the default connection information.

How to do it...

1. Create a new project called `hedis-trie` with a `simple` stack template:

   ```
   stack new hedis-trie simple
   ```

2. Add a dependency on the *hedis* library in the `build-depends` sub-section of the `executable` section:

   ```
   executable hedis-trie
     hs-source-dirs:      src
     main-is:             Main.hs
     default-language:    Haskell2010
     build-depends:       base >= 4.7 && < 5
                        , hedis
                        , bytestring
   ```

3. Open `src/Main.hs`. We will be adding our source here.

4. Add the initial module declaration and import the required headers. Enable OverloadedStrings as we will be dealing with ByteString in this recipe:

```
{-# LANGUAGE OverloadedStrings #-}
module Main where

import Prelude as P
import Database.Redis
import Data.ByteString.Char8 as B
import Data.Char
import Data.Monoid
import Control.Monad
import Control.Monad.IO.Class
```

5. Write a function to take a sentence, break it into words, and return prefixes of all the words:

```
prefixes :: B.ByteString -> [[B.ByteString]]
prefixes = P.map (P.tail . B.inits) . B.words
```

6. Write a function that take two input values, a list of prefixes for each word (a list of a list), and the key of the Redis hash set where we are storing data. . The function returns the number of keys updated. Since we are working with a list of lists, we use two foldM. Each prefix contributes a sorted set, and we add the input key to each of these sorted set with default score of 0.0:

```
addKeys :: (RedisCtx m f, Applicative f) => [[B.ByteString]]
->
B.ByteString -> m (f Integer)
addKeys prefixes hashkey =
  let addtrie i p = do
        rs <- zadd p [(0.0, hashkey)]
        pure $ (+) <$> i <*> rs
      addtries ps = foldM addtrie (pure 0) ps
      addtriesS s ps = do
        rs <- addtries ps
        pure $ (+) <$> s <*> rs
  in foldM addtriesS (pure 0) prefixes
```

7. Create a hash for the stock symbol and its name:

```
addSymbol :: (RedisCtx m f, Applicative f) => B.ByteString ->
B.ByteString -> m (f Bool)
addSymbol symbol name = do
  hset symbol "NAME" name
```

8. Prepare some data to be added to *Redis*. We will add all symbols from the *Singapore* exchange. The symbols and their names are embedded in the code:

```
stockData :: [(B.ByteString, B.ByteString)]
stockData = [ ("MT1", "Dragon Group International Ltd")
            , ("BKV", "Dukang Distillers Holdings Ltd")
            ,("CZ4", "Dutech Holdings Ltd")
            ,("5SO", "Duty Free International Ltd")
            ,("NO4", "Dyna-Mac Holdings Ltd")
            ,("D6U", "Dynamic Colours Ltd")
            ,("BDG", "Eastern Holdings Ltd")
            ,("BWCU", "EC World Real Estate Investment Trust")
            ,("5CT", "EcoWise Holdings Ltd")
            ,("5HG", "Edition Ltd")
            ,("42Z", "Eindec Corporation Ltd")
            ,("E16", "Elec & Eltek International Co Ltd")
            ,("BIX", "Ellipsiz Ltd")]
```

9. Take the preceding data and add it to the *Redis* server. The symbol and its name is added to the hash set, whereas all the prefixes for the name (by separating into words) are added to sorted sets. Each prefix will create a new sorted set:

```
addData :: (RedisCtx m f, Applicative f) => [(B.ByteString,
B.ByteString)] -> m ()
addData stocks = do
  forM_ stocks $ \(stock, name) -> do
    addSymbol stock name
    -- convert name into lower case so that we can do a
    generic
    search
    let nameL = B.map toLower name
        namePs = prefixes nameL
    addKeys namePs stock
```

10. Search the stock and return the list of stocks:

```
searchStocks :: B.ByteString -> Redis [B.ByteString]
searchStocks search = do
  stocks <- zrange search 0 (-1)
  case stocks of
    Right ss -> forM ss $ \s -> do
      n <- hget s "NAME"
      case n of
        Right (Just name) -> return $ s <> ": " <> name
        _                 -> return $ s <> ": name not found
    ***error***"
```

```
main :: IO ()
main = do
 conn <- checkedConnect defaultConnectInfo
 runRedis conn $ do
    liftIO $ B.putStrLn "Adding stocks to the redis trie index"
    addData stockData
    liftIO $ B.putStrLn "Seaching for strings"
    found1 <- searchStocks "holdi"
    liftIO $ do
       B.putStrLn "Results for \"holdi\""
       forM_ found1 B.putStrLn
    found2 <- searchStocks "dyna"
    liftIO $ do
       B.putStrLn "Results for \"dyna\""
       forM_ found2 B.putStrLn
```

11. Build and execute the project:

    stack build
    stack exec -- hedis-trie

12. You should see the following output:

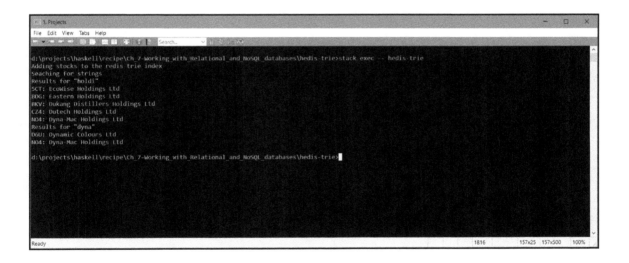

How it works...

In this recipe, we used a Redis sorted set for storing the search data. A *sorted set* stores the data sorted with a score. Each score should be attached with only a single value. Here, we get the name of the stock, such as *EcoWise Holdings Ltd*, or *Eastern Holdings Ltd*. We convert them into prefixes, as discussed earlier. Since both the names contain the word "Holdings", we will have a sorted set with a `holdi` key (remember that we convert all names to lowercase), and two values:

```
holdi - score = 0.0, value = 5CT
holdi - score = 0.0, value = BDT
```

When we search for the string `hold`, both the values should be returned. From the values, we find the name from the hash set, and return the set of names. We can further optimize the search by increasing the score for commonly searched stocks. Further, if multiple strings are searched, then we can also take the intersection of two sorted sets, and create a temporary sorted set (with TTL specifying time to live) and search from the new temporary set.

8
Working with HTML and Templates

In this chapter, we will work with the following recipes:

- Using blaze to create an HTML template
- Using blaze to reverse engineer an HTML page
- Use blaze-html with Bootstrap to create HTML template
- Using heist as a template engine
- Working with splice in Heist

Introduction

In this chapter, we will work with HTML. We will be looking at two libraries, *blaze* and *heist*, to author and manipulate HTML. While *blaze* is a generic HTML DSL, *heist* provides HTML templates for various purposes. We will look at how we can leverage both these libraries to manipulate HTML contents.

Using blaze to create an HTML template

In this recipe, we will be using the *blaze-html* library to construct HTML documents. The *blaze-html* library provides very efficient and fast DSL for constructing HTML documents. It is very lightweight and supports efficient UNICODE support. Being that it is embedded inside Haskell, one can also take full advantage of *Haskell* while constructing HTML documents. It also supports HTML5 and HTML4 strict syntax.

Note that the aim of the recipe is not to showcase HTML, but the interoperability between Haskell and HTML through *blaze-html*.

How to do it...

1. Create a new project, `working-with-blaze-html`, with `simple` stack template:

   ```
   stack new working-with-blaze-html simple
   ```

2. Add a dependency on the `blaze-html` library in the `build-depends` sub-section of the `executable` section:

   ```
   executable blaze-html
     hs-source-dirs:    src
     main-is:           Main.hs
     default-language:  Haskell2010
     build-depends:     base >= 4.7 && < 5
                      , blaze-html
   ```

3. Open `src/Main.hs`. We will be adding our source here.

4. Add the extension `OverloadedStrings`. This will enable us to work with many strings that we will use in this recipe. Also add the `Main` module definition:

   ```
   {-# LANGUAGE OverloadedStrings #-}
   module Main where
   ```

5. Import `blaze-html` modules for creating HTML5 elements and attributes:

   ```
   import Control.Monad
   import Text.Blaze.Html5 as H hiding (main)
   import Text.Blaze.Html5.Attributes as A
   import Text.Blaze.Html.Renderer.Pretty (renderHtml)
   ```

6. Create a data type to represent a user and his interest in equity stocks:

   ```
   data User = User { firstName :: String, lastName :: String }
   deriving Show
   data Stock = Stock { symbol :: String, exchange :: String,
   description :: String } deriving Show
   data UserStocks = UserStocks { user :: User, stocks :: [Stock]
   }
   deriving Show
   ```

7. Create some data:

```
sampleUser :: User
sampleUser = User "Jerry" "McQuire"

sampleStocks :: [Stock]
sampleStocks = [ Stock "D05" "SGX" "DBS Group"
               , Stock "GOOGL" "NASDAQ" "Alphabet Inc"
               , Stock "INFY" "BSE" "Infosys Ltd"
               ]

sampleData :: UserStocks
sampleData = UserStocks sampleUser sampleStocks
```

8. Use the *blaze* HTML5 primitives to create an HTML. Use a CSS on cloud for styling. The user's stocks are represented by a table:

```
sampleHtml (UserStocks user stocks) = html $ do
  header $ do
   H.title $ toHtml $ "Stock Data for " ++ lastName user ++ ",
   " ++ firstName user
   link ! rel "stylesheet" ! type_ "text/css" ! href
"https://cdnjs.cloudflare.com/ajax/libs/aegis/1.3.3/aegis.css"
   body $ do
   h1 $ toHtml $ "Stock Data for " ++ lastName user ++ ", " ++
   firstName user
   p $ table $ do
     thead $ do
       th $ H.span $ toHtml ("Stock"::String)
       th $ H.span $ toHtml ("Exchange"::String)
       th $ H.span $ toHtml ("Description"::String)
     forM_ stocks $ \s -> do
       tr $ do
         td $ toHtml $ symbol s
         td $ toHtml $ exchange s
         td $ toHtml $ description s
```

9. Use `main` to create an HTML page:

```
main :: IO ()
main = do
 putStr $ renderHtml $ sampleHtml sampleData
```

10. Build and execute the project:

```
stack build
stack exec -- working-with-blaze-html  > example.html
```

11. If you open `example.html` in the browser, you should see the following HTML page:

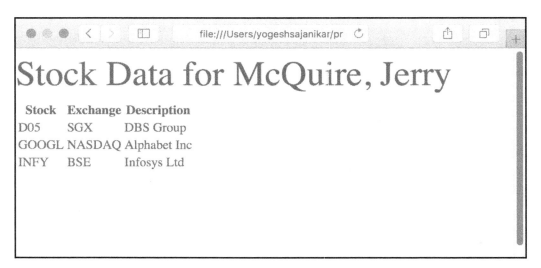

How it works...

The *blaze-html* library is derived from *blaze*, an amazingly fast text builder library that constructs text data in chunks. The *blaze-html* library provides a DSL for representing HTML. In fact, it provides three HTML DSLs-- HTML5, HTML4 (Strict and Transitional), and XHTML.

All of them offer a monadic way of combining different HTML elements and creating an HTML as a structure represented by data type *Html* (an alias of *Markup*). Once created, one can *render* the *Html* element using different renderers (such as Pretty, String, Text, and Utf8).

The *Html* data type itself is an alias of *Text.Blaze.Internal.Markup*. Using *Markup*, it is possible to create custom HTML elements.

One of the important things to note in the recipe is how smoothly we can combine a user's data type into templates. We can create composable functions to render an *Html* element from the given data structure.

Using blaze to reverse engineer an HTML page

In this recipe, we will use a package *blaze-from-html* to reverse engineer an existing HTML page, to create `Haskell` code that uses *blaze-html*.

How to do it...

1. Install `blaze-from-html` using stack. Here we use the resolver `lts-9.1`. Feel free to use the latest or your favorite resolver:

       stack --resolver lts-9.1 install blaze-from-html

2. Check the location of the tool using `stack`:

       stack path --local-bin

3. Use `curl` to download the home page from haskell.org (http://www.haskell.org/):

       curl -X GET http://www.haskell.org -o index.html

4. Use `blaze-from-html` to engineer the blaze DSL from the HTML page:

       blaze-from-html -v html5 -s index.html > index.hs

5. You will need to tweak the code.

6. Correct the encoding of the copyright message in the footer class (find the code `H.div ! class_ "footer"`). Find the message "`2014-2017 haskell.org`". Either correct the encoding or remove the characters that create problems.

7. Add the module for rendering at the top:

```
import Text.Blaze.Html.Renderer.Pretty (renderHtml)
```

8. Hide the main function exported by the `Html5` module at the top:

```
import Text.Blaze.Html5 hiding (main)
```

9. Add the `main` function to render the html page:

```
main :: IO ()
main = putStr $ renderHtml index
```

10. Run the file using `stack` and `runhaskell`. The `runhaskell` utility runs the haskell file directly:

```
stack --resolver lts-9.1 exec -- runhaskell index.hs > index-
out.html
```

11. Open `index-out.html` in the browser. You will find that the links are still pointing to the relative path from the base URL, `www.haskell.org`. Change the URLs in `index.hs` to point to the fully qualified URL `http://www.haskell.org/static...`

12. Run the stack with `runhaskell` again. Open the HTML `index-out.html` in the browser. You will see something like the following:

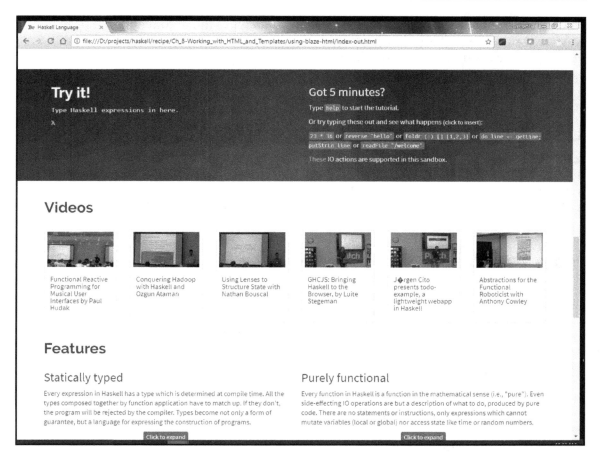

13. Not all elements will render as the original page. For example, the top will show that the code is not rendered correctly. But the reverse engineered page reflects the structure and contents of the original page very well.

How it works...

Blaze-from-html is an extremely useful, though not a perfect, solution. It can be used with an advantage for capturing the skeleton of a page. For example, it can be used to capture the designs from the skeleton or bootstrap (http://getbootstrap.com) examples.

Once reverse engineered, it is easier to hook user data types into it to render the page the way we want it. Other tools which are useful in this context are pandoc (`https://pandoc.org` - a generic document converter for many document types) and hakyll (`https://jaspervdj.be/hakyll/` - static website generator).

Use blaze-html with Bootstrap to create HTML template

In this recipe, we will use Blaze HTML to create bootstrap based HTML. In this recipe, we will create a Navbar (which is actually one of the examples at `http://getbootstrap.com`).

How to do it...

1. Create a new folder `blaze-html`. We will not be creating a separate project. Instead, create a new file called `index.hs` file. Open the file and enable the extension `OverloadedStrings` for being able to use a generic string syntax for supporting text as well as `ByteString`:

   ```
   {-# LANGUAGE OverloadedStrings #-}
   ```

2. Add the necessary imports:

   ```
   import Prelude
   import qualified Prelude as P
   import Data.Monoid (mempty,(<>))

   import Text.Blaze.Html5 hiding (main)
   import qualified Text.Blaze.Html5 as H
   import Text.Blaze.Html5.Attributes
   import qualified Text.Blaze.Html5.Attributes as A
   import Text.Blaze.Html.Renderer.Utf8 (renderHtml)
   import qualified Data.ByteString.Lazy.Char8 as BC
   ```

3. Define the functions to represent often used URLs:

   ```
   -- Attribute value
   -- Point to CDNJS library
   cdnjs :: AttributeValue
   cdnjs = "https://cdnjs.cloudflare.com/ajax/libs/"
   ```

```
-- Bootstrap 4.0 base for example
bootstrapUrl :: AttributeValue
bootstrapUrl = "http://getbootstrap.com/docs/4.0/"
```

4. We will be creating the navigation bar example from bootstrap, Create Header, for our purpose:

```
-- Create Header
navHeader :: Html
navHeader = H.head $ do
 meta ! charset "utf-8"
 meta ! name "viewport" ! content "width=device-width,
initial-
   scale=1, shrink-to-fit=no"
 meta ! name "description" ! content "Navigator example from
 Bootstrap"
 meta ! name "author" ! content "Haskell Cookbook"
 H.title "Top navbar example for Bootstrap Using Blaze-Html"
 link ! href (cdnjs <> "twitter-bootstrap/4.0.0-
 beta/css/bootstrap.min.css") ! rel "stylesheet"
 --  Point to bootstrap example css
 link ! href (bootstrapUrl <> "examples/navbar-top/navbar-
 top.css") ! rel "stylesheet"
```

5. Now create a body with the navigation bar and the container pointing to some text:

```
navBody :: Html
navBody = body $ do
  -- Create navigator bar
  nav ! class_ "navbar navbar-expand-md navbar-dark bg-dark
mb-
   4" $ do
   a ! class_ "navbar-brand" ! href "#" $ "Top navbar"
   button ! class_ "navbar-toggler" ! type_ "button" !
   dataAttribute "toggle" "collapse" ! dataAttribute "target"
   "#navbarCollapse" $ H.span ! class_ "navbar-toggler-icon" $
   mempty
   H.div ! class_ "collapse navbar-collapse" ! A.id
   "navbarCollapse" $ do
     ul ! class_ "navbar-nav mr-auto" $ do
       li ! class_ "nav-item active" $ a ! class_ "nav-link" !
   href "#" $ do
         "Home"
         H.span ! class_ "sr-only" $ "(current)"
       li ! class_ "nav-item" $ a ! class_ "nav-link" ! href
```

```
                "http://www.haskell.org" $ "Haskell"
                    li ! class_ "nav-item" $ a ! class_ "nav-link disabled"
!
        href "#" $ "Disabled"
          H.form ! class_ "form-inline mt-2 mt-md-0" $ do
            input ! class_ "form-control mr-sm-2" ! type_ "text" !
             placeholder "Search"
            button ! class_ "btn btn-outline-success my-2 my-sm-0"
!
        type_ "submit" $ "Search"

        H.div ! class_ "container" $ H.div ! class_ "jumbotron" $
do
        h1 $ do
          "Navbar example using "
          b $ "blaze-html"
          p ! class_ "lead" $ do
          "This example shows how to use blaze-html with bootstrap
           framework using "
          i $ "Text.Blaze.Html5"
          " and bootstrap defined classes and tags"
        a ! class_ "btn btn-lg btn-primary" ! href ( bootstrapUrl
<>
          "components/navbar/") $ "View navbar docs"
```

6. Combine the header and body with scripts in *Html5* DSL:

```
index :: Html
index = docTypeHtml ! lang "en" $ do
  navHeader
  navBody
  -- Bootstrap core JavaScript
  --    ======================================================
  -- Placed at the end of the document so the pages load
faster
  script ! src "https://code.jquery.com/jquery-
  3.2.1.slim.min.js" $ mempty
  script "window.jQuery || document.write('<script
  src=\"https://cdnjs.cloudflare.com/ajax/libs/jquery/3.2.1/j
  query.min.js\"><\\/script>')"
  script ! src (cdnjs <> "popper.js/1.12.3/esm/popper.min.js")
$
  mempty
  script ! src (cdnjs <> "twitter-bootstrap/4.0.0-
  beta/js/bootstrap.min.js") $ mempty
```

7. Use a `ByteString` to render the HTML from the `index` function:

```
main :: IO ()
main = BC.putStr $ renderHtml index
```

8. Run `stack` to create an HTML file. Use `runhaskell` to get the HTML content. The command `runhaskell` is used to run a Haskell file directly, without compilation. Here we use the resolver so that `runhaskell` is called for a specific version of GHC and packages:

```
stack --resolver lts-9.1 exec -- runhaskell index.hs > index-out.html
```

9. Open `index-out.html` in the browser. You should see the following:

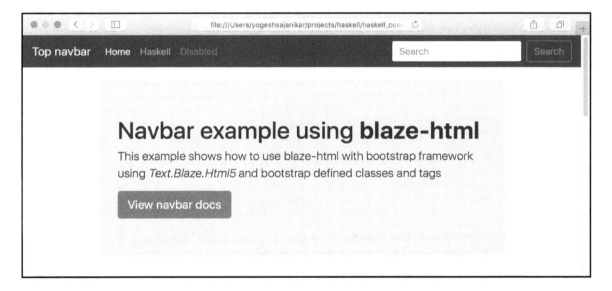

How it works...

In this very simple recipe, we have used *blaze-html* HTML5 DSL to create the Navbar example from bootstrap. Do note how we can compose different components (such as headers, body, and scripts) together to create a single HTML file.

Using heist as a template engine

In this recipe, we will work with *heist*, a templating framework that can work with HTML or XML documents. The *heist* framework is also a default templating framework used for the *Snap* web development framework. At the same time, *heist* does not have any dependency on *Snap* and can be used independently.

In this recipe, we will create a template and bind a value to the template.

How to do it...

1. Create a new project, `working-with-heist`, with a `simple` stack template.

   ```
   stack new working-with-heist simple
   ```

2. Add a dependency on the `heist` library in the `build-depends` sub-section of the `executable` section:

   ```
   executable working-with-heist
     hs-source-dirs:      src
     main-is:             Main.hs
     default-language:    Haskell2010
     build-depends:       base >= 4.7 && < 5
                        , heist
                        , text
                        , bytestring
                        , lens
                        , xmlhtml
   ```

3. The `heist` library does not exist in the stackage LTS. Thus, we need to run the following command to update the dependencies automatically:

   ```
   stack solver --update-config
   ```

4. Open `src/Main.hs`. We will be adding our source here. Enable the `OverloadedStrings` extension, and define the `Main` module:

   ```
   {-# LANGUAGE OverloadedStrings #-}
   module Main where

   import Heist
   import Heist.Interpreted
   import Data.ByteString.Char8 as B
   ```

```
import Data.ByteString.Builder
import Data.Text as T
import Control.Lens
import System.IO
import qualified Text.XmlHtml as X
```

5. Now we will create a few heist templates. Heist templates are XML documents. Create a subdirectory *templates* in the project folder. Create a file HelloWorld.tpl (the *tpl* extension stands for template).

```
<h1> Hello <name/> </h1>
<p>
 In this example, we will look at templates and bindings. You,
 <familyname/>, <name/> will be creating some templates, and
then
 using these templates to generate something wonderful.

 In heist, you can always bind with a tag.
</p>
```

Note the use of <name/> and <familyname/>. These are the parameters which are filled at runtime.

6. Create a configuration for loading the templates. We do not use any namespaces, so initialize the Heist configuration with an empty namespace. Load the templates from the "templates" directories. Set the loaded templates in the configuration. The name of the template file will serve as the name of the template. In this case, HelloWorld will be the name of the template.

```
loadTemplateState :: IO (Either [String] (HeistState IO))
loadTemplateState = do
 -- Load all templates in the directory "templates"
 loc <- loadTemplates "templates"
 -- Create a config without a namespace
 let ex  = over hcNamespace (const "") emptyHeistConfig
     ex1 = over hcTemplateLocations (const [return loc]) ex
 initHeist ex1
```

7. *HeistT* is a monad for manipulating tests. We use *HeistT* with `HeistState`. In the *HelloWorld* template we need to evaluate two parameters-- `name` and `familyname`. Let's bind their values with state:

```
bindValues :: HeistState IO -> HeistState IO
bindValues s = let s1 = bindString "name" "Tom" s
                   s2 = bindString "familyname" "Bombadil" s1
               in s2
```

8. In the main function, load the templates to get the state, and then bind the values to the `name` and `familyname` tags. Finally, evaluate the template to produce the evaluated result which substitutes the values for `name` and `familyname`.

```
main :: IO ()
main = do
  Right st <- fmap bindValues <$> loadTemplateState
  -- Eval the template "HelloWorld" in the context
  (Just template) <- evalHeistT (evalTemplate "HelloWorld")
  (X.Element "html" [] []) st
  -- Get the evaluated template, and then render it on the
  console
  let builder = X.renderHtmlFragment X.UTF8 template
  hPutBuilder stdout builder
```

9. Build and execute the project:

```
stack build
stack exec -- working-with-heist
```

10. You should see the following output, with the substituted values:

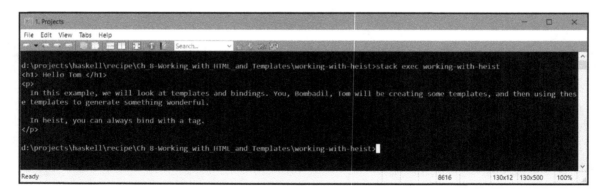

How it works...

This recipe looks at *heist* as a template framework where we loaded a template *HelloWorld* from a `template` directory. The template requires the arguments `name` and `familyname`. The values of these arguments or tags are inserted in the `HeistState`. Then we run the *HeistT* monad with the `evalHeistT` function by supplying the state.

The *heist* framework inserts the splices (named *HeistT*), and runs the evaluation for the template by using values supplied in the state.

In this recipe, we used the `Heist.Interpreted` module. The *heist* library also provides the `Heist.Compiled` library. The major difference is that the interpreted module evaluates the DOM at runtime, whereas the compiled module does DOM evaluation at the load time, reducing the overhead during the runtime. Both the `Heist.Interpreted` and `Heist.Compiled` modules export the same functions.

Working with splice in Heist

In the previous recipe, we created a template and externally attached bindings to a tag, and rendered the template using these bindings. This is useful when we have simple bindings. But what if we have to do some calculation and bind the calculation to the tag, rather than a simple string binding? In this recipe, we will be binding a tag to the local time on the server (or actually, a place where the template will be rendered).

How to do it...

1. Create a new project, `working-with-splice`, with a `simple` stack template:

   ```
   stack new working-with-splice simple
   ```

2. Add a dependency on the *heist* library in the `build-depends` sub-section of the `executable` section. In addition, also add a dependency on additional libraries required for this recipe. In addition to `text`, `bytestring`, `lens`, and `xmlhtml`, also add the `time` library:

   ```
   executable working-with-splice
     hs-source-dirs:      src
     main-is:             Main.hs
     default-language:    Haskell2010
     build-depends:       base >= 4.7 && < 5
   ```

```
                         , heist
                         , text
                         , bytestring
                         , lens
                         , xmlhtml
                         , time
```

3. Open `src/Main.hs`. We will be adding our source here. Add the support for `OverloadedStrings`. Also add the required modules after the definition of the `Main` module:

```haskell
{-# LANGUAGE OverloadedStrings #-}
module Main where

import Heist
import Heist.Interpreted
import Data.ByteString.Char8 as B
import Data.ByteString.Builder
import Data.Text as T
import Control.Lens
import System.IO
import qualified Text.XmlHtml as X
import Data.Time
import Control.Monad.IO.Class
import System.Info
```

4. Create a splice for getting a time and returning a node as a result of processing:

```haskell
currentTime :: MonadIO m => Splice m
currentTime = do
  formatnode <- getParamNode
  let format = T.unpack $ X.nodeText formatnode
  utc <- liftIO $ getCurrentTime
  let ctime = formatTime defaultTimeLocale format utc
  return [ X.TextNode $ T.pack ctime ]
```

5. Write a splice to get the `os` name and architecture:

```haskell
osSpecs :: MonadIO m => Splice m
osSpecs = do
  let specs = os ++ " : " ++ arch
    return [ X.Element "em" [] [X.TextNode (T.pack specs)]]
```

6. Create a template `welcome.tpl` in the `templates` folder in the project directory. We will bind `<currentTime/>` with the current time:

```
<html>
  <body>
    <h1> Heist Framework </h1>

    <p> Welcome to Haskell built on <b> <osspec/> </b> </p>

    <p> This page binds two tags, viz.,  &lt;osspec&gt; and
&lt;currenttime&gt; to the splices. The username is simply a
text node bound to current OS architecture, whereas
currenttime
  is bound to a splice that fetches the current time of the
  system, and formats it using the format string specified in
the
  tag.
    <p> This page was rendered on <b> <currenttime>%B %d,
%Y</currenttime> </b>. </p>
  </body>
</html>
```

7. Write a function to load the templates:

```
loadTemplateState :: IO (Either [String] (HeistState IO))
loadTemplateState = do
-- Load all templates in the directory "templates"
loc <- loadTemplates "templates"
-- Create a config without a namespace
let ex  = over hcNamespace (const "") emptyHeistConfig
    ex1 = over hcTemplateLocations (const [return loc]) ex
initHeist ex1
```

8. Bind the splice with the correct tags:

```
bindLocalSplices :: MonadIO m => HeistState m -> HeistState m
bindLocalSplices =
bindSplice "osspec" osSpecs . bindSplice "currenttime"
currentTime
```

9. Implement the `main` function to load and run the `heist`:

```
main :: IO ()
main = do
  Right st <- fmap bindLocalSplices <$> loadTemplateState
  Just (b, mimeType) <- renderTemplate st "welcome"
  hPutBuilder stdout b
```

10. Build and execute the project:

```
stack build
stack exec -- working-with-splice > out.html
```

11. When you open `out.html` in the browser, you should see following output:

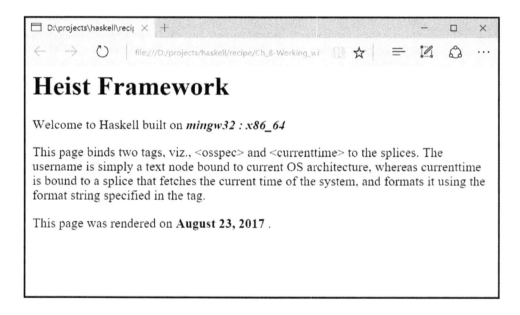

How it works...

In this recipe, rather than binding to a static string, we created a splice (which is a monadic computation). We created a binding between a tag and the splice, and inserted this binding into a `HeistState`. The templates that are rendered in the given *HeistState* will dynamically apply these bindings and call the splice to create a resultant template.

It is thus possible to embed an arbitrary computation, such as doing a database query, calling a backend microservice, and so on, and populate the template using the splices. In this recipe, we bound a `<currenttime/>` tag. The contents of this tag serve as an input to the splice. In this case, it is a time format in which the time should be output.

Working with Snap Framework

9

In this chapter, we will look at the Haskell-based web framework, **Snap**. We will look at the following recipes:

- Getting started with Snap
- Routing in Snap
- Serving static contents in Snap
- Form handling in Snap
- Creating and composing snaplets
- Session handling in Snap
- Authentication in Snap
- File upload with Snap

Introduction

Haskell offers many choices to work with web programming. The most popular choices are listed here:

- Yesod (http://www.yesodweb.com/)
- Happstack (http://www.happstack.com/)
- Snap (http://snapframework.com/)

Because of the modularity and compositional nature of Haskell, it is possible to easily use many libraries, including parts of web frameworks with other web frameworks, interoperably. In addition to this, the **Web Application Interface (WAI)** `https://hackage.haskell.org/package/wai`, allows for the sharing of code among different web frameworks with minimal changes.

In this chapter, we will primarily work with Snap Framework. A Snap Framework consists of reusable blocks called snaplets. It is possible to compose snaplets together to create a web application. In this chapter, we will start with a Snap application generated from Snap templates. In later recipes, we will work with different aspects of a web application in the context of Snap Framework. We will look at routing, forms, sessions, and authentication in Snap Framework. Later, we will create our own snaplet, composing it with existing snaplets. In the end, we will look at uploading the data in parts.

The recipe authentication in Snap is a complete web application, which shows integration between databases, session management, HTML template processing, and authentication.

Getting started with Snap

In this recipe, we will install Snap and create our first Snap application. The Snap Framework is not (yet) part of the official list of packages on Stackage. Hence, to get started with Snap, we will have to build the Snap Framework ourselves.

How to do it...

1. Open a console, change the directory to the desired location, and clone the `snap-templates` framework, as follows:

   ```
   git clone https://github.com/snapframework/snap-templates.git
   ```

2. The `snap-templates` package does not have a `stack.yaml` file generated. Generate a new one.

   ```
   stack --resolver lts-9.1 init --solver --ignore-subdirs
   ```

At the moment, `lts-9.1` is the latest LTS available with `stack`. We also need to ignore the subdirectories, as otherwise, `stack` will include all the subdirectories and cabal files in the `stack` project file.

3. Build and install the project using the following commands:

```
stack build
stack install
```

4. The snap executable will be installed in the local bin folder. On Unix systems, this path will be `$HOME/.local/bin`. You can also get this path by running the following command:

```
stack path --local-bin
```

5. Add this path to the `$PATH` variable, or run snap by providing the full path.
6. Change into a new directory, `starting-with-snap` and `snap` to create a default Snap application template.

```
snap init
```

7. Again, since this project is not created with `stack`, we need to create a `stack` project, as follows:

```
stack --resolver lts-9.1 init --solver
```

`stack` will show a warning, but should be able to use the resolver to create a project with some external dependencies added, as `lts-9.1` will not be able to resolve the exact versions of some of the dependencies.

8. Build and run the project using these commands:

```
stack build
stack exec -- starting-with-snap
```

9. Point the browser to `http://localhost:8000`. You should see the following screen:

10. Create a new user, and log in. You should see the default page, as seen in this screenshot:

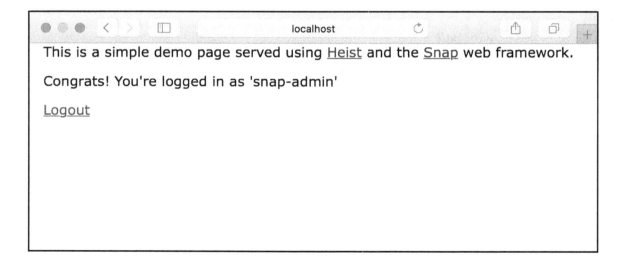

How it works...

In this recipe, we generated a default Snap application using `snap-templates`. The default application integrates the snaplets login, the session, and Snap's templating engine, Heist. A snaplet is a *modular* component of Snap, which allows us to add our own functionality and integrate with existing snaplets.

With Snap, there are the following important components:

- **snap-core**: This core defines the *Snap* monad and various web handlers
- **snap-server**: This is an HTTP web server with various handlers for running snap handlers
- **snap**: This is a utility package which allows you to work with the snap skeleton
- **heist**: This is a templating library for HTML/XML, based on the `xmlhtml` library

 A unit in Snap is called a **snaplet**. A snaplet provides a unit functionality (such as templating, session, and so on). It is possible to compose multiple snaplets together to create a web application.

Routing in Snap

In this recipe, we will add `routes` using the Snap Framework. We will add plain routes and routes with parameters.

How to do it...

1. Create a new project, `routing-in-snap`, with a `simple` stack template. We use `lts-9.1` as a resolver package archive. You can use the latest one available on Stackage. Just make sure that you use the same `resolver` later to solve the dependency constraints:

```
stack --resolver lts-9.1 new routing-in-snap simple
```

2. Add a dependency on the following libraries in the `build-depends` subsection of the `executable` section, as follows:

```
executable routing-in-snap
hs-source-dirs:      src
```

```
main-is:              Main.hs
default-language:     Haskell2010
build-depends:        base >= 4.7 && < 5
                  , snap-server
                  , snap-core
                  , snap
                  , lens
                  , bytestring
                  , text
```

3. Use the following command to solve the dependency constraints to update the `stack.yaml` file:

```
stack --resolver lts-9.1 solver --update-config
```

4. Open `src/Main.hs`. We will add our source here. Add the imports for Snap:

```
{-# LANGUAGE OverloadedStrings #-}
module Main where

import Data.Monoid
import Control.Applicative
import Snap
import Snap.Core
import Snap.Http.Server
```

5. Add the routes. We will add two routes. The first route, `hello`, is where we will respond with a standard `Hello World!` greeting. The second route, `greet/:nameparam`, has a parameter embedded in the route. The parameter `nameparam` is embedded in the route path with a colon:

```
routes = [ ("hello", writeBS "Hello World!")
         , ("greet/:nameparam", greetHandler)
         ]
```

6. Next, we will add a handler for the `greet/:nameparam` route. We access the named parameter with the `getParam` function. This *may* fetch us the value of the parameter. We write an error message if the parameter value is not specified:

```
greetHandler = do
 name <- getParam "nameparam"
 maybe (writeBS "nameparam not specified") (\n -> writeBS
 ("Welcome " <>n)) name
```

7. Compose the routes in a single site. The top route and other routes are combined with `</>` (an instance of the `Alternative` type class), as shown here:

```
site =
  ifTop (writeBS "Serving from root") <|>
  route routes
```

8. Use the `quickHttpServe` method to serve the site:

```
main :: IO ()
main = quickHttpServe site
```

9. Build and execute the project. Also create a folder, `log`, in the project directory. The access/error logs are stored in this folder:

```
stack build
stack exec -- routing-in-snap
```

10. The server will run at `0.0.0.0:8000`; connect to the local host by pointing the browser to `http://localhost:8000/greet/snap`. You should see the following message:

How it works...

In this recipe, we explained how we can do routing. A URL (for example, `http://example.com:8080/some/path?param`) has these two main parts:

- The first part locates the server and service, and is composed of a scheme (such as HTTP/HTTPS), a host name (`example.com`), and a port.
- The second part is composed of a `path` or `routes`, and `query parameters`. (`/some/path?param`).

The generic schema is explained at `https://en.wikipedia.org/wiki/URL`.

In a web application, we are interested in the HTTP/HTTPS schema and path. Each path can be connected by a remote user through a verb such as `GET`, `POST`, `PUT`, or `DELETE`. Combined with HTTP verbs and paths, the web application delivers web content.

In this recipe, we worked with `GET` requests (which are default ones) that are associated with different routes. In the Snap Framework, the route is a list of path/route names and the corresponding handlers. The `route` function takes this table and allows us to construct a site. The special function `ifTop` handles dealing with the root (`/`) path.

In the REST (`https://en.wikipedia.org/wiki/Representational_state_transfer`) philosophy, the path acts as a state, and hence, the path fragment can be a parameter uniquely determining a state. In the Snap Framework, a parameter is identified by the prefix `':'`, and the string that follows this name (till the path separator or `'/'` character) is the parameter name. The Snap Framework allows us to access this parameter using the `getParam` function.

We use the `quickHttpServe` function to run the built-in HTTP server. By default, it runs the HTTP server at port `8000`.

Serving static contents in Snap

A website consists of two types of contents, **static contents** and **dynamic contents**. The static contents are the HTML files, images, a folders containing these files. These contents do not change per request. The dynamic contents depend upon *route*, *parameters*, and *request type*. The Snap Framework allows us to serve static contents seamlessly with the dynamic contents. In this recipe, we will look at how we can serve static contents with the Snap Framework.

How to do it...

1. Create a new project, `static-contents-in-snap`, with the `simple` stack template:

```
stack --resolver lts-9.1 new static-contents-in-snap simple
```

2. Add a dependency on the following libraries in the `build-depends` subsection of the `executable` section:

```
executable static-contents-in-snap
  hs-source-dirs:     src
  main-is:            Main.hs
  default-language:   Haskell2010
  build-depends:      base >= 4.7 && < 5
                    , snap-server
                    , snap-core
                    , snap
                    , lens
                    , bytestring
                    , text
```

3. Add a directory, `static`, in the project folder. Add `index.html` in this directory, as follows:

```
<!DOCTYPE HTML5>
<html>
  <body>
    <p> This file is served as a static content. You may add
    links to subfolder as well. But the folder ".." and
absolute
    path are not honoured while serving the directory. </p>

    <p> This is a link to <a href="subfolder">subfolder</a>
</p>
  </body>
</html>
```

4. Also add a subfolder named `subfolder`, and add the following contents to the file `subfolder/example.html`:

```
<!DOCTYPE HTML5>
<html>
  <body>
    <p>
      This content is served from the folder
<em>subfolder</em>
    </p>
  </body>
</html>
```

5. Open `src/Main.hs`. We will add our source here. Add the `Main` module and the necessary imports:

```
{-# LANGUAGE OverloadedStrings #-}
module Main where

import Data.Monoid
import Control.Applicative
import Snap
import Snap.Core
import Snap.Http.Server
import Snap.Util.FileServe
```

6. Serve the static contents using the `serveDirectory` function. The directory listing will be stylized by `fancyDirectoryConfig`:

```
main :: IO ()
main = quickHttpServe $ serveDirectoryWith
fancyDirectoryConfig   "static"
```

7. Build and execute the project:

```
stack build
stack exec -- static-contents-in-snap
```

8. Point the browser to `http://localhost:8000/subfolder`. You should see the following output:

How it works...

In this recipe, the `static` folder is served by `quickHttpServe`.

Note that in the absence of any route, the static folder serves the contents from the `root` path. The subfolders are automatically mapped to the subpath.

Snap prevents access to the parent folder of the static directory, and the absolute paths are also not allowed. The `defaultMimeTypes` function in the module `Snap.Util.FileServe` gives a list of the default mime types. It is possible to add your own mime types to the list and serve the directory.

The `fancyDirectoryConfig` function uses its own built-in style for the listing directory. The `defaultDirectoryConfig` function shows the directory listing in a plain manner.

Note that the files `index.html`, `index.htm`, `default.html`, and others are automatically recognized as default indexes. In case these files are not present, Snap shows the directory contents with file types recognized with the mime types.

Form handling in Snap

In this recipe, we will look at how forms can be handled in the Snap Framework. We will also look at HTTP redirection and handling GET and POST methods.

How to do it...

1. Create a new project, `form-handling-in-snap`, with the `simple` stack template:

   ```
   stack --resolver lts-9.1 new form-handling-in-snap simple
   ```

2. Add a dependency on the following libraries in the `build-depends` subsection of the `executable` section, as follows:

   ```
   executable form-handling-in-snap
     hs-source-dirs:      src
     main-is:             Main.hs
     default-language:    Haskell2010
     build-depends:       base >= 4.7 && < 5
                        , snap-server
                        , snap-core
                        , snap
                        , lens
                        , bytestring
                        , text
                        , containers
   ```

Once the dependency is added, solve the dependency constraints by using the same resolver and allowing `stack` to update the `stack.yaml` file:

   ```
   stack --resolver lts-9.1 solver --update-config
   ```

3. Open `src/Main.hs`. We will add our source here. After the `Main` module header, add the necessary imports. Also enable the `OverloadedStrings` extension, as shown here:

```
{-# LANGUAGE OverloadedStrings #-}
module Main where

import Data.Monoid
import Control.Applicative
import Snap
import Snap.Core
import Snap.Http.Server
import Snap.Util.FileServe
import Data.Map.Lazy as M
import qualified Data.ByteString.Char8 as BC
```

4. Create a folder, `static`, in the project directory, and add `form.html` to it with the following contents. The following HTML document shows a form where a user can enter his/her first and last names, and his/her favorite Haskell web framework to work with:

```
<!DOCTYPE HTML5>
<html>
  <body>
    <p> The form shown below takes the the input, and submits
it to the action defined in Snap. Snap processes the action,
and produces a page showing the processed input. </p>

    <form action="/survey" method="post">
      <fieldset>
        First Name :
        <input type="text" name="firstname"><br>
        Last Name :
        <input type="text" name="lastname"><br>
        Your favorite Haskell Web Framework
        <select name="framework">
          <option value="snap">Snap Framework</option>
          <option value="yesod">Yesod Framework</option>
          <option value="happstack">Happstack </option>
        </select>
        <br><hr>
        <input type="submit" value="Complete Survey">
      </fieldset>
    </form>
  </body>
</html>
```

We will serve this preceding directory with `static` as the root folder.

5. Next, add a handler for the `GET` method. We will redirect to the form defined earlier:

```
getSurvey :: MonadSnap m => m a
getSurvey = method GET (redirect "/form.html")
```

6. Also add a handler for handling the `POST` method for the form. We will grab the contents of the form, and write them as text, as follows:

```
postSurvey :: MonadSnap m => m ()
postSurvey = method POST $ do
  rq <- getRequest
  params <- getParams
  let fullName = extractName params
  let favorite = extractFavorite params

  maybe (writeBS "Hello Anonymous") (\n -> writeBS ("Hello " <>
n)) fullName
  maybe (writeBS "No preference") (\n -> writeBS ("Your
favorite framework : " <> n)) favorite

  where
    extractName :: Params -> Maybe BC.ByteString
    extractName params = do
      firstname <- M.lookup "firstname" params
      lastname  <- M.lookup "lastname" params
      return $ (head firstname) <> " " <> (head lastname) <>
"\n"

    extractFavorite = fmap head . M.lookup "framework"
```

7. Create routes for handling the survey. Add a separate route for handling the `GET` and `POST` methods:

```
routes = [ ("/survey", postSurvey)
         , ("/survey", getSurvey) ]
```

8. Create a site for the combined static and survey handler, like this:

```
site = route routes <|> serveDirectoryWith fancyDirectoryConfig
"static"
```

9. Start the HTTP server with aforementioned site:

```
main :: IO ()
main = quickHttpServe site
```

10. Build and execute the project:

```
stack build
stack exec -- form-handling-in-snap
```

11. Point the browser to `http://localhost:8000/survey`. You should see the following form:

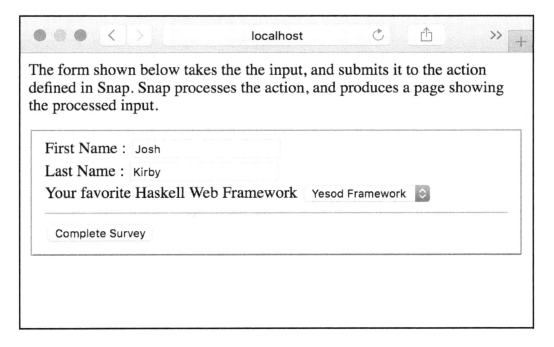

The form shown below takes the the input, and submits it to the action defined in Snap. Snap processes the action, and produces a page showing the processed input.

First Name : Josh
Last Name : Kirby
Your favorite Haskell Web Framework Yesod Framework

Complete Survey

After submission, the output will show the selection done through the form, as seen in the following screenshot:

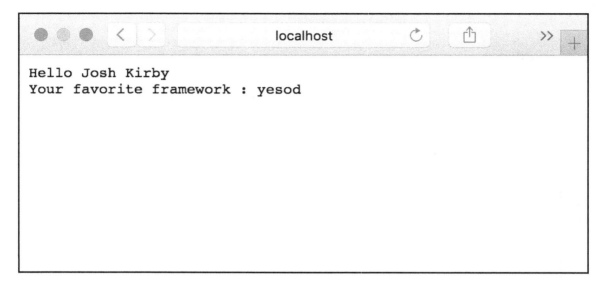

How it works...

In this recipe, the same route serves both GET and POST methods. We have used the same route twice, once with a GET handler (getSurvey) and another with the handler for the POST request (postSurvey).

In the GET handler, we use the redirect function to redirect to another location. The redirect function generates an HTTP 302 redirection request to another location.

In the POST handler, we use getParams to get the form parameters. The getParams function extracts the parameters from the HTTP request and makes it available as a Map of parameter names against their values. The POST handler extracts the necessary parameters, and then prints the results.

Creating and composing snaplets

In this recipe, we will create a snaplet and build the Snap application around it. We will also use the `heist` snaplet for serving the HTML templates. This recipe will demonstrate the following:

- How to create a snaplet
- How to use an existing snaplet inside another existing snaplet
- How the snaplet data is structured and placed
- How to access snaplet data

How to do it...

1. Create a new project, `working-with-snaplets`, with the `simple` stack template:

   ```
   stack new working-with-snaplets simple
   ```

2. Add a dependency on the `snap-core` library in the `build-depends` subsection of the `executable` section, as follows:

   ```
   executable working-with-snaplets
       hs-source-dirs:     src
       main-is:            Main.hs
       default-language:   Haskell2010
       build-depends:      base >= 4.7 && < 5
                         , snap-core
                         , snap-server
                         , snap
                         , lens
                         , bytestring
                         , text
                         , mtl
   ```

3. Open `src/Main.hs`. We will add our source here. After the initial `Main` module definition, add the necessary imports. Enable the `OverloadedStrings` and `TemplateHaskell` extensions, as Snap uses the `Lens` Template Haskell library:

```
{-# LANGUAGE TemplateHaskell, OverloadedStrings #-}
module Main where

import Control.Applicative
import Control.Lens
import Control.Lens.TH
import Control.Monad.State.Class (gets)
import Data.ByteString.Char8
import Data.Maybe
import Data.Monoid
import Snap
import Snap.Core
import Snap.Http.Server
import Snap.Snaplet.Session
import Snap.Snaplet.Heist
```

4. Create a data type, `MyData`. It contains a `ByteString` list. This is done as follows:

```
data MyData = MyData { _someData :: [ByteString] }
```

5. Create lenses for our data type. Note that lenses are covered in detail in Chapter 11, *Working with Lens and Prism*. In the context of this recipe, it is sufficient to know that while creating lenses, template haskell will remove an underscore ("_") from the record field and will create a lens. In the aforementioned type, `MyData`, a lens called `someData` will be created.

```
makeLenses ''MyData
```

6. Create a `Snaplet` for `MyData`. We create a snaplet that can be used in other Snap applications, as follows:

```
-- Initialize the snaplet
myDataInit :: SnapletInit b MyData
myDataInit = makeSnaplet "myData" "Snaplet with MyData" Nothing
$ do
  return (MyData ["My Data is initialized"])
```

7. Create an application composed of the `Heist` and `MyData` snaplets, as shown here:

```
data MyApp = MyApp { _heist :: Snaplet (Heist MyApp)
                   , _myData :: Snaplet MyData
                   }
```

8. Create lenses for `MyApp`:

```
makeLenses ''MyApp
```

9. Create a Snap handler function, `snapletName`, which will access the current snaplet name, and will print it as a text:

```
snapletName :: Handler b MyData ()
snapletName = method GET $ do
  name <- getSnapletName
  let snapletname = fromMaybe "Cannot get snaplet name" name
  writeText $ "Name of the snaplet : " <> snapletname
```

10. Create a Snap handler function, `snapletData`, which will access the data stored in `MyData`, and print it as a text:

```
snapletData :: Handler b MyData ()
snapletData = method GET $ do
  mydata <- gets _someData
  writeBS $ mconcat mydata
```

11. Now create the snaplet for `MyApp`. This snaplet will initialize the `heist` and `MyData` snaplets, and will also add routes for getting the name of the snaplet and for accessing the data inside `MyDatasnaplet`. It will also allow static serving of templates through `heist`:

```
myAppInit :: SnapletInit MyApp MyApp
myAppInit = makeSnaplet "myApp" "My First Snaplet" Nothing $ do
  hst <- nestSnaplet "heist" heist $ heistInit "templates"
  myd <- nestSnaplet "mydata" myData $ myDataInit
  addRoutes [ ("/mysnaplet", with myData snapletName)
            , ("/mysnaplet/data", with myData snapletData)
            ]
  wrapSite (<|> heistServe)
  return (MyApp hst myd)
```

12. Create an instance of the `HasHeist` type class. This will simplify accessing `heist` for binding templates, and so on:

```
instance HasHeist MyApp where
   heistLens = subSnaplet heist
```

13. Use the `MyApp` snaplet to be served as the web application, as follows:

```
main :: IO ()
main = serveSnaplet defaultConfig myAppInit
```

14. We will still need to add some templates for *Heist*. Create a directory, *snaplets*, in the project directory, and create a `heist/templates` subpath inside the `snaplets` directory.

15. Add the default template in the `snaplets/heist/templates` directory, as follows:

```
<html>
  <head>
    <title>Creating and composing Snaplets</title>
  </head>

  <apply-content/>
</html>
```

16. Add the index template in the same `templates` directory. The index template uses the `default` template:

```
<apply template="default">
  <h1> Welcome to Heist </h1>
  <p>
    This page is displayed through <em>Heist</em> snaplet.
  </p>
</apply>
```

17. Build and execute the project:

```
stack build
stack exec -- working-with-snaplets
```

The Snap server will serve at port 8000. Pointing the browser to http://localhost:8000, you should see the following HTML output:

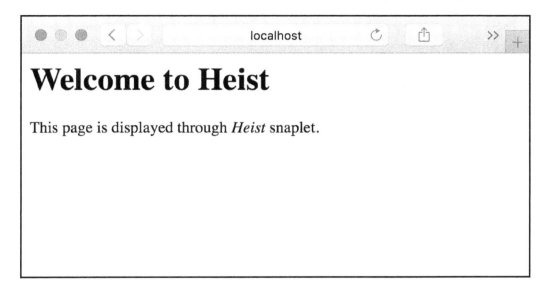

If you enter http://localhost:8000/mysnaplet, you will see the name of the snaplet. The output should look like the following:

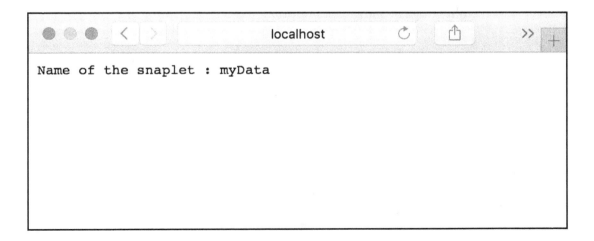

You can see the following output when you load the URL
`http://localhost:8000/mysnaplet/data`:

How it works...

In this recipe, we created two snaplets for two data types: one for `MyData`, and another for `MyApp`. The following list shows the important aspects of creating and composing snaplets:

- The `MyData` contains a list of strings. The field `_someData` starts with an underscore. This is done so that `makeLenses` (a Haskell Template function) can generate a *lens* for accessing and setting the field. More information about lenses is covered in `Chapter 11`, *Working with Lens and Prism*. Note that, in this recipe, we do not use *lens* as such, and the use of lenses is strictly restricted to only where Snap APIs demand.

- The `makeSnaplet` function takes the snaplet name, description, and an optional data directory on the disc. Here we have used the default option (`Nothing`) for the data directory. The `makeSnaplet` function takes the initializer function. In the case of `MyData`, we have written `myDataInit`, which creates the initial data for `MyData`.

- The data type `MyApp` represents the web application we are building. It has two fields--one points to `Snaplet Heist`, and another points to `Snaplet MyData`. This is how snaplets can be composed together. Also note that the names of the record fields in this data type start with an underscore so that a *lens* can be generated for each field.

- In the initializer `myAppInit` for `MyApp`, notice the following things:

- The `nestSnaplet` function is used for initializing and nesting snaplets.

- The nesting is done with the following syntax:

  ```
  nestSnaplet "mydata" myData $ myDataInit
  ```

- Here, the first parameter, `"mydata"`, is the name given for an *instance* of the snaplet. The second parameter, `myData`, is the *lens* generated for `MyData` for `MyApp` field *_myData*, and `myDataInit` is the snaplet initialization function for the MyData snaplet.

- In the `myAppInit` function, we use `addRoutes` to add routes for the `MyApp` snaplet. Each snaplet can have its own set of routes.

- We use `wrapSite (<|> heistServe)` in the `myAppInit` function. This is used for writing an initializer which has to be called before the site is served. Here, we use `heistServe` to serve `heisttemplates`.

- In the handlers `snapletName` and `snapletData`, notice the signature of the function. The following is the type signature for these handlers:

  ```
  Handler b MyData ()
  ```

In the preceding signature, `b` is the snaplet inside which we are working. In the current recipe, this is `MyApp`. The second type parameter, `MyData`, denotes the current Snaplet data type. The third parameter `()` is the return type of the `Monad Handler b MyData`.

- Handlers in Snap are `State` monads, and it is possible for *gets* and *puts* to be used inside the Handler. Here we use `getSnapletName` to get the name of the snaplet, and *gets* to get the data *_someData* inside `MyData`.

- Each snaplet can expect the data in the path `snaplets/`. In the current recipe, the `heist` data is located in the `snaplets/heist` directory. `Heist` has a convention to put all the templates in the `templates` subdirectory in its assigned path.

- In the template, we use two templates--*default* and *index*. Notice that the `index` template defines only the specific data for the index page, whereas, `default` represents a generic HTML structure. The `apply-content` tag in the `default` template embeds the contents of the `apply` tag in the *index* template to serve the *index* file.

- Since we have not defined the `root` path handler, the default home page will be served through the `index` heist template.

Session handling in Snap

In this recipe, we will work with session manager data type, `SessionManager` in Snap. The HTTP is a connection-less protocol, and the concept of a session has to be built on top of the interaction between client and server. The session is usually represented by some *key-value* pair that can be persisted across the interactions between a client and the server. In HTTP, this can be done in multiple ways--one of the most popular ways of handling a session is to set the session cookies. The session cookies are retained by the browser for a particular interaction duration.

In this recipe, we will set session cookies through cookie based the session manager in Snap.

How to do it...

1. Create a new project, `session-in-snap`, with a `simple` stack template:

   ```
   stack new session-in-snap simple
   ```

2. Add a dependency on the `snap-core` library in the `build-depends` subsection of the `executable` section. Add the other libraries necessary for working with Snap:

   ```
   executable session-in-snap
     hs-source-dirs:      src
     main-is:             Main.hs
   ```

```
default-language:    Haskell2010
build-depends:       base >= 4.7 && < 5
                   , snap-core
                   , snap-server
                   , snap
                   , lens
                   , bytestring
                   , text
```

3. Use the following command to solve the constraints within the current resolver. For this recipe, we have used lts-9.1 as a resolver:

```
stack --resolver lts-9.1 solver --update-config
```

4. Open src/Main.hs. We will add our source here. Enable the GHC extensions, OverloadedStrings and TemplateHaskell. After the Main module definition, add the necessary imports:

```
{-# LANGUAGE OverloadedStrings, TemplateHaskell #-}
module Main where

import Snap
import Snap.Core
import Snap.Http.Server
import Snap.Snaplet.Session
import Snap.Snaplet.Session.Backends.CookieSession
import Control.Lens
```

5. Create our own application that nests the session manager:

```
data MyApp = MyApp { _session :: Snaplet SessionManager }
```

6. Use lens macros to create a lens for our application, as follows:

```
makeLenses ''MyApp
```

7. Write a handler to print `Hello World!` as a text response. In addition to printing a message, we also use the `withSession` function to use the session inside our handler. We also use the handler also to set a key `user` inside the session:

```
greetings :: Handler MyApp MyApp ()
greetings = withSession session $ do
  with session $ setInSession "user" "Haskell Web Developer"
  writeBS "Hello World"
```

8. Write a handler where we get the key stored in the session and show it as an output, like this:

```
welcome :: Handler MyApp MyApp ()
welcome = withSession session $ do
  message <- with session $ do
    name <- getFromSession "user"
    return $ maybe "You are not registered" id name
  writeText $ message
  writeText "\n"
```

9. Initialize the application by providing the session manager. Initialize the cookie manager, and embed it as a session manager in our application, `MyApp`. Add two routes, `greet` and `welcome`, for the functions `greetings` and `welcome`, respectively:

```
initMyApp = makeSnaplet "sessionDemo" "Demonstrating session
with Snaplet" Nothing $ do
  -- site_key is the name of the file where cookie session
manager will store the site key.
  -- demo-session is the name of the session cookie
  sess <- nestSnaplet "session" session $
initCookieSessionManager "site_key.txt" "demo-session" Nothing
(Just 3600)
  addRoutes [ ("/greet", greetings)
            , ("/welcome", welcome)]
  return (MyApp sess)
```

10. Now serve the snaplet through the `serveSnaplet` function, as follows:

```
main :: IO ()
main = serveSnaplet defaultConfig initMyApp
```

11. Build and execute the project. The server should run at port `8000`:

```
stack build
stack exec -- session-in-snap
```

Open the browser, and point it to `http://localhost:8000/welcome`; you should see a message, **You are not registered**, as shown in the following screenshot:

Now, visit `http://localhost:8000/greet`. This should set the cookie in the session. If you now visit `http://localhost:8000/welcome`, you should see the message, **Haskell Web Developer**:

How it works...

In the preceding recipe, we took the following steps to store information in a session:

- The `withSession` function introduces the `session` lens into the handler. At the end of the request, the `withSession` function commits the changes to the session.
- The `with` function allows us to use the `session` functions in the handler.
- The function `setInSession` allows us to set a key to the value that we would like.
- The function `getFromSession` allows us to get a key if it is present in the session.
- We use `initCookieManager` to initialize the cookie-based session manager supplied with the snap framework. The cookie manager is configured with `site_key.txt`, a file where a private encoding key for the session manager will be stored, the name of the session key, and the expiry time for the session.

You can use `curl` to see the cookie generated. Start the snap server as mentioned in the previous section, and connect to the `greet` endpoint using the following command:

```
curl -X GET http://localhost:8000/greet --verbose --cookie-jar
cookies.txt
```

You should see the following output:

```
session-in-snap — -bash — 126×30

session-in-snap $ curl -X GET http://localhost:8000/greet --verbose --cookie-jar cookies.txt
Note: Unnecessary use of -X or --request, GET is already inferred.
*   Trying ::1...
* Connection failed
* connect to ::1 port 8000 failed: Connection refused
*   Trying 127.0.0.1...
* Connected to localhost (127.0.0.1) port 8000 (#0)
> GET /greet HTTP/1.1
> Host: localhost:8000
> User-Agent: curl/7.49.0
> Accept: */*
>
< HTTP/1.1 200 OK
* Added cookie demo-session="LORoyeL5C0HOCBpU+R6gQpdUj3wNEU9WA2WruNyl4Ax2tvqeMgiEGYT1HxD80uR/eqw4Milir11mYdCvuz1Z2OiZ8D6klp+YQ
2LP/a8MsDZIpEClt34XWbq7/JxPpwbHuQGZS2xJFSkvrkWCGBOSdVagjJ2iVTX6swOv8Cc482FYnnLnQqJdpws/s4FGtL5CuIV/GEiPDMwhcmd2vb0=" for domai
n localhost, path /, expire 1505165548
< set-cookie: demo-session=LORoyeL5C0HOCBpU+R6gQpdUj3wNEU9WA2WruNyl4Ax2tvqeMgiEGYT1HxD80uR/eqw4Milir11mYdCvuz1Z2OiZ8D6klp+YQ2L
P/a8MsDZIpEClt34XWbq7/JxPpwbHuQGZS2xJFSkvrkWCGBOSdVagjJ2iVTX6swOv8Cc482FYnnLnQqJdpws/s4FGtL5CuIV/GEiPDMwhcmd2vb0=; path=/; exp
ires=Mon, 11-Sep-2017 21:32:28 GMT; HttpOnly
< server: Snap/1.0.3.0
< date: Mon, 11 Sep 2017 20:32:28 GMT
< transfer-encoding: chunked
<
* Connection #0 to host localhost left intact
Hello World
session-in-snap $
```

The cookie that is acquired from the preceding interaction is stored by the user client, such as `curl` and `browser`. This session cookie is again shared with the server when interacting the next time. Hence, the next time, when you connect with the endpoint `http://localhost:8000/welcome`, the session cookie is decoded, and the embedded message is displayed.

To run the same endpoint with `curl`, run the next command:

```
curl -X GET http://localhost:8000/welcome --verbose -b cookies.txt --
cookie-jar cookies.txt
```

The `curl` command will show the following output. You can see that the cookie is now sent to the server, and we will get the welcome message from the endpoint, `http://localhost:8000/welcome`:

```
● ● ●                    session-in-snap — -bash — 126×30
session-in-snap $ curl -X GET http://localhost:8000/welcome --verbose -b cookies.txt --cookie-jar cookies.txt
Note: Unnecessary use of -X or --request, GET is already inferred.
*   Trying ::1...
* Connection failed
* connect to ::1 port 8000 failed: Connection refused
*   Trying 127.0.0.1...
* Connected to localhost (127.0.0.1) port 8000 (#0)
> GET /welcome HTTP/1.1
> Host: localhost:8000
> User-Agent: curl/7.49.0
> Accept: */*
> Cookie: demo-session=LORoyeL5C0HOCBpU+R6gQpdUj3wNEU9WA2WruNy14Ax2tvqeMgiEGYTlHxD80uR/eqw4Milirl1mYdCvuz1Z2OiZ8D6klp+YQ2LP/a8
MsDZIpEC1t34XWbq7/JxPpwbHuQGZS2xJFSkvrkWCGBOSdVagjJ2iVTX6swOv8Cc482FYnnLnQqJd;ws/s4FGtL5CuIV/GEiPDMwhcmd2vb0=
>
< HTTP/1.1 200 OK
* Replaced cookie demo-session="YCKVvUUrCMPky5BT0t5nJUHXx/jFX0bUNeEMp/cfPFfROgFpuCilA0y63mfipJo9RiNsbA9LY/ppc621Et7sljrxmLWuTU
TolIZsOpdOgY7EhhDqnVvldekoTT/4T7/GaqA8q3eqsRDnUSnF0BW5F/p5Q3f6o7rSiRDveIwKiySzJlFqa0yGENHrAyFBMAr390np79xYDpUOxHkVtw8=" for do
main localhost, path /, expire 1505165626
< set-cookie: demo-session=YCKVvUUrCMPky5BT0t5nJUHXx/jFX0bUNeEMp/cfPFfROgFpuCilA0y63mfipJo9RiNsbA9LY/ppc621Et7sljrxmLWuTUTolIZ
sOpdOgY7EhhDqnVvldekoTT/4T7/GaqA8q3eqsRDnUSnF0BW5F/p5Q3f6o7rSiRDveIwKiySzJlFqa0yGENHrAyFBMAr390np79xYDpUOxHkVtw8=; path=/; exp
ires=Mon, 11-Sep-2017 21:33:46 GMT; HttpOnly
< server: Snap/1.0.3.0
< date: Mon, 11 Sep 2017 20:33:46 GMT
< transfer-encoding: chunked
<
Haskell Web Developer
* Connection #0 to host localhost left intact
session-in-snap $ ▊
```

Authentication in Snap

In this recipe, we will work with authentication with help of the built-in authentication manager in snap. Snap provides a framework that can be tied to HTML templates to provide a customizable authentication mechanism. In this recipe, we will have a few routes requiring authentication, and a few without it. We will see how transitioning from one route to another requiring authentication kicks in the authentication framework.

We will also work with the SQLite backend for storing user credentials.

How to do it...

1. Create a new project, `auth-in-snap`, with a `simple` stack template:

```
stack new auth-in-snap simple
```

2. Add a dependency on the `snap-core` library in the `build-depends` subsection of the `executable` section.

```
executable auth-in-snap
  hs-source-dirs:      src
  main-is:             Main.hs
  default-language:    Haskell2010
  build-depends:       base >= 4.7 && < 5
                     , snap-core
                     , snap-server
                     , snaplet-sqlite-simple
                     , heist
                     , snap
                     , lens
                     , bytestring
                     , text
                     , map-syntax
```

3. Use the following command to solve the constraints within the current resolver. For this recipe, we have used `lts-9.1` as a resolver:

```
stack --resolver lts-9.1 solver --update-config
```

4. Copy the archive from `https://www.dropbox.com/s/hsprdjk5221r83c/auth-in-snap-templates.tar.gz?dl=0`. It is a set of templates and heist templates to be used in this recipe. The archive contains templates for the index page and the login page. Expand the archive in the project folder.

5. Open `src/Main.hs`. We will add our source here. Enable the extensions `OverloadedStrings` and `TemplateHaskell` for working with the snaplet:

```
{-# LANGUAGE OverloadedStrings, TemplateHaskell #-}
module Main where

import Snap
import Snap.Core
import Snap.Http.Server
import Snap.Snaplet.Session
import Snap.Snaplet.Session.Backends.CookieSession
import Snap.Snaplet.SqliteSimple
import Snap.Snaplet.Auth.Backends.SqliteSimple
import Control.Lens
import Snap.Snaplet.Heist
import Snap.Snaplet.Auth
import Snap.Util.FileServe
```

```
import Data.ByteString.Char8
import Data.Text
import Heist.Interpreted
import Data.Monoid
import Data.Map.Syntax ((##))
import Control.Applicative
import Control.Monad.IO.Class
```

6. Create your own application that nests the session manager, `auth` manager, and `heist` snaplets. We use the `SQLite` database for storing user credentials:

```
data MyApp = MyApp { _heist :: Snaplet (Heist MyApp)
                   , _mysession :: Snaplet SessionManager
                   , _auth :: Snaplet (AuthManager MyApp)
                   , _authdb :: Snaplet Sqlite
                   }
```

7. Let's create lenses for our application so that we can use them in the snaplet composition:

```
makeLenses ''MyApp
```

8. For our convenience, we'll create the `HasHeist` instance for our application so that we can use `heist` transparently:

```
instance HasHeist MyApp where
  heistLens = subSnaplet heist
```

9. Handle the logout event. After the logout, redirect the user to the home page:

```
signoutUser :: Handler MyApp (AuthManager MyApp) ()
signoutUser = logout >> redirect "/"
```

10. Show the login form to the user. Take an additional parameter to show the error message in case there was an error logging in before:

```
signinUserForm :: Maybe Text -> Handler MyApp (AuthManager
MyApp) ()
signinUserForm errorMsg =
  let errSplice msg = "loginError" ## textSplice msg
      err = maybe mempty errSplice errorMsg
  in heistLocal (bindSplices err) (render "signin")
```

11. Handle the login form. The names of the input elements handling the user name and password need to be provided to the handler. Also note that we will provide a parameter as a route that we will be redirected to. Upon error, we show the form again, showing the login error:

```
signinUser :: ByteString -> Handler MyApp (AuthManager MyApp)
()
signinUser route = loginUser "username" "password" Nothing
(const (signinUserForm err)) (redirect route)
  where
    err = Just "Invalid user name or password"
```

12. Combine the sign-in form rendering and submitting together in a single handler. Display the form for the GET request, and submit the login request for the POST request:

```
signin :: ByteString -> Handler MyApp (AuthManager MyApp) ()
signin route = method GET (signinUserForm Nothing) <|> method
POST (signinUser route)
```

13. Handle new user sign up. After signing up, redirect the user to the home page:

```
signupUser :: Handler MyApp (AuthManager MyApp) ()
signupUser = method POST $ do
  registerUser "susername" "spassword"
  redirect "/"
```

14. Add a protected route tour which can be accessed only if the user has signed in:

```
tour :: Handler MyApp (AuthManager MyApp) ()
tour = do
  authorised <- isLoggedIn
  if authorised
    then
      render "tourpage"
    else
      redirect "/signin"
```

15. Construct the routes for signing in, signing out, signing up, and the home page. Also add a route for *tour* to display a custom page, and serve the directory *static* for serving static contents.

```
routes :: [(ByteString, Handler MyApp MyApp ())]
routes = [ ("signin", with auth (signin "/"))
         , ("signout", with auth signoutUser)
         , ("signup", with auth signupUser)
         , ("tour", with auth tour)
         , ("",   serveDirectory "static")
         ]
```

16. Initialize the application with all the snaplets. For the session, use initCookieSessionManager:

```
initMyApp :: SnapletInit MyApp MyApp
initMyApp = makeSnaplet "myApp" "My snaplet with auth, db,
session and auth" Nothing $ do
  hst <- nestSnaplet "" heist $ heistInit "templates"
  ses <- nestSnaplet "session" mysession $
initCookieSessionManager "site_key.txt" "session" Nothing (Just
3600)
  adb <- nestSnaplet "authdb" authdb sqliteInit
  ath <- nestSnaplet "auth" auth $ initSqliteAuth mysession adb
  addRoutes routes
  addAuthSplices hst auth
  return $ MyApp hst ses ath adb
```

17. Serve the snaplet from the command line as follows:

```
main :: IO ()
main = serveSnaplet defaultConfig initMyApp
```

18. Build and execute the project, like this:

```
stack build
stack exec -- auth-in-snap
```

The server will start at port 8000. If you point your browser to http://localhost:8000, you should see the following output:

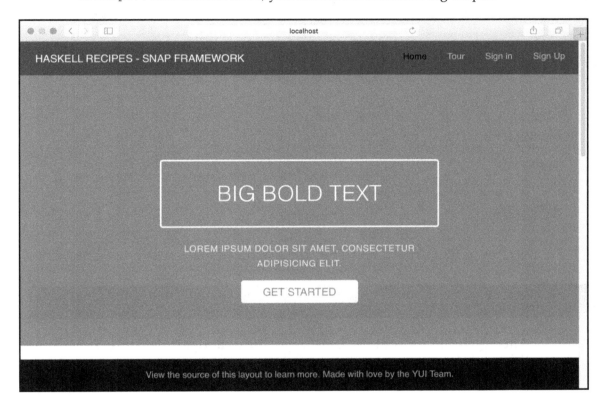

The server will create default configurations for the SQLite database, and tables required for auth. If you click on the sign-up form, you can add the user.

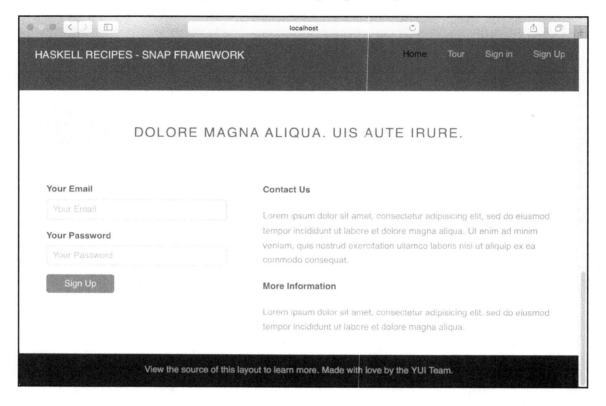

After signing in, you can visit the X page. The web page should take cognizance of the fact that you have logged into the portal.

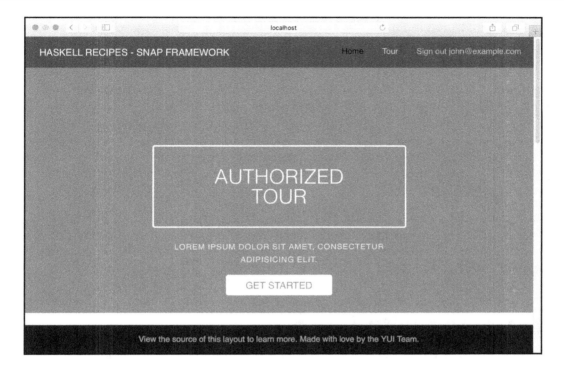

How it works...

In this last recipe, we combined a database, auth framework, a session backend, and heist templating together. We created a web application that renders heist templates based on `https://purecss.io/CSS`. The application stores user data in the SQLite database, `test.db`, located in the project directory.

When the application starts for the first time, the SQLite database snaplet and its auth backend create configuration files in the directories `snaplets/sqlite-simple` and `snaplets/sqlite-auth`, respectively. These directories contain the default configuration files for initializing databases and authorization. One can modify these files or create new ones for differentiating between development and production databases.

During the application initialization, we used `addAuthSplices` along with routes. This adds the required heist splices, such as `ifLoggedIn` and `ifLoggedOut`, which we have used in the `default.tpl` template to check if the user has already logged in.

The authentication happens through the `loginUser` and `logout` functions. The function `registerUser` is required for signing up the user. Both the `loginUser` and `registerUser` functions take the names of the usernames and passwords in the associated HTML form. In addition to verifying the user's credentials with the database backend, these functions also take advantage of the session and store the user login data in the session cookie; this allows us to implement the *remember me* feature (not implemented in this recipe).

All the handlers which require authentication have the signature with `auth <>`. This enables us to call the authentication functions that the Snap framework provides. Note that the `auth` framework also encapsulates the session, and hence, there is no separate need to pass session information to the `with auth ...` handlers.

File upload with Snap

File upload is a very basic HTTP operation handled through `Content-type: multipart/form-data`. In this recipe, we will create an HTML form and upload a file through it. While the file is being uploaded, we will dynamically process the contents, and report the summary.

How to do it...

1. Create a new project, `file-upload`, with a `simple` stack template:

   ```
   stack new file-upload simple
   ```

2. Add a dependency on the `snap-core` library in the `build-depends` subsection of the `executable` section, as follows:

   ```
   executable file-upload
     hs-source-dirs:      src
     main-is:             Main.hs
     default-language:    Haskell2010
     build-depends:       base >= 4.7 && < 5
                        , snap-core
                        , snap-server
   ```

```
, heist
, snap
, lens
, bytestring
, io-streams
, text
```

3. Use the following command to solve the constraints within the current resolver. For this recipe, we have used `lts-9.1` as a resolver:

```
stack --resolver lts-9.1 solver --update-config
```

4. Open `src/Main.hs`. We will add our source here. Enable the GHC extensions `OverloadedStrings` and `TemplateHaskell`. After the `Main` module definition, add the necessary imports:

```
{-# LANGUAGE OverloadedStrings, TemplateHaskell #-}
module Main where

import Snap
import Snap.Core
import Snap.Http.Server
import Control.Lens
import Data.ByteString.Char8 as B
import Snap.Util.FileUploads
import Snap.Util.FileServe
import Data.Monoid
import qualified System.IO.Streams as Streams
```

5. Create a directory, `static`, in the project `root` folder. Create a form `form.html` in the `static` directory. Add the following contents to the `form.html` file:

```
<!DOCTYPE HTML5>
<html>
  <body>
    <form enctype="multipart/form-data" action="/upload"
method="POST">
      <input name="file" type="file" />
      <input type="submit" value="Upload File" />
    </form>
  </body>
</html>
```

6. Write a handler for processing the file contents. The file contents in parts are processed by the part handler, which is implemented later:

```
uploadHandler :: Snap ()
uploadHandler = do
  (_, lines) <- foldMultipart defaultUploadPolicy partHandler 0
  writeBS $ "Number of lines uploaded : " <> B.pack (show lines)
```

7. Now implement the part handler for counting the number of lines in the uploaded file as it is being uploaded. The end of the input is signalled by Nothing, as returned by read function:

```
partHandler :: PartFold Int
partHandler info inp seed = do
  part <- Streams.read inp
  case part of
    Nothing -> return seed
    Just p  -> partHandler info inp (seed + Prelude.length (B.lines p))
```

8. Create routes for uploading the file, and serving the form:

```
routes :: [(ByteString, Snap ())]
routes = [ ("/upload", uploadHandler)
         , ("", serveDirectory "static") ]
```

9. Write the main function to start the server to serve the aforementioned routes:

```
main :: IO ()
main = quickHttpServe $ route routes
```

10. Build and execute the project:

```
stack build
stack exec -- file-upload
```

11. The server runs at `http://localhost:8000`. Point your browser to `http://localhost:8000/form.html`. You should see the following form:

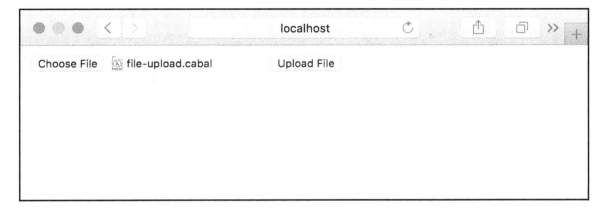

Choose the file, say `file-upload.cabal`, and press the `upload` button. You should see the following lines printed in the browser window:

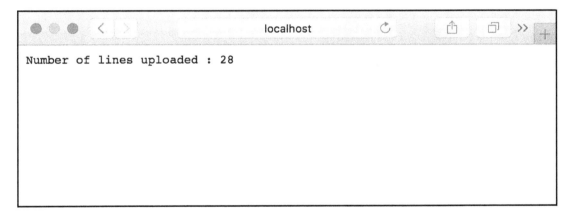

How it works...

The file uploader in the preceding recipe uses the function called `foldMultipart`. It handles `Content-type: multipart/form-data`, and handles each chunk. It takes `PartFold` as an argument. The type `PartFold a` is defined as follows:

```
type PartFold a = PartInfo -> InputStream ByteString -> a -> IO a
```

The data type `InputStream` can be worked upon by a
function `read` (`System.IO.Streams` module). This function waits for the data being
uploaded, and spits out the contents in part. At the end of the data being
uploaded, `read` produces `Nothing`, signalling the end of data.

In the preceding recipe, the function `foldMultipart` works similar to `foldr`, except that at
each folding operation, we can use *read* to wait for the data being chunked and handed over
to us. This kind of processing is very useful if we would like to parse the contents as the file
is being uploaded. Indeed, the package `io-streams`, which provides
the `InputStream` data type, also contains a
module, `Systems.IO.Streams.Attoparsec`, for dynamically parsing the data as it is
uploaded.

If the developer is interested in looking at all the data after it is uploaded, then there is a
function, `handleFileUploads`, which can handle whole file uploads.

10
Working with Advanced Haskell

In this chapter, we will be looking at following recipes:

- Working with existentially quantified type
- Working with Rank-N type
- Working with type family
- Working with GADTs

Introduction

Haskell has numerous extensions (Visit `https://downloads.haskell.org/~ghc/latest/docs/html/users_guide/` for a comprehensive list of extensions and features), which can be used through `{-# LANGUAGE <pragma> #-}`. In this chapter, we will be looking at some advanced GHC extensions, and advanced language features such as type-families, rank-n-types, existential types and **Generic Algebraic Data Types** (**GADT**). The selection is offered from a usefulness point of view, and it is in no way complete, but it should be representative.

Working with existentially quantified type

In this recipe, we will create a list of heterogeneous types which are instances of the type class `Show`. We will use an `ExistentialQuantification` extension to show the list. We will use `StandaloneDeriving` extension to derive a type class instance.

How to do it...

1. Create a new project `working-with-existentials` with a `simple` stack template:

   ```
   stack new working-with-existentials simple
   ```

2. Open `src/Main.hs`. We will be adding our source here.

3. Enable the existential support, and define the `Main` module. Also add `StandaloneDeriving` extension.

   ```
   {-# LANGUAGE ExistentialQuantification, StandaloneDeriving #-}

   module Main where
   ```

4. Define an existential type:

   ```
   data Display = forall a . Show a => Display a
   ```

5. Create a standalone instance of `Show Display`:

   ```
   deriving instance Show Display
   ```

6. Create a list of Displays, and, call it in the `main` function:

   ```
   displayList :: [Display]
   displayList = [ Display 10
                 , Display ["One","Two","Three"]
                 , Display 10.0
                 , Display (Just "Something")
                 , Display True ]

   main :: IO ()
   main = do
     putStrLn "Printing heterogenous showable list"
     print displayList
   ```

7. Build and execute the project:

   ```
   stack build
   stack exec -- working-with-existentials
   ```

8. You should see the following output:

```
working-with-existentials — -bash — 96×7
working-with-existentials $ stack exec working-with-existentials
Printing heterogenous showable list
[Display 10,Display ["One","Two","Three"],Display 10.0,Display (Just "Something"),Display True]
working-with-existentials $
```

How it works...

In this recipe, we have primarily used the ExistentialQuantification extension. Note how we have defined the data type, Display:

```
data Display = forall a . Show a => Display a
```

An important thing to note here is that the type variable a does not appear on the left-hand side. It only appears on right-hand side expressions. It also appears with a construct forall a . Show a. It is a way of embedding information about the type class that is embedded inside the data type. In this case, it tells us that Display is defined for all a which are instances of Show. In this way, the data constructor Display a embeds a value of type a. But the only information that is available to us is about the type class Show. This means that we can only call functions of type class Show here. This is how we could encode, an Int, List, Maybe and so on, in the same list in the preceding example, and show it too!

We have also used another extension called StandaloneDeriving. Here, because, Display is an existential type, we cannot say *deriving Show* for Display. However, we can create a standalone deriving instance by saying deriving instance Show Display (without the where clause). The standalone deriving instance can be defined in another file as well. Also note that the standalone deriving instance can be for a specific data type (or constraint) as well.

Working with Rank-N type

We will be using *ST s a* monad to convert imperative actions into pure actions. ST Monad provides a strictly isolated mutability. ST monad allows access to mutable memory to be strictly inside the ST monad itself. Once we *run* an ST monad, the mutability goes away, and we get a referentially transparent function. Thus ST monad is very useful in creating an efficient isolated computation where mutability is strictly isolated from outside world, and, by running it, we can embed it as a pure function.

To be able to isolate ST monad, we will use higher ranked data type in this recipe.

How to do it...

1. Create a new project `working-with-rank-n-type` with a `simple` stack template:

   ```
   stack new working-with-rank-n-type simple
   ```

2. Open `src/Main.hs`. We will be adding our source here.

3. Add the language extension `Rank2Types`, and define `Main` module:

   ```
   module Main where
   ```

4. Import the `ST` monad module:

   ```
   import Control.Monad.ST
   import Data.STRef
   import Control.Monad
   ```

5. Use the `ST` monad to calculate:

   ```
   factorialST :: (Num t, Eq t) => t -> STRef s t -> ST s t
   factorialST 0 x = readSTRef x
   factorialST n x = do
     x' <- readSTRef x
     writeSTRef x $! x' * n
     factorialST (n-1) x
   ```

6. Convert the preceding factorial function from `ST s t` to a pure function:

```
factorial n = runST $ do
  x <- newSTRef 1
  factorialST n x
```

7. Call the `factorial` in `main`:

```
main :: IO ()
main = do
  putStr "100! = "
  print $ factorial 100
  putStrLn ""
  putStr "500! = "
  print $ factorial 500
  putStrLn ""
```

8. Build and execute the project:

stack build
stack exec -- working-with-rank-n-type

9. You should see the following output:

How it works...

In this recipe, we will use `ST s a`, which is defined as follows:

```
newtype ST s a = GHC.ST.ST (GHC.ST.STRep s a)
```

The ST is a special monad that lets us update in place. But it allows us to do this without explicit *IO*, by allowing us to escape ST. This is done by using runST. The function runST has a peculiar type:

```
runST :: (forall s. ST s a) -> a
```

This is a rank 2 type, as the function runST must take an argument of type ST s and this argument should be universal in terms of s. Also note that the quantification (forall s . ST s a) helps runST escape ST.

In fact, all functions of rank 1, such as map can be used with quantifiers for example

```
map :: forall a b . (a -> b) -> [a] -> [b]
```

However, with runST, by specifying (forall s . ST s a), we increase the rank to 2, because now we need one more quantifier. The actual type of runST is as follows:

```
runST :: forall a . (forall s . ST s a) -> a
```

We stop at the rank-2 level, but you can imagine how we can move up the rank.

Working with type family

In this recipe, we will work with *type family* or associated types. In *type family*, we associate a data type with another data type. In this particular recipe, we will work with a package *vector-space*, which beautifully show the association between types which defining *vector* and *scalar* types.

How to do it...

1. Create a new project working-with-type-family with a simple stack template:

```
stack new working-with-type-family simple
```

2. Add a dependency on vector-space library in the build-depends sub-section of executable section:

```
executable working-with-type-family
   hs-source-dirs:      src
   main-is:             Main.hs
```

```
default-language:    Haskell2010
build-depends:       base >= 4.7 && < 5
                   , vector-space
```

3. Open `src/Main.hs`. We will be adding our source here.

4. Define the module `Main`, and import `Data.VectorSpace`:

```
module Main where

import Data.VectorSpace
```

5. Define vectors in three dimensions by using a tuple:

```
diagonal :: (Double, Double, Double)
diagonal = (1, 1, 1)

xaxis :: (Double, Double, Double)
xaxis = (1, 0, 0)
```

6. Scale the diagonal vector, and take an inner product with `xaxis`:

```
scaleanddotx :: Double -> (Double, Double, Double) -> (Double,
Double, Double) -> Double
scaleanddotx s p q = (s *^ p) <.> q
```

7. Print the values in `main` by invoking the preceding functions:

```
main :: IO ()
main = do
  putStrLn $ "Vector operation :- ((1,1,1) * 10) . (1,0,0)"
  print $ scaleanddotx 10.0 diagonal xaxis
  putStrLn $ "Midpoint of (1,1,1) and (1,0,0)"
  print $ lerp diagonal xaxis 0.5
```

8. Build and execute the project:

```
stack build
stack exec -- working-with-type-family
```

9. You should see the following output:

How it works...

The preceding example is rather simple, but it cleverly uses the `type` *family*. Look at the definition of `VectorSpace` type-class. We know that we can scale a *vector* by a *scalar*. The type class `VectorSpace` allows us to define our data structure as a *vector*. however, we should also be able to customize which *scalar* we would like to associate with this type.

The `VectorSpace` type class is defined as follows:

```
class AdditiveGroup v => VectorSpace v where
    type Scalar v :: *
```

In the preceding class definition, the type `Scalar` is defined as `type Scalar v :: *`. The type `Scalar v` means that, for a data type v, which is an instance of `VectorSpace`, there is a scalar associated with it. And this type `Scalar` can be defined as we define the instance.

In the preceding recipe, we use (`Double, Double, Double`) as an instance of `VectorSpace`. This instance is defined as follows:

```
instance ( VectorSpace u, s ~ Scalar u
         , VectorSpace v, s ~ Scalar v
         , VectorSpace w, s ~ Scalar w )
      => VectorSpace (u,v,w) where
    type Scalar (u,v,w) = Scalar u
```

This means that, if u, v, and w are vector spaces, and they share a common scalar value s, then we can define (u,v,w) as an instance of `VectorSpace`, and its `Scalar` value is s.

Working with GADTs

In this recipe, we will work with GADTs. GADTs extend the data constructors, and allow us more expressivity for representing a complex structure such as a DSL. In this recipe, we will use GADTs to create an expression representation, and a simple parser.

How to do it...

1. Create a new project `working-with-GADTs` with `simple` stack template:

   ```
   stack new working-with-GADTs simple
   ```

2. Open `src/Main.hs`. We will be adding our source here.

3. Enable `GADTs`, and `StandaloneDeriving`:

   ```
   {-# LANGUAGE GADTs, StandaloneDeriving #-}
   module Main where

   import Control.Monad
   import Data.Char
   import Control.Applicative
   ```

4. `GADTs` take an algebraic data type one step further, and allow us to write data constructors explicitly. For example, we can represent a set of expressions as follows:

   ```
   data Expr where
     Value :: Int -> Expr
     Add :: Expr -> Expr -> Expr
     Mult :: Expr -> Expr -> Expr

   deriving instance Show Expr
   ```

5. We can evaluate the preceding expression as follows:

   ```
   eval :: Expr -> Int
   eval (Value i) = i
   eval (Add e1 e2) = eval e1 + eval e2
   eval (Mult e1 e2) = eval e1 * eval e2
   ```

6. Create some expression:

```
sampleExpr :: Expr
sampleExpr = Add (Value 10) (Mult (Add (Value 20) (Value 10))
(Value 20))
```

7. In fact, we can also represent `Parser` monad with GADTs:

```
data Parser a where
  Return :: a -> Parser a
  Unparser :: (String -> [(a,String)]) -> (a -> Parser b) ->
Parser b
```

8. Instantiate a `Functor`, `Applicative`, and `Monad` instance for our `Parser`:

```
instance Functor Parser where

  fmap f (Return x) = Return (f x)
  fmap f (Unparser parseFn afb) = Unparser parseFn (fmap f .
afb)

instance Applicative Parser where

  pure = Return

  Return f <*> Return x = Return (f x)
  Return f <*> Unparser parseFn cfa = Unparser parseFn (fmap f
.
  cfa)
  Unparser pc cfab <*> pa = Unparser pc (\c -> cfab c <*> pa)

instance Monad Parser where

  return = Return

  Return x >>= f = f x
  Unparser parseFn afb >>= f = Unparser parseFn ((>>= f) .
afb)
```

9. Similar to `Expr`, we can also write an evaluator for our `Parser`:

```
parse :: Parser a -> String -> [(a, String)]
parse (Return x) s = [(x, s)]
parse (Unparser parseFn afb) s =
  case parseFn s of
    (a,s'):_ -> parse (afb a) s'
    _        -> []
```

10. Write a set of parsing functions. Create a `digit` parser:

```
conditional :: (Char -> Bool) -> String -> [(Char,String)]
conditional _ [] = []
conditional f (x:xs) | f x = [(x,xs)]
conditional _ _ = []

digit :: Parser Char
digit = Unparser (conditional isDigit) Return
```

11. Use the preceding functions in `main` to evaluate `Expr` and run `Parser`:

```
main :: IO ()
main = do
  putStrLn $ "Sample Expression - " ++ (show sampleExpr) ++ " =
"
  print $ eval sampleExpr

  -- Create a parser for ditit
  putStrLn "Parsing digit from \"1abc\" should be successful"
  print $ parse digit "1abc"

  putStrLn "Parsing digit from \"abc\" should fail"
  print $ parse digit "abc"
```

12. Build and execute the project:

```
stack build
stack exec -- working-with-GADTs
```

13. You should see the following output:

```
working-with-GADTs $ stack exec -- working-with-GADTs
Sample Expression - Add (Value 10) (Mult (Add (Value 20) (Value 10)) (Value 20)) =
610
Parsing digit from "1abc" should be successful
[('1',"abc")]
Parsing digit from "abc" should fail
[]
working-with-GADTs $
```

How it works...

We have looked at Generalized Algebraic Data Types. They allows us to create a domain-specific language, and evaluate it the way we want it. We can use this DSL to simulate, or execute, or for any other purpose.

In the second part, we have created a `Parser` with GADTs. In fact we can generalize it to a generic monad:

```
data Parser a where
  Return :: a -> Parser a
  Unparser :: (String -> [(a,String)]) -> (a -> Parser b) -> Parser b
```

Here the data constructors `Return` and `Unparser` look very similar to `return` and bind `>>=` of a monad. In fact, we can actually represent a generic instance of a monad in terms of data constructors. This is equivalent to *Free* monad. For more information, have a look at (https://www.andres-loeh.de/Free.pdf).

11
Working with Lens and Prism

In this chapter, we will be looking at the following recipes:

- Creating lenses
- Working with lenses
- Working with Traversal
- Working with Iso
- Working with Prism
- Working with predefined lenses

Introduction

If you have worked with object-oriented programming, then you must be aware of the properties (such as in C# or Python, or even in managed C++). Usually, we can access the properties inside an object and also set the property to some value:

```
Point point = Point(1.0, 2.0);
double x = point.x; // Should be 1.0
point.x = 3.0;      // Now point x is changed to 3.0
```

Though the preceding code mutates the data, it is very convenient to get and set a property. Imagine doing the same with Haskell:

```
data Point = Point Double Double

x :: Point -> Double
x (Point xv _) = xv

setx :: Point -> Double -> Point
setx (Point _ y) x = Point x y
```

We need to de-construct a type, and reconstruct it again. If we had some generic way of accessing a field inside the data, and then accessing it back, then we will get the lost convenience of getting and setting a property back.

It is said that *Lens* and *Prism* are some of the most complex pieces of code written in Haskell, thanks to the use of existential quantification, rank 2 types and many operators that can work with each other. Thankfully, working with Lens and Prism is not that hard, and definitely very productive due to their usefulness.

We will be using Edward Kmett's original lens library for this chapter. We will start by manufacturing our own lenses in the first recipe. We will quickly move on to the lens library, working with *Lens, Traversal, Iso*, and *Prism*.

Creating lenses

In this recipe, we will look at how we can define a generic property getter and setter. We will write a data type and we will write a generic type that will achieve both getting and setting a field inside the data type.

How to do it...

1. Create a new project `creating-lenses`, with a `simple` stack template:

```
stack new creating-lenses simple
```

2. Open `src/Main.hs`. We will be adding our source here. Define the `Main` module. Enable extension `Rank2Types` before the `Main` module. Also, add `StandaloneDeriving` and `DerivingFunctor`. We will use `DerivingFunctor` to automatically derive the `Functor` definition:

```
{-# LANGUAGE Rank2Types, StandaloneDeriving, DeriveFunctor #-}
module Main where
```

3. Define a data type `Point`, which represents a two-dimensional point:

```
data Point = Point Double Double deriving Show
```

4. Now define a generic structure *s*, and we need to get a field of type a from the structure. Its type would be `s -> a`. Now imagine we need to change some property of structure s with value b, and the result will be another structure, t. This will have a type `s -> b -> t` (actually, this is generic type for the specific setter `s -> b -> s`). Let's now define types for these getter and setter functions:

```
type Getter s a = s -> a
type Setter s b t = s -> b -> t
```

5. We will combine getter and setter in one type, `Lens` :

```
type Lens s t a b = forall f . Functor f => (a -> f b)
-> s -> f t
```

The preceding type is a rank 2 type, as it should work for any `Functor f`, and f is not included on the left-hand side. Note that *s* is an input data type and, t is the output data type. a corresponds to some property of s, whereas b is some property type associated with t.

6. Let's now see if we can combine getter and setter to create a combined lens:

```
lens :: Getter s a -> Setter s b t -> Lens s t a b
lens getter setter f x = fmap (setter x) $ f $ getter x
```

7. Now define lenses for x and y coordinates in the `Point`. Since, in our case, we would like to have the output data type be the same as the input data type, with the same property type, we can define `Lens'` to be a restricted version of `Lens`:

```
type Lens' s a = Lens s s a a

 x :: Lens' Point Double
```

```
x = lens getter setter
where
getter (Point xv _) = xv
setter (Point _ yv) xv = Point xv yv

y :: Lens' Point Double
y = lens getter setter
where
getter (Point _ yv) = yv
setter (Point xv _) yv = Point xv yv
```

8. Define an identity functor:

```
newtype Access a s = Access { access :: a } deriving Show
```

9. Define an instance of `Functor`:

```
deriving instance Functor (Access a)
```

10. Define a function to get field, given a lens:

```
view :: Lens' s a -> s -> a
view l = access . l Access
```

11. Similarly, define a generic function to set a field.

```
newtype Binder a = Binder { bound :: a }

deriving instance Functor Binder
set :: Lens' s a -> a -> s -> s
set l d = bound . l (const (Binder d))
```

12. Use the preceding lenses in the `main` function:

```
main :: IO ()
main = do
 -- Create a point
 let p = Point 3 5
 putStrLn $ "Initial Point = " ++ show p
 putStrLn $ "Getting x and y coordinates using lenses x and y"
 print $ view x p
 print $ view y p
 putStrLn $ "Setting x and y coordinates alternatively using
 lenses x and y"
 print $ set x 7 p
 print $ set y 7 p
```

13. Build and execute the project:

```
stack build
stack exec -- creating-lenses
```

14. You should see the following output:

```
creating-lenses $ stack exec -- creating-lenses
Initial Point = Point 3.0 5.0
Getting x and y coordinates using lenses x and y
3.0
5.0
Setting x and y coordinates alternatively using lenses x and y
Point 7.0 5.0
Point 3.0 7.0
creating-lenses $
```

How it works...

In this recipe, we have defined a generic lens Lens s t a b which expands to the following:

```
fmap (setter x) $ f (getter x)
```

Here, x is some structure, getter x gets a field from x, and setter x is a function that takes an argument, sets the same field, and returns a modified x. In the lens, they are connected together by fmap, with f transforming the value of the field to a Functor.

Since, the lens is a rank 2 type, through the choice of f, if made wisely, we can achieve both generic get and set at the same time. Thus, when creating a generic getter view function, we use Access as a Functor. Access captures the field value, and ignores fmap mapping. On the other hand, the setter set function, uses Binder, which takes the input field value, and submits itself to the fmap by replacing the field value in the given input x.

Working with lenses

In this recipe, we will be working with the lens library. This library provides a whole battery of functions. We will be using some of those functions. We will also create lenses for our own data type.

How to do it...

1. Create a new project `working-with-lenses`, with a `simple` stack template:

    ```
    stack new working-with-lenses simple
    ```

2. Add a dependency on `lens` library in the `build-depends` sub-section of the `executable` section:

    ```
    executable working-with-lenses
      hs-source-dirs:      src
      main-is:             Main.hs
      default-language:    Haskell2010
      build-depends:       base >= 4.7 && < 5
                         , lens
    ```

3. Open `src/Main.hs`. We will be adding our source here. Add a `TemplateHaskell` extension for creating lenses for the user-defined data types. Define the `Main` module, and import the necessary imports:

    ```
    {-# LANGUAGE TemplateHaskell #-}

    module Main where

    import Control.Lens.TH
    import Control.Lens
    ```

4. Define a data type, `Line`, which is composed of two end `Point`s. Note that we used `*_*` for naming the fields:

    ```
    data Point a = Point { _x :: a, _y :: a } deriving Show
    data Line a = Line { _start :: Point a, _end :: Point a }
    deriving Show
    ```

5. Create lenses for `Point` and `Line`. We use `TemplateHaskell` support in lens to automatically create the lenses for `Point` and `Line`:

```
makeLenses ''Point
makeLenses ''Line
```

This will remove the *underscores* from the field names, and make lenses out of them.

6. Use the data types, and lenses in the `main` function:

```
main :: IO ()
main = do
  let line = Line (Point 5 7) (Point 11 13)
  putStrLn $ "Line " ++ show line
  putStrLn $ "Using lenses"

  -- Get the x coordinates of the start point
  putStrLn "Start point of line"
  print $ view start line
  putStrLn "Composing lenses"
  putStrLn "X of end of the line"
  print $ view (end . x) line

  putStrLn "Using setters"
  putStrLn "Setting Y coordinate of end of the line"
  -- Supply a function to modify the coordinate (const 17)
  print $ over (end . y) (const 17) line

  putStrLn "Making it fancier with ^."
  putStrLn "Access X of start of line"
  print $ line ^. (start . x)
```

7. Build and execute the project:

```
stack build
stack exec -- working-with-lenses
```

8. You should see the following output:

```
working-with-lenses — -bash — 139×10
working-with-lenses $ stack exec -- working-with-lenses
Line Line {_start = Point {_x = 5, _y = 7}, _end = Point {_x = 11, _y = 13}}
Using lenses
Start point of line
Point {_x = 5, _y = 7}
Composing lenses
X of end of the line
11
Using setters
Setting Y coordinate of end of the line
Line {_start = Point {_x = 5, _y = 7}, _end = Point {_x = 11, _y = 17}}
Making it fancier with ^.
Access X of start of line
5
working-with-lenses $
```

How it works...

In our last recipe, we manufactured our own lenses. A lens is defined as follows:

```
type Lens s t a b = forall f . Functor f => (a -> f b) -> s -> f t
```

The creation of the lens is achieved via the creation of `getter` and `setter` for a particular field in a data type.

```
lens :: (s -> a) -> (s -> b -> t) -> Lens s t a b
lens getter setter f x = fmap (setter x) $ f (getter x)
```

We have to write `getter` and `setter` manually for each field to supply lenses. Using `TemplateHaskell` we can create these lenses. Also, note the use of "_" while defining the data type.

Working with Traversal

In this recipe, we will work with traversals, where we can use lens for traversing many fields.

How to do it...

1. Create a new project `working-with-traversal` with a `simple` stack template.

   ```
   stack new working-with-traversal simple
   ```

2. Add a dependency on the `lens` library in the `build-depends` sub-section of the executable section. Also add `containers`, as we will be using *Map* in this recipe:

   ```
   executable working-with-traversal
     hs-source-dirs:     src
     main-is:            Main.hs
     default-language:   Haskell2010
     build-depends:      base >= 4.7 && < 5
                       , containers
                       , lens
   ```

3. Open `src/Main.hs`. We will be editing this file for this recipe. Add the module definition for `Main`. Also import the required modules.
   Enable `TemplateHaskell` at the top, as we will be creating lenses using the template Haskell:

   ```
   {-# LANGUAGE TemplateHaskell #-}
   module Main where

   import Data.Map
   import Control.Lens
   import Control.Lens.TH
   ```

4. Add a data type for maintaining list of exchanges and symbols. We keep symbols as a map between the unique symbol ID and generic symbol name:

   ```
   data Symbol = Symbol { _sid :: String, _sname :: String }
   deriving Show
   type Symbols = Map String Symbol
   data Exchange = Exchange { _exchange :: String, _symbols ::
   Symbols } deriving Show
   ```

5. Make the lenses for the preceding data types:

```
makeLenses ''Symbol
makeLenses ''Exchange
```

6. Populate symbols from two exchanges, viz., Singapore and National Stock Exchange, India:

```
singExchange :: Exchange
singExchange =
  let symbols = [ Symbol "1A1" "AGV Group Ltd"
                , Symbol "D05" "DBS Group Holding"
                , Symbol "CC3" "StarHub Ltd." ]
    in Exchange "SGX" $ fromList $ zip (_sid <$> symbols)
symbols

nseExchange :: Exchange
nseExchange =
  let symbols = [ Symbol "3MINDIA" "3M India Ltd"
                , Symbol "HINDALCO" "Hindalco Industries Ltd"
                , Symbol "HCLTECH" "HCL Technologies Ltd" ]
    in Exchange "NSE" $ fromList $ zip (_sid <$> symbols)
symbols

exchanges :: [Exchange]
exchanges = [singExchange, nseExchange]
```

7. Use the preceding data types in the traversals:

```
main :: IO ()
main = do
  putStrLn $ "Just traverse the exchanges, should get back
same
  input"
  print $ toListOf traverse exchanges

  putStrLn $ "Traverse and modify names of the exchanges,
  prepend 'X' to the exchange names"
  putStrLn $ "Traversal is a valid lens, and can be combined
  with other lenses"
  print $ over (traverse . exchange) ('X':) exchanges

  putStrLn $ "Traverse and get combined list symbols across
  exchanges"
  print $ view (traverse . symbols) exchanges
```

```
putStrLn $ "Get all symbol IDs in all exchanges"
print $ toListOf (traverse . symbols . traverse . sid )
exchanges

putStrLn $ "Same as above but with 'view' rather than
'toListOf'"
print $ view (traverse .symbols . traverse . sid ) exchanges

putStrLn $ "Use 'set' to set everything in the traversal to
the same value"
print $ set traverse 8 [1..10]
```

8. Build and execute the project.

```
stack build
stack exec -- working-with-traversal
```

9. You should see the following output:

How it works...

We have looked at *lens* in the preceding recipe. A lens applies to a field in a data structure. If we have a `Traversable` field type somewhere, then we can use traverse to browse over the collection. An important fact must be remembered, if we view the traverse, then the target field must be an instance of Monoid. For example, `toListOf` *traverse exchanges* will be successful, and will fetch same list of exchanges back but *view traverse exchanges* will fail with a complaint that *Exchange is not an instance of Monoid*. This happens because, traversal tries to summarize the target values by assuming that the target type is an instance of Monoid. Hence it starts with an empty value (*mempty*) and then starts appending values *mappend/mconcat*.

It is also possible combine traversal with lenses. In fact, to get to the list of all symbols we used the following lens:

```
traverse . symbols . traverse . sid
```

Here first traverse applies to a list of exchanges, [Exchange], and the second element in the preceding composition `symbols` will lead us to symbol Map. Since Map is an instance of *Traversable*, we can also use `traverse` to browse through the map values. This is where the third element `traverse` comes from. In the end, we are interested in the symbol ID of each symbol. Hence, the last element in the preceding composition is `sid`. Thus you can see that traversals can be easily composed with lenses. (You should read the preceding composition from left to right).

 Since traversal is a valid lens, we can also use *over* to set or modify the value in the data structure. If we would like to change all the fields visited to a single value, then we can use *set* (as we have used earlier).

Working with Iso

So far, we have looked at *lens* and *traversals* which are aimed at focusing on a particular field(s) from the context of accessing or changing its value. In this recipe, we will look at *Iso* which represents isomorphism between two types. It is possible to go back and forth between two types. For example, we can convert from *Text* to *String* and vice versa.

How to do it...

1. Create a new project `working-with-iso` with a `simple` stack template:

```
stack new working-with-iso simple
```

2. Add a dependency on the *lens* library in the `build-depends` sub-section of the `executable` section. Also, add a dependency on `text` and `bytestring` and add the `quicklz` library for compression utility:

```
executable working-with-iso
  hs-source-dirs:      src
  main-is:             Main.hs
  default-language:    Haskell2010
  build-depends:       base >= 4.7 && < 5
                     , lens
                     , text
                     , bytestring
```

 Note that, at the time of writing this recipe, the library `quicklz` is not included in the stack package repository. We need to add it explicitly to the `stack.yaml` in the project directory. Explicitly add the following packages in the `extra-deps` section in *stack.yaml*. We have used a **lts-9.0** resolver for package resolution for this recipe.

```
extra-deps:
  - quicklz-1.5.0.11
```

3. Open `src/Main.hs`. We will be adding our source here. Add the `OverloadedStrings` extension before writing the `Main` module definition:

```
{-# LANGUAGE OverloadedStrings #-}
module Main where

import Control.Lens
import Data.Text.Strict.Lens
import qualified Codec.Compression.QuickLZ as LZ
import qualified Data.ByteString.Char8 as B
import Data.ByteString.Lens
```

4. Use `Iso` to convert between `text`, `string`:

```
stringConvertTest :: IO ()
stringConvertTest = do
```

```
let str = "A string to text" :: String
    text = str ^. packed
    str1 = text ^. unpacked
-- You can also do (from packed)
let str2 = text ^. (from packed)

putStrLn $ "String -> Text -> String round trip successful?
"
++ show (str == str2)
```

5. Create a lens for the compression and decompression of a `ByteString`:

```
compress :: Iso' B.ByteString B.ByteString
compress = iso LZ.compress LZ.decompress
```

This represents a one-to-one correspondence between the original string, its compression, and the uncompressed string

6. Now convert `string` to `bytestring`. Compress it, and then convert it back to string by uncompressing it:

```
strCompressRoundTrip :: String -> String
strCompressRoundTrip s = s ^. (packedChars . compress . from
compress . unpackedChars)
```

7. Now test it with some messages:

```
-- Sample string for compression
message :: String
message = "The quick brown fox jumps over the lazy dog"

strCompressRoundTripTest :: IO ()
strCompressRoundTripTest = do
  let str1 = strCompressRoundTrip message
  putStrLn ("Compressing and uncompressing \"" ++ message ++
  "\"")
  putStrLn ("Test Successful? " ++ show (str1 == message))
```

8. Use the `isos` and *lens*es in the `main` function:

```
main :: IO ()
main = do
  stringConvertTest
  strCompressRoundTripTest
```

9. Build and execute the project:

```
stack build
stack exec -- working-with-iso
```

10. You should see following output:

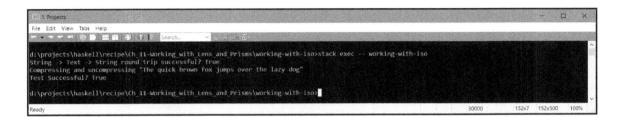

How it works...

Iso represent an isomorphic lens. It represents a bidirectional lens. So, if you can use *Iso compress* to convert from `ByteString` to a compressed `ByteString`, then you can use *from* compress to convert compressed `ByteString` back to original `Bytestring`. An *Iso* is also a lens, and it is possible to combine it with other lenses as we have done in the case of compress.

 Isos are more convenient if we often convert between different string types (`text`, `bytestring`, and `String`).

Working with Prism

Lens gives you the ability to focus on a particular field in a data type. *Traversal* will do the same thing for a traversable (something that you can traverse and collect). But these data types were *product* types.

In this recipe, we will work with *Prism*, where we will work with *sum type* data.

How to do it...

1. Create a new project `working-with-prism` with a `simple` stack template:

   ```
   stack new working-with-prism simple
   ```

2. Add a dependency on the `lens` library in the `build-depends` sub-section of the `executable` section:

   ```
   executable working-with-prism
     hs-source-dirs:    src
     main-is:           Main.hs
     default-language:  Haskell2010
     build-depends:     base >= 4.7 && < 5
                      , lens
   ```

3. Open `src/Main.hs`. We will be adding our source here.
   Enable `TemplateHaskell`, as we will produce *Prism* using the template Haskell. Add the `Main` module. Import the *template haskell* module for lens, alongwith other imports:

   ```
   {-# LANGUAGE TemplateHaskell #-}

   module Main where

   import Control.Lens
   import Control.Lens.TH
   ```

4. Define the sum data type:

   ```
   data Point = Point { _x :: Double, _y :: Double } deriving Show
   data Shape = Rectangle { _leftTop :: Point, _rightBottom ::
                  | Point }
                  Circle { _centre :: Point, _radius :: Double }
                  deriving Show
   ```

5. Make the *lens* and *prism* out of it:

   ```
   makeLenses ''Point
   makeLenses ''Shape
   makePrisms ''Shape
   ```

6. Create some shapes. Write two functions, one to create a rectangle of some size, and another to make a circle, with some radius value and a center:

```
makeRectangle :: Shape
makeRectangle = Rectangle (Point 0 0) (Point 100 100)

makeCircle :: Shape
makeCircle = Circle (Point 0 0) 25.0
```

7. Work with Shape using prism and lenses

```
usePrism :: IO ()
usePrism = do
 let rect = makeRectangle
     circ = makeCircle
 putStrLn "Create two shapes"
 print rect
 print circ

 -- Check if we are dealing with rectangle
 putStrLn "Are we dealing with a rectangle"
 print $ rect ^? _Rectangle

 putStrLn "Get first point of rectangle"
 print $ rect ^? _Rectangle . _1

 putStrLn "Get Y coordinate of the right bottom point of
 rectangle"
 print $ rect ^? _Rectangle . _2 . y

 putStrLn "Get the rectangle back from two points"
 print $ _Rectangle # (Point (-1) (-1), Point 1 1)

 putStrLn "Get radius of a circle"
 print $ circ ^? _Circle . _2

 putStrLn "Create circle from center and point"
 print $ (Point 0 0, 10.0) ^. re _Circle

 putStrLn "Change radius of the circle (from 25 to 3)"
 print $ over (_Circle . _2) (const 3) circ

 putStrLn "Get details of rectangle back from rectangle by
 traversing"
 print $ rect ^.. _Rectangle
 -- This is equivalent to toListOf
 print $ toListOf _Rectangle rect
```

```
-- Create list of shapes
let shapes = [rect, circ]

putStrLn "Return result if all are rectangles"
print $ shapes ^.. below _Rectangle

putStrLn "Now try with all rectangles"
let rects = [rect, rect]
print $ rects ^.. below _Rectangle
```

8. Use the *lens*es and *prism*s in the `main` function:

```
main :: IO ()
main = usePrism
```

9. Build and execute the project:

stack build
stack exec -- working-with-prism

10. You should see the following output:

How it works...

Prism represents a traversal for a sum type. For a sum type, different alternatives are available for creating the data type. The *Prism* explores these alternatives. It also allows us to traverse to internals. Note the use of *_* for using makePrisms template. The generated prism will create a tupled representation (as we have the sum of product types). One can combine *Prism* and *lens* as *Prism* is a valid traversal. Similarly, we can also use *over* to change the internals of the data.

Working with predefined lenses

In this recipe, we will work with predefined lenses. We will use a library `lens-aeson` for dealing with JSON data. The *aeson* library is a popular library for parsing and writing JSON instances for the user-defined data. Often, we have to deal with JSON, and parse it on the fly to extract the desired data.

Getting ready

In this recipe, we will use the generic JSON parser provided by *aeson*, and then use *lens-aeson* to dig through the JSON to extract the data.

How to do it...

1. Create a new project, `working-with-aeson-lens`, with a `simple` stack template.

   ```
   stack new working-with-aeson-lens simple
   ```

2. Add a dependency on the lens library in the `build-depends` sub-section of the `executable` section. Also add dependency on `aeson` and `lens-aeson` libraries. Also add `bytestring` and *text*, as *aeson* uses `bytestring` for parsing and `text` for string values. Add `vector`, as we need to work with arrays in JSON:

   ```
   executable working-with-aeson-lens
     hs-source-dirs:      src
     main-is:             Main.hs
     default-language:    Haskell2010
     build-depends:       base >= 4.7 && < 5
   ```

```
                                           , lens
                                           , lens-aeson
                                           , aeson
                                           , bytestring
                                           , text
                                           , vector
```

3. Open `src/Main.hs`. We will be adding our source here. Use the `OverloadedStrings` extension and define the `Main` module. Import the required modules:

```
{-# LANGUAGE OverloadedStrings #-}

module Main where

import Control.Lens
import Data.Aeson.Lens
import Data.Aeson
import Data.ByteString.Lazy.Char8 as BC
import Data.Vector hiding ((++))
import Data.Text
```

4. Let us consider a decoded JWT token (`https://jwt.io/`). We have added a few permissions to the JWT token:

```
jwtToken :: ByteString
jwtToken = "{ \"header\" : { \"alg\": \"HS256\", \"typ\":
\"JWT\" }, \"payload\" : { \"sub\": \"1234567890\", \"name\":
 \"John Doe\", \"admin\": true, \"permissions\": [ \"status\",
  \"user:read\", \"user:write\" ]} }"
```

5. Now find the attributes for different fields:

```
isJWT :: ByteString -> Bool
isJWT tok = case (decode tok :: Maybe Value) of
        Nothing -> False
        Just v  -> let typ = v ^? key "header" . key "typ"
                   in typ == Just (String "JWT")
```

6. In fact, we need not explicitly pass the JSON data:

```
isAdmin :: AsValue v => v -> Bool
isAdmin tok = (tok ^? key "payload" . key "admin") == Just
(Bool True)
```

7. We can also access an element of an array:

```
permission0 :: AsValue v => v -> Maybe Value
permission0 tok = (tok ^? key "payload" . key "permissions" .
nth 0)
```

8. Get all the `permissions`:

```
permissions :: AsValue v => v -> [Text]
permissions tok = Prelude.head (tok ^. key "payload" . key
"permissions" . _Array . to toList ^.. below
 Data.Aeson.Lens._String)
```

9. Use the token function to test our tokens to print permissions, admin access and type of token:

```
main :: IO ()
main = do
  BC.putStrLn "Analyzing token"
  BC.putStrLn jwtToken

  Prelude.putStrLn $ "Is JWT Token? " ++ (show $ isJWT
jwtToken)
  Prelude.putStrLn $ "Is Admin? " ++ (show $ isAdmin jwtToken)

  Prelude.putStrLn $ "Permissions = " ++ (show $ permissions
jwtToken)
```

10. Build and execute the project:

```
stack build
stack exec -- working-with-aeson-lens
```

11. You should see following output:

How it works...

This recipe shows just one aspect of usefulness. Here we have used the *lens*es created for JSON using the *aeson* library. This helps us parse arbitrary JSON without actually writing an instance of `FromJSON` or `ToJSON` required to represent the user-defined data. The *lens* can be similarly used for simplifying the manipulation of large data structures required for certain libraries.

12
Concurrent and Distributed Programming in Haskell

In this chapter, we will be looking at the following recipes:

- Working with IORef
- Working with MVar
- Working with STM
- Working with strategies
- Working with monad-par
- Working with Cloud Haskell
- Using Cloud Haskell to start master and slave nodes
- Using closure to communicate between nodes

Introduction

The fact that Haskell is a pure language, that is, there are no unintended side effects, helps a lot in parallel and concurrent programming. The library and compiler both have a lot of options for optimizing and tuning the performance since it can (mostly!) correctly guess the intention of the program and how a program can be tuned to run concurrently.

Haskell gives a set of primitives for concurrent programming. These primitives enable programmers to build concurrency around them. These basic primitives are *IORef*, *MVar*, and *STM*. In this chapter, we will start with primitives, and then also work with *strategies*, and `monad-par` libraries which are built around these primitives to provide a higher-level abstraction for specifying concurrency within a program.

With the Cloud Haskell library, we move into the distributed world. In Cloud Haskell, we create logical nodes, which represent a logical process that may be present in a same physical process or can be spanned across multiple processes or even machines across a network. We will start with a logical node in the same process, and then move to communicating across the process boundary.

Working with IORef

In this recipe, we will work with IORef, a mutable reference in the *IO* monad. We will use *IORef Int* as a counter for the progress that can be tracked from a separate thread, while we do the *work* in the *main* thread.

How to do it...

1. Create a new project called `working-with-ioref` with the `simple` stack template:

   ```
   stack new working-with-ioref simple
   ```

2. Add the `ghc-options` subsection in the section `executable`. Add the `-threaded` option for GHC compilation. If it's not provided, any foreign call will block all Haskell threads. Foreign calls are calls made outside the Haskell runtime (typically by calling functions in external functions):

   ```
   executable working-with-type-family
     hs-source-dirs:    src
     main-is:           Main.hs
     ghc-options:       -threaded
     default-language:  Haskell2010
     build-depends:     base >= 4.7 && < 5
   ```

3. Open `src/Main.hs`. We will be adding our source here. Define the `Main` module:

   ```
   module Main where
   ```

4. Import the module `Data.IORef` for `IORef`, and multithreading (`Control.Concurrent`):

```
import Data.IORef
import Control.Concurrent
```

5. Define the `work` function. The `work` function atomically modifies `IORef` by adding 1 to the existing counter. Also use threadDelay to wait for half a second after each modification. Note that the threadDelay function expects the time to be in microseconds. The work function is supplied a count. At every modification, the work function decreases the counter by 1. The work terminates when the count goes down to zero. The work function returns the value of the previous count:

```
work :: Int -> IORef Int -> IO Int
work count i = work' count 0
  where
    work' count retval | count <= 0 = return retval
    work' count _ = do
      retval <- atomicModifyIORef' i (\j -> (j+1,j))
      threadDelay (500*1000)
      putStrLn $ "Work: Modifying progress to " ++ show retval
      work' (count-1) retval
```

6. Write a `tracker` function. It takes `IORef` and, after every second (by using `threadDelay` as a waiting time in-between), checks the value of the counter and prints it:

```
tracker :: IORef Int -> IO ()
tracker i = do
  threadDelay (1000*1000)
  counter <- readIORef i
  putStrLn $ "Tracker: Counting " ++ show counter
  tracker i
```

7. In the `main` function, create a new `IORef` by using the `newIORef` function. Use `forkIO` to create a new thread for the tracker. Do the work in the main thread, and once we are done with the work, we kill the tracker using `killThread` function:

```
main :: IO ()
main = do
  counter <- newIORef 0
```

```
trackerId <- forkIO (tracker counter)
howmuch <- work 10 counter
killThread trackerId
putStrLn $ "Work completed with counter " ++ show howmuch
```

8. Build and execute the project:

   ```
   stack build
   stack exec -- working-with-ioref
   ```

9. You should see the following output:

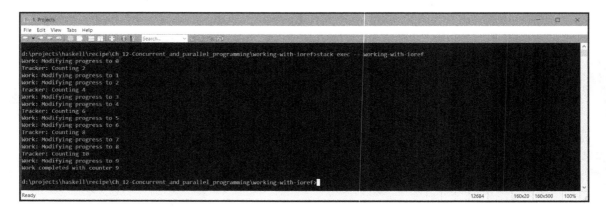

How it works...

The `IORef` a represents a mutable reference in an the IO monad. In this recipe, we used `forkIO` run an `IO()` action for *tracker* in a separate thread. The function *work* runs in the main thread. It uses `atomicModifyIORef'` to atomically increment the counter. This function will prevent race conditions for one `IORef`. Note that there are two versions of `atomicModifyIORef`. The `atomicModifyIORef` version is a lazy version (the operation done may not be evaluated immediately), whereas `atomicModifyIORef'` is a strict version. Finally, we kill the tracker thread with the `killThread` function.

Working with MVar

In this recipe, we will look at *MVar* and *Chan* as the basic ingredients of a concurrent pipeline. We will create a Forex Order processing system, in which the orders to buy or sell currency are sent to an exchange. The exchange backend will process the orders, and print the summary.

How to do it...

1. Create a new project called `working-with-mvar` with the `simple` stack template:

   ```
   stack new working-with-mvar simple
   ```

2. Add dependencies on the `containers` and `random` libraries in the `build-depends` sub-section of the `executable` section. Also add the `-threaded` option to the `ghc-options` subsection:

   ```
   executable working-with-mvar
     hs-source-dirs:     src
     main-is:            Main.hs
     ghc-options:        -threaded
     default-language:   Haskell2010
     build-depends:      base >= 4.7 && < 5
                       , containers
                       , random
   ```

3. Open `src/Main.hs`. We will be adding our source here. Define the main module, and import headers for using *MVar* and *Chan:*

   ```
   module Main where

   import Control.Concurrent
   import Control.Concurrent.Chan
   import Data.Map
   import Control.Monad
   import System.Random
   ```

4. Represent an order as a `Currency` and the associated amount as `Int`. We represent a positive amount as buy and a negative amount as `**sell`. An `Exchange*` is a channel that can accept orders. We need to stop the Exchange at some point of time, hence we represent `ProcessOrder` as a message sent to the Exchange. If `StopExchange` is sent to the `Exchange`, the exchange stops processing orders:

```
type Currency = String
type Amount = Int

data Order = Order Currency Amount deriving Show
data ProcessOrder = ProcessOrder Order | StopExchange
  deriving Show
type Exchange = Chan ProcessOrder
```

5. Define an backend for `Exchange` that will receive the order, and maintains a register of Currency and Amount showing the current status. We represent the current status with MVar. MVar stores a Map of Currency and Amount:

```
type Catalog = Map Currency Amount
type Register = MVar Catalog
```

6. Add functions for managing the catalog. We would like to add currency and amount to the catalog. Add `addOrder` to add an order to a catalog. The `modifyOrder` function will do the same thing as `addOrder`, but will return the tuple of modified `Catalog`. This will be used further in modifying `Register`:

```
addOrder :: Order -> Catalog -> Catalog
addOrder (Order c a) = insertWith (+) c a

modifyOrder :: Monad m => Order -> Catalog -> m (Catalog,
  Catalog)
modifyOrder order cat = let cat' = addOrder order cat
  in return (cat',cat')
```

7. Add a function to print the `Catalog` details:

```
printCatalog :: Catalog -> IO ()
printCatalog cat = forM_ (toAscList cat) $ \(c,a) -> do
  putStrLn $ "Currency : " ++ c ++ ", Amount : " ++ show a
```

8. Once we receive an order, we open the `Register` and add the order into it. Use `modifyOrder` for extracting `Catalog` from `Register` and modifying an order. The `processOrders` function will continue to process orders and modify `Reigster` until the `StopExchange` message is received:

```
processOrders :: Exchange -> Register -> IO ()
processOrders exch reg = do
  po <- readChan exch
  case po of
    ProcessOrder o -> do
      cat' <- modifyMVar reg (modifyOrder o)
      putStrLn "Summary of orders"
      printCatalog cat'
      processOrders exch reg
    StopExchange -> return ()
```

9. Prepare for random data generation. Let consider three currencies, AUD--Australian Doller, SGD--Singapore Dollar and USD--US Dollar:

```
currencies :: [Currency]
currencies = ["AUD","SGD","USD"]
```

10. Generate a random sequence of currencies:

```
currenciesM :: Int -> IO [Currency]
currenciesM i | i <= 0 = return []
currenciesM i = do
  c <- randomC
  cs <- currenciesM (i-1)
  return (c : cs)
    where
      randomC = (currencies !!) <$> randomRIO (0,2)
```

11. Similarly, generate a set of order amounts (either sell or buy):

```
amounts :: Int -> IO [Amount]
amounts i | i <= 0 = return []
amounts i = do
  sellOrBuy <- randomIO :: IO Bool
  amount <- randomRIO (1,1000)
  let orderAmount = if sellOrBuy then amount else (-1) * amount
  orderAmounts <- amounts (i-1)
  return (orderAmount:orderAmounts)
```

12. Now get the set of random `orders`:

```
orders :: Int -> IO [Order]
orders i = zipWith Order <$> currenciesM i <*> amounts i
```

13. Write a function to send orders every second to the `Exchange`:

```
sendOrders :: [Order] -> Exchange -> IO ()
sendOrders [] _ = return ()
sendOrders (o:os) exch = do
  putStrLn $ "Sending order " ++ show o
  writeChan exch (ProcessOrder o)
  threadDelay (1000*1000)
  sendOrders os exch
```

14. In the `main` function, create three order generators:

```
main :: IO ()
main = do
  exch <- newChan :: IO Exchange
  reg <- newMVar empty
  -- Start the order processing backend
  forkIO $ processOrders exch reg
  -- Start order generators
  forM_ [1..3] $ \_ -> forkIO $ do
    os <- orders 10
    sendOrders os exch

  -- Wait for all orders to finish, and stop the exchange
  threadDelay (1000*1000*15)
  writeChan exch StopExchange

  cat <- readMVar reg
  putStrLn "Printing Final Summary of orders"
  printCatalog cat
```

15. Build and execute the project:

```
stack build
stack exec -- working-with-mvar
```

You should see the following output:

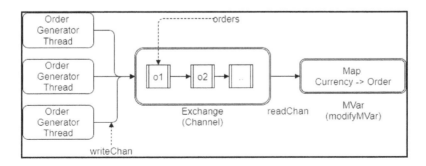

How it works...

We use MVar t as a mutable location, that is either empty or contains a value of type t. We also use Chan which wraps up MVar as a stream. A Chan represents a FIFO stream. In this recipe, we use Chan to send orders simultaneously from multiple threads to a single channel Exchange. We then use backend processor processOrder which uses an MVar for aggregating all these orders by in a single Map. The following diagram, explains the order processing system:

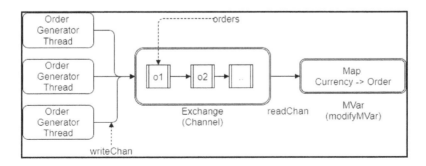

Working with STM

In this recipe, we will work with **STM (Software Transactional Memory)** which provides atomic blocks for executions. It provide more guarantees the about atomicity of the operation than *MVars*. We will work with an example of a bank account, where simultaneous transactions are trying to do the transaction with the same bank account.

How it works...

1. Create a new project called `working-with-STM` with the `simple` stack template:

   ```
   stack new working-with-STM simple
   ```

2. Add the `ghc-options` subsection to the `executable` section. Set the option to `-threaded`. Also add `stm` to the build-depends subsection:

   ```
   executable working-with-STM
     hs-source-dirs:    src
     main-is:           Main.hs
     ghc-options:       -threaded
     default-language:  Haskell2010
     build-depends:     base >= 4.7 && < 5
                      , stm
   ```

3. Open `src/Main.hs`. We will be adding our source here. Import `Control.Concurrent.STM` to importing STM module:

   ```
   module Main where

   import Control.Concurrent.STM
   import Control.Concurrent
   ```

4. Define the account type which points to `TVar Int`, which represents the current balance:

   ```
   newtype Account = Account (TVar Int)
   ```

5. Define a *transact function* where the balance in the account can be modified. The transaction is not permitted if the balance would become less than zero. In such a case, the transaction is retried:

```
transact :: Int -> Account -> STM Int
transact x (Account ac) = do
  balance <- readTVar ac
  let balance' = balance + x
  case balance' < 0 of
    True -> retry
    False -> writeTVar ac balance'
  return balance'
```

6. Initialize the bank account with any amount:

```
openAccount :: Int -> STM Account
openAccount i = do
  balance <- newTVar i
  return (Account balance)
```

7. Write a function to print the balance:

```
printBalance :: Account -> IO ()
printBalance (Account ac) = do
  balance <- atomically (readTVar ac)
  putStrLn $ "Current balance : " ++ show balance
```

8. Do the bank transaction in the `main` function. Open an account with initial balance `100`. Let's then try to debit `200` from a thread. Since we do not have that much balance, this should wait until there is a sufficient balance. From another thread, we do two credits of `75` each. After the sufficient balance has been made available, the debit should be allowed:

```
main :: IO ()
main = do
  ac <- atomically $ openAccount 100
  printBalance ac
  forkIO $ do
    balance <- atomically $ transact (-200) ac
    putStrLn $ "Balance after debit : " ++ show balance

  forkIO $ do
    balance1 <- atomically $ transact 75 ac
    putStrLn $ "Balance after credit of 75 : " ++ show balance1
```

```
        balance2 <- atomically $ transact 75 ac
        putStrLn $ "Balance after credit of 75 : " ++ show balance2

        threadDelay (1000*1000) -- Wait for above actins to finish
        printBalance ac
```

9. Build and execute the project:

```
stack build
stack exec -- working-with-STM
```

10. You should see the following output:

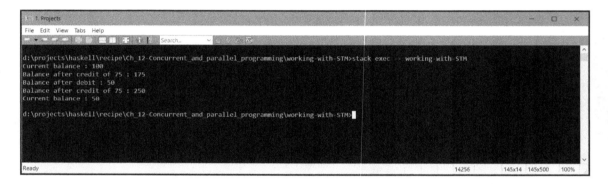

How it works...

With *MVar*, where there is no control over the subsequent options as far as atomicity is concerned. For example, reading the account balance and doing a transaction have to be done separately with *MVar* and not together. *STM* on the other hand, fully guarantees the atomicity of transactions in an *STM* monad.

In the preceding recipe, we use *TVar* (which is like *MVar* but is used in the context of *STM*). We use *readTVar* and *writeTVar* for reading and writing *TVars*. But all operations are enclosed in an *STM* monad. We have to use function *atomically* to run *STM* in the *IO* context.

In the *transact* function, we use *retry* in the context of *STM*. This tells *STM* to retry the same action. In this case, it will result in a blocked action until it becomes successful.

Working with strategies

In this recipe, we will use the `parallel` library. This library provides a set of strategies to allow us to program concurrent tasks easily.

How to do it...

1. Create a new project called `working-with-eval` with the `simple` stack template:

   ```
   stack new working-with-eval simple
   ```

2. Add a dependency on the `parallel` library in the build-depends sub-section of the executable section. Also add `-threaded` and `-fprof-auto -rtsopts -eventlog` to enable multithreading and profiling:

   ```
   executable working-with-eval
     hs-source-dirs:    src
     main-is:           Main.hs
     ghc-options:       -threaded -fprof-auto -rtsopts -eventlog
     default-language: Haskell2010
     build-depends:     base >= 4.7 && < 5
                      , parallel
   ```

3. Open `src/Main.hs`. We will be adding our source here. Add the `Main` module and import the relevant modules:

   ```
   module Main where

   import Control.Parallel.Strategies
   ```

4. Create a data type for the binary tree:

   ```
   data BTree a = BTree (BTree a) a (BTree a) | Empty
     deriving Show
   ```

5. Add a function to split a list in the middle. We will partition the list into two two parts, a *Left* list, a *right* list and a *middle* element:

```
split :: [a] -> ([a], Maybe a, [a])
split xs    = split' xs xs []
  where
    split' []                      =  ([], Nothing, [])
    split' (x:xs) (_:[])    ls  =  (reverse ls, Just x, xs)
    split' (x:xs) (_:_:[])  ls  =  (reverse ls, Just x, xs)
    split' (x:xs) (_:_:ys)  ls  =  split' xs ys (x:ls)
```

6. Now using a *parallel* strategy, build a balanced binary tree from the list:

```
fromList :: [a] -> Eval (BTree a)
fromList xs = do
  (ls,m,rs) <- rseq (split xs)
  ltree     <- rpar (runEval $ fromList ls)
  rtree     <- rpar (runEval $ fromList rs)
  case m of
    Just x   -> return (BTree ltree x rtree)
    Nothing  -> return Empty
```

7. Use the code in the `main` function:

```
main :: IO ()
main = do
  let tree = runEval $ fromList [1..1000]
  print tree
```

8. Build and execute the project. We run with a different runtime profiling output to generate an event log. We use four cores (-*N2* options). You should feel free to modify this option to your hardware:

```
stack build
stack exec -- working-with-eval +RTS -N4 -l
```

Typically, you should see a `working-with-eval.eventlog` file. If this file is not generated (the sometimes happens on Windows), then you should run the executable directly by locating it in the `.stack-work` directory.

If you open the event log in the *threadscope* (https://wiki.haskell.org/ThreadScope), you should see the following output (or similar):

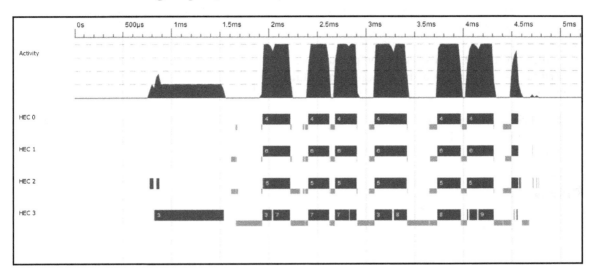

It should show all four cores being engaged. It also shows number of SPARKS generated. Though there is scope for improvement (as you can still see gaps in the activity), this is a good start point for us. Note that, initially, only one core is engaged when we split the list for the first time.

How it works...

There are two primitives--rpar, which immediately returns, and rseq, which forces the argument into **weak headed normal form** *(WHNF)* . WHNF is related to lazy evaluation in Haskell, and usually points to a minimally evaluated thunk. In WHNF, only a part of the thunk is evaluated, whereas in **normal form** (**NF**), the whole thunk is evaluated (or reduced). Both rpar and rseq work as *Strategies*. We specify the work in terms of *Strategies* in an Eval monad. The runEval function takes the Eval monad and parallelizes the computation.

This recipe also shows how to profile the project, and look at the event log. This comes in very handy especially when dealing with concurrency.

Working with monad-par

The `monad-par` library provides a way to specify the job in both pure as well as IO contexts. The `monad-par` library implements a work-stealing scheduler. Using `monad-par`, we can define a future value, that is, a context where a value is expected to be evaluated sometime in future, and specify the point where to fork the computation. The `monad-par` library takes care of scheduling these computation on threads and fulfilling the context for where the computed value should be kept.

In this recipe, we compute *fibonacci* number using two methods, first with a naive recursive method, and second implementing the same recursion using the `monad-par` library.

How to do it...

1. Create a new project called `working-with-monad-par` with the `simple` stack template:

   ```
   stack new working-with-monad-par simple
   ```

2. Add a dependency on the `monad-par` library in the `build-depends` sub-section of the `executable` section. Also add `-threaded -fprof-auto -rtsopts -eventlog` to the `ghc-options` subsection:

   ```
   executable working-with-monad-par
     hs-source-dirs:      src
     main-is:             Main.hs
     ghc-options:         -threaded -fprof-auto -rtsopts -eventlog
     default-language:    Haskell2010
     build-depends:       base >= 4.7 && < 5
                        , monad-par
   ```

3. Open `src/Main.hs`. We will be adding our source here. After the `Main` module, add the relevant imports:

   ```
   module Main where

   import Control.Monad.Par
   import Data.Int
   ```

4. Write a simple *fibonacci* number calculator:

```
fib :: Int64 -> Int64
fib 0 = 0
fib 1 = 1
fib n = let x = fib (n-1)
            y = fib (n-2)
        in (x `seq` x) + (y `seq` y)
```

5. Now write a *parallel* fibonacci with a threshold. This implementation is taken from http://www.cse.chalmers.se/edu/year/2015/course/pfp/lectures/lecture2/Marlow14.pdf:

```
pfib :: Int64 -> Int64 -> Par Int64
pfib n threshold | n <= threshold = return (fib n)
pfib n threshold = do
  n_1f <- spawn $ pfib (n-1) threshold
  n_2f <- spawn $ pfib (n-2) threshold
  n_1  <- get n_1f
  n_2  <- get n_2f
  return (n_1 + n_2)
```

6. Try a parallel version, `pfib` in the `main` function:

```
main :: IO ()
main = do
  putStrLn "Run pfib 30 with some threshold"
  print $ runPar $ pfib 30 15
```

7. Build and execute the project, with four cores, and with the -l option to produce an event log:

```
stack build
stack exec -- working-with-monad-par +RTS -N4 -l
```

8. You should see the following output:

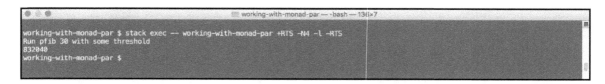

The threadscope should show the activity distributed throughout the cores:

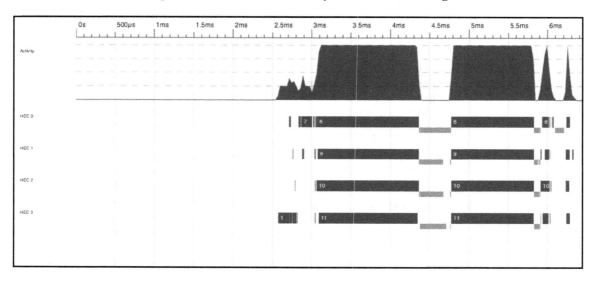

How it works...

`monad-par` defines the *Par* monad which defines the following primitives:

- *new*: Define a new empty *IVar*
- *get*: Wait for having some value in *IVar*
- *put*: Put some value into *IVar*
- *fork*: Signal that the input *Par* action can be run in parallel
- *spawn*: A function to run an action in parallel to produce an *IVar*

Internally, monad-par implements a way to balance these activities across threads by scheduling and balancing them. monad-par allows us to specify parallel tasks without getting into the nitty-gritty of actually scheduling tasks.

Also note that, in this recipe, we have used a threshold to run the task sequentially. This is to increase the granularity of the tasks. This speeds up more speedup when there is no threshold. As because when there is no threshold, the tasks become too small to gain any advantage from parallelism.

Working with Cloud Haskell

So far, we have seen multi-threaded concurrency. In this recipe, we will look at distributed concurrency, where the concurrency can be achieved through multiple processes either on the same machine or a cluster of machines. In this recipe, we will create a *local* node and communicate with it using *tcp* transport.

Getting ready

We will use cloud-haskell libraries for this.

How to do it...

1. Create a new project called working-with-cloud-haskell with the simple stack template:

   ```
   stack new working-with-cloud-haskell simple
   ```

2. Add a dependency on the distributed-process library in the build-depends sub-section of executable section. Also add support libraries and the -threaded option to ghc-options:

   ```
   executable working-with-cloud-haskell
       hs-source-dirs:     src
       main-is:            Main.hs
       ghc-options:        -threaded
       default-language:   Haskell2010
       build-depends:      base >= 4.7 && < 5
                         , binary
                         , distributed-process
   ```

```
, network-transport
, network-transport-tcp
```

At the time of writing this recipe, the Cloud Haskell libraries are not part of *LTS stack*. Hence we need to add more dependencies to `stack.yaml` in the extra-deps section. Note that the version numbers may change in future, and you might have to adjust them:

```
extra-deps:
  - distributed-process-0.6.6
  - syb-0.6
  - network-transport-tcp-0.5.1
```

3. Open `src/Main.hs`. We will be adding our source here. Add the `DeriveGeneric` extension to auto-derive the Binary instance:

```
{-# LANGUAGE DeriveGeneric #-}
module Main where

import Control.Concurrent
import Control.Monad
import Control.Distributed.Process
import Control.Distributed.Process.Node
import Network.Transport.TCP
import Network.Transport (Transport)
import Data.Binary (Binary)
import GHC.Generics
```

4. Create a transport serving on port `10501`:

```
localTransport :: IO Transport
localTransport = do
  Right t <- createTransport "127.0.0.1" "10501"
   defaultTCPParameters
  return t
```

5. Create a *Process* to welcome the user with a greeting:

```
type UserId = String

data UserIntimation = UserIntimation ProcessId UserId deriving
(Show, Generic)

instance Binary UserIntimation
```

```
welcome :: UserIntimation -> Process ()
welcome (UserIntimation pid uid) = send pid $ "Welcome to Cloud
 Haskell, " ++ uid
```

6. Create a *Process* to define some distributed work. Accept a message and give back a reply:

```
greet :: Process ()
greet = forever $ receiveWait [match welcome]
```

7. Run the nodes in the `main` function:

```
main :: IO ()
main = do
  t <- localTransport
  node <- newLocalNode t initRemoteTable

  runProcess node $ do
    self <- getSelfPid

    greetPid <- spawnLocal greet

    -- Continue with greetings
    say "Greeting Rudy!"
    send greetPid (UserIntimation self "Rudy")

    greeting <- expectTimeout 1000000
    case greeting of
      Nothing -> die "Greet server not up?"
      Just g  -> say $ "Greetings says : " ++ g

    -- Wait for all distributed messages to finish exchanging
     befor exiting
    liftIO $ threadDelay 1000000
```

8. Build and execute the project:

```
stack build
stack exec -- working-with-cloud-haskell
```

9. You should see following output:

```
working-with-cloud-haskell $ stack exec — working-with-cloud-haskell
Tue Aug 15 15:30:49 UTC 2017 pid://127.0.0.1:10501:0:10: Greeting Rudy!
Tue Aug 15 15:30:49 UTC 2017 pid://127.0.0.1:10501:0:10: Greetings says : Welcome to Cloud Haskell, Rudy
working-with-cloud-haskell $
```

How it works...

You will notice a few peculiar things in this recipes:

- The *UserIntimation* data is required to be an instance of *Binary*. This is required for serialization between the calling process and called process.
- We first create a transport. In this case, we start the *backend* on a local server at port 10501.
- We create a node where we would like to run the processes.
- We use the Process monad to define what we want to do at the node.
- The runProcess function takes the Process monad and converts it to IO action.
- The receiveWait and match functions are used to wrap up the kind of messages we expect to run in Process.
- We declare our expectation using either expect or expectTimeout. We use expectTimeout to showcase that if we do not get a message within a certain period of time, we will start further processing.
- The say function is used for logging.

Using Cloud Haskell to start master and slave nodes

In this recipe, we will use *simplelocalnet* to create *master* and *slave* nodes. We will start *slave* nodes and a *master* node, and use the *master* node learn about the slave nodes.

How to do it...

1. Create a new project called `master-slave` with the `simple` stack template:

   ```
   stack new master-slave simple
   ```

2. Add a dependency on the `distributed-process` and `distributed-process-localnet` libraries in the `build-depends` sub-section of the `executable` section:

   ```
   executable master-slave
     hs-source-dirs:     src
     main-is:            Main.hs
     default-language:   Haskell2010
     build-depends:      base >= 4.7 && < 5
                       , distributed-process
                       , distributed-process-simplelocalnet
   ```

3. Note that you might have to add the dependent library specifically to the `extra-deps` section, as these libraries are not part of stackage LTS at the time of writing this recipe. Add the following to `stack.yaml`:

   ```
   extra-deps:
     - distributed-process-0.6.6
     - distributed-process-simplelocalnet-0.2.3.3
     - syb-0.6
   ```

4. Open `src/Main.hs`. We will be adding our source here. Add the `Main` module, and the relevant imports:

   ```
   module Main where

   import System.Environment (getArgs)
   import Control.Distributed.Process
   import Control.Distributed.Process.Node
   import Control.Distributed.Process.Backend.SimpleLocalnet
   ```

5. Create the `Process` that we will run on the master node:

   ```
   masterTask :: Backend -> [NodeId] -> Process ()
   masterTask backend slaves = do
     liftIO $ putStrLn $ "Initial slaves: " ++ show slaves
     terminateAllSlaves backend
   ```

6. Use `main` to start either the master or slave node:

```
main :: IO ()
main = do
  args <- getArgs

  case args of

    "-m":h:p:[] -> do
      backend <- initializeBackend h p initRemoteTable
      startMaster backend (masterTask backend)
    "-s":h:p:[] -> do
      backend <- initializeBackend h p initRemoteTable
      startSlave backend
```

7. Build and execute the project:

```
stack build
stack exec -- master-slave -s 127.0.0.1 10501 &
stack exec -- master-slave -s 127.0.0.1 10502 &
stack exec -- master-slave -s 127.0.0.1 10503 &
stack exec -- master-slave -s 127.0.0.1 10504 &
stack exec -- master-slave -m 127.0.0.1 10505
```

You should see the following output:

How it works...

In this recipe, we use the *simplelocalnet* backend to start both *master* and *slave* nodes. It is possible to use different backends such as the *p2p* (peer to peer) or *Azure* backend. When we are closing the *master*, we close all *slave* nodes.

Using closure to communicate between nodes

In this *recipe*, we will start two separate processes, one master and one slave. We will use the *master* process to spawn a subprocess on a *slave* node.

How to do it...

1. Create a new project called `master-slave` with the `simple` stack template:

   ```
   stack new using-closure simple
   ```

2. Add a dependency on the `distributed-process` and `distributed-process-localnet` libraries in the `build-depends` sub-section of the `executable` section:

   ```
   executable using-closure
     hs-source-dirs:      src
     main-is:             Main.hs
     ghc-options:         -threaded
     default-language:    Haskell2010
     build-depends:       base >= 4.7 && < 5
                        , distributed-process
                        , distributed-process-simplelocalnet
   ```

   At the time of writing this recipe, some of the dependencies are not resolved through *stackage LTS*. Add the following to `stack.yaml`:

   ```
   extra-deps:
     - distributed-process-0.6.6
     - distributed-process-simplelocalnet-0.2.3.3
     - syb-0.6
   ```

3. Open `src/Main.hs`. We will be adding our source here. Add the `Main` module and the relevant imports. Enable `TemplateHaskell`:

```
{-# LANGUAGE TemplateHaskell #-}
module Main where

import System.Environment (getArgs)
import Control.Distributed.Process
import Control.Distributed.Process.Closure
import Control.Distributed.Process.Node
import Control.Distributed.Process.Backend.SimpleLocalnet
import Control.Monad
import Control.Concurrent
```

4. Create a `Process`. This process receives a message, and returns an acknowledgment:

```
ack :: Int -> Process ()
ack i = do
  self <- getSelfPid
  say $ "Started the process at " ++ show self
  forever $ do
    receiveWait [match (acknowledge self), matchAny (\_ -> say
    "Message received") ]

  where
    acknowledge :: ProcessId -> (ProcessId, String) ->
     Process ()
    acknowledge self (pid, message) = do
      liftIO $ threadDelay (i*1000*1000)
      send pid $ ("Ack from : " ++ show self ++ ", message : "
       ++ message :: String)
```

5. Create a remote table. This table has entries that enables Cloud Haskell to spawn a process remotely:

```
remotable ['ack]
```

6. Create the master table. The *remoteable* macro creates the table in the current module. Let's combine `initRemoteTable` with the preceding table:

```
masterTable :: RemoteTable
masterTable = Main.__remoteTable initRemoteTable
```

7. Create the `Process` that we will run on the master node. First create a closure around `ack`, so that we can serialize the Process along with any arguments:

```
ackClosure :: Int -> Closure (Process ())
ackClosure = $(mkClosure 'ack)

masterTask :: Backend -> [NodeId] -> Process ()
masterTask backend slaves = do
  liftIO $ putStrLn $ "Initial slaves: " ++ show slaves
  self <- getSelfPid
  case slaves of
    [] -> liftIO $ putStrLn $ "No slaves"
    (s:_) -> do
      pid <- spawn s $ ackClosure 1
      say $ "Spawned " ++ show pid ++ " on " ++ show s
      send pid (self, "Remote confirmation" :: String)
      m <- expectTimeout (1000000*3)
      case m of
        Nothing -> say "No message confirmation from
          remote node"
        Just r  -> say $ "Remote confirmation: " ++ r
        terminateAllSlaves backend
```

8. Use `main` to start either the master or *slave* node:

```
main :: IO ()
main = do
  args <- getArgs

  case args of

    "-m":h:p:[] -> do
      backend <- initializeBackend h p masterTable
      startMaster backend (masterTask backend)
    "-s":h:p:[] -> do
      backend <- initializeBackend h p masterTable
      startSlave backend
```

9. Build and execute the project:

```
stack build
stack exec -- master-slave -s 127.0.0.1 10501 &
stack exec -- master-slave -m 127.0.0.1 10502
```

You should see the following output, showing that we are able to start the process on a remote node, and get an acknowledgment from it:

How it works...

In this recipe, we uses the *simplelocalnet* backend to start both *master* and *slave* nodes. We then created a table using template Haskell based on the *remoteable macro*. In this table, we registered all the functions (resulting in *Process*) that need to be serialized across.

Cloud Haskell uses the *static pointer* extension, which allows *Cloud Haskell* to find a fingerprint of a function and then compose the *serializable* arguments along with the *fingerprint*. On the remote node, using the information contained in the closure, it is possible for the remote node to recreate the *function call* with arguments. The *static pointer* extension, however, can only be used for rank-1 types. For higher ranks, *Cloud Haskell* converts it in to the *Data.Dynamic* type so that it can cast the function back into the original function on the remote node with the help of remote table.

Index